VOCATION TO VIRTUE

KENT J. LASNOSKI

VOCATION TO VIRTUE

*Christian Marriage as a
Consecrated Life*

The Catholic University of America Press
Washington, D.C.

Copyright © 2014
The Catholic University of America Press
All rights reserved

Library of Congress Cataloging-in-Publication Data
Lasnoski, Kent J.
Vocation to virtue : Christian marriage as a consecrated life /
Kent J. Lasnoski.
pages cm
Includes 978-0-8132-3646-9 (pbk)

1. Marriage—Religious aspects—Catholic Church.
2. Catholic Church—Doctrines.   I. Title.
BX2250.L357 2014
248.8'44—dc23   2014009586

To Caitlin

In our Father's house there are many rooms.

Together let us fill them with saints.

CONTENTS

Acknowledgments	ix
Introduction	xi
1. Speaking of Marriage—Relationship or Practice?	1
2. Is Marriage Made in a Monastery?	35
3. Foundations for a Consecrated Way	55
4. Something New from Someone Old—Augustine	88
5. Everyone's Doing It—Householding with God	132
6. Consecrating Conjugal Life— A Construction Site	171
Bibliography	225
Index	243

ACKNOWLEDGMENTS

Caitlin and our children (Aquinas John Paul, Hope Julian, Innocence Francis, Gabriel Benedict, Magdalena Grace, Maksymilian Paul, and Augustine Francis) deserve first acknowledgment and thanks for making this work possible. We daily form each other in the virtues (and sometimes the vices) of marriage as consecrated way; may God grant that we be ever more conformed to the life, death, and resurrection of Christ the poor, chaste, and obedient. Second acknowledgment must go to our Christian households of origin (Joseph and Robin Lasnoski and Donna and David Lukens), as well as to our friends and relatives working with us toward practices and principles of marriage as a consecrated way in Christ.

As for professional acknowledgments, a first belongs to M. Therese Lysaught, who diligently, charitably, and skillfully directed the dissertation that bore fruit in this present work. Her encouragements, insight, love for the Church, and excellence in the practice of scholarship have provided integral support for this project. Second, all the theology faculty at Marquette University deserve acknowledgment for having shaped my habits of thought and research practices by introducing me to the

Acknowledgments

subjects and authors near to their own hearts, minds, bookshelves, and keyboards.

Finally, St. Augustine, St. Thomas Aquinas, St. Benedict of Nursia, St. Francis of Assisi, St. Alphonsus Liguori, St. John the Evangelist, St. Joseph, and Mary the Mother of God, I thank you for the witness of your lives in faith, hope, charity, and for the writings you left to our edification, and most especially for your continued prayers to God the Father, through Christ the Son, in the Spirit. May we all come to share in the many rooms of our Father's house.

INTRODUCTION

I could begin by saying that marriage is in crisis, but that much is obvious. Besides, marriage has always been in crisis. I could jump into this work by decrying the lacuna of scholarship on marriage and family, but that would just be a lie. No, the problem necessitating this book is not that marriage is in crisis or that the scholarship on marriage has gaping holes. The goal of my book is not to fix marriage or save the scholarship. I could never accomplish that task, and, moreover, I do not believe marriage itself requires any fixing. Instead, I intend to be "like a householder who brings out of his treasure things new and things old" (Mt 13:51). Saying something "new" is not all that difficult, though. The real challenge is that in Catholic theology we must say something both *nova et vetera* all at once. The goal of this book, therefore, is to offer for the scholarly community at the service of the Church a "new" grammar for speaking about marriage simultaneously rooted in the Church's tradition while faithfully synthesizing and developing traditional voices. I will argue that there is a whole body of language waiting to be dusted off and put to work speaking into the current challenges facing marriage and family.

The central thesis of this book is that the language of the evangelical virtues (poverty, chastity, and obedience), a rule of life, and a robust preparation period (e.g., a novitiate) belongs as properly to conjugal life as it does to consecrated religious life. I seek to establish this fact and constructively apply this language to conjugal life. Consecrated religious life and Christian married life are two specifications of one consecrated way in Christ—unique shares in the ecclesial practice of householding with God so as to be conformed to Christ the poor, chaste, and obedient bridegroom living in a communion of persons who images the trinitarian communion of persons.

How do I achieve this end? What is the book's method? First, the book makes a number of assumptions. As a study in Catholic systematic and moral theology, the work assumes the veracity of the Church's dogmas and presumes in favor of all its doctrines. The work is at the service of the Church. It seeks to understand systematically what is believed and taught about marriage, family, and consecrated life and offer insight into decisions Christians make to enact what is believed, specifically relating to married life.

Second, since I am writing about the location of marriage as a practice and a relationship within the Church, I must offer a clear ecclesiology up front. When I use the word "Church" with a uppercase "C" I follow *Lumen gentium* 8 in referring to that one, holy, catholic, and apostolic people of God, which is at once the Mystical Body of Christ and a society structured with hierarchical organs, at once a visible assembly and a spiritual community, at once an earthly communion and a communion enriched with heavenly things, at once inhabited by sinners and saints while being the living organ of salvation, the sacrament of Christ on earth. The Church is "the community of faith, hope, and charity, as an entity with visible delineation through which He communicated truth and grace to all."[1] Furthermore, the one Church of Christ "subsists in the Catholic Church, which is governed by the successor of Peter and by the Bishops in communion with him, although many elements of sanc-

---

1. *Lumen gentium* (hereafter *LG*) 8.

Introduction

tification and truth are found outside its visible structure."[2] When I mean something else, "church" will be qualified with terms such as "domestic church" or Catholic Church.

Having made explicit my assumptions, I will do the same with my argumentative strategy. I begin with a brief explanation of the current crisis in marriage and the linguistic paradigms for speaking about Christian marriage, suggesting that they point in the direction of my thesis. The second chapter considers how modern scholars have construed the relationship between conjugal life and consecrated religious life, wherein I argue that a competitive narrative remains in place despite the best efforts of these theologians. The third chapter lays out the fundamental theological groundwork in Christ and the Trinity for considering a deeper, noncompetitive, dialogical relationship between the consecrated religious life and married life. Both ways of life are specifications of a common consecration to Christ the poor, chaste, and obedient bridegroom. The fourth chapter moves from theory into tradition to begin supplanting the competitive narrative with an alternative account of the ecclesial connection between the states of life found in the thought of Augustine. The fifth chapter extends the ecclesial connection between the states with recourse to John's Gospel, which sees all of Christian life in terms of a practice common to both married and consecrated religious life—householding. Turning to history, we see consecrated religious life has expressed its own practices and identity by relying on domestic and familial language common to all who inhabit the Church, the household of God. Just as appropriation of this language is not "domesticizing" religious life, the appropriation of language typically reserved for consecrated religious life need not be considered a "monasticization" of marriage. This is because the use of the language is not an effort to make marriage more like

2. *LG* 8.

Introduction

religious life but to make the practice of marriage better conform spouses to the origin and exemplar of both ways of life—Christ the poor, chaste, and obedient bridegroom inhabiting the household of God. In the final chapter, free from any accusation of "monasticizing" marriage, I develop practices of Christian householding for conjugal life using the language of poverty, chastity, and obedience, a rule of life, and a novitiate.

VOCATION TO VIRTUE

1

SPEAKING OF MARRIAGE—RELATIONSHIP OR PRACTICE?

"Houston, We Have a Problem": Marriage in the United States, 1965–2010

Since the Second Vatican Council's end, the world has seen radical changes in the practice and theory of marriage, divorce, and sexuality at the cultural, religious, and political levels. At least six major shifts have taken place: (1) 50 percent fewer people are marrying;[1] (2) people marry at a later age; (3) cohabitation has exploded, moving from virtually none in 1960 to more than 60 percent of marriages being preceded by cohabitation in 2009;[2] (4) marriage has lost child-centeredness—only 33 percent of American households contained children; (5) fewer children are growing up in married homes—in general only 66.7 percent of children live with married parents, and 39 percent of nonmarried cohabitors are raising chil-

---

1. See Bradford Wilcox, ed., *The State of Our Unions, Marriage in America 2010: When Marriage Disappears; The New Middle America,* National Marriage Project (Charlottesville, Va.: University of Virginia Press, 2010), 62–68, http://www.stateofourunions.org, accessed February 7, 2011.

2. Ibid., 13–61; Wilcox, *The State of Our Unions 2009,* National Marriage Project (Charlottesville, Va.: University of Virginia Press, 2009), 83–85.

Speaking of Marriage—Relationship or Practice?

dren;³ and (6) teens do not believe marriage is better than the alternatives—only one-third of teens think marriage is more beneficial to individuals than the alternatives.⁴ Despite a recent decline in the divorce rate, approximately one out of two couples who do marry will divorce.⁵ Scholarly and popular opinions across the political and theological spectrum generally agree that these demographic changes have been harmful to persons and society; it is generally agreed that marriage needs reform and renewal.⁶

Within this context social institutions of all kinds have made an effort to renew and support the theory and practice of marriage and family.⁷ For their part, theologies of marriage have seen many and

---

3. Wilcox, *State of Our Unions 2010*, 75, 90, 92. This percentage is just down from 2008, when it was over 40 percent; Wilcox, *State of Our Unions 2009*, 83–85; and Judith S. Wallerstein, Julia M. Lewis, and Sandra Blakeslee, *The Unexpected Legacy of Divorce: A 25 Year Landmark Study* (New York: Hyperion, 2000).

4. Wilcox, *State of Our Unions 2010*, 95–102.

5. Divorce statistics are contested owing to multiple calculation methods. One compares the number of divorces per annum to the number of marriages per annum. A second inspects the total number of people who have been married and counts the number who have divorced; see Steven Martin, "Women's Changing Attitudes Toward Divorce, 1974–2002: Evidence for an Educational Crossover," *Journal of Marriage and Family* 68, no. 1 (2006): 29–40; and Dan Hurley, "Divorce Rate: It's Not as High as You Think," *New York Times*, April 19, 2005, http://www.divorcereform.org/nyto5.html, accessed November 17, 2009.

6. See, for example, Lawrence Stone, "The Family Crisis Today," in *The Family, Civil Society, and the State*, ed. Christopher Wolfe, 17–21 (Lanham, Md.: Rowman and Littlefield, 1998); Allan Carlson, "The State's Assault on the Family," in *The Family, Civil Society, and the State*, 39–51; David Popenoe, *Life without Father: Compelling New Evidence That Fatherhood and Marriage Are Indispensable for the Good of Children and Society* (New York: Martin Kessler, 1996); and National Commission on Children, *Beyond Rhetoric: A New American Agenda for Children and Families* (Washington, D.C.: U.S. Government Printing Office, 1991).

7. Among secular institutions' attempts, see the U.S. Department of Health and Human Services' Administration for Children and Families' "Healthy Marriage Initiative," http://www.acf.hhs.gov/healthymarriage, accessed April 26, 2013. Their $150 million budget funds programs such as the "National Healthy Marriage Resource Center"; http://www.healthymarriageinfo.org. Some type of marital education, preparation, and restoration program is available in nearly every state. A program named "Think Marriage" (http://www.thinkmarriage.org) has a list of websites of local efforts to renew marriage in almost every state. Explicitly secular efforts use the language of "healthy relationships" and are goal-oriented: reduce divorce, reduce nonmarried cohabitation (for nonreligious reasons), increase the well-being of children and married persons, and give dating people techniques for finding a good mate.

Speaking of Marriage—Relationship or Practice?

varied attempts at authentic reform in theory and practice: from Rome's Pontifical Council for the Family, to the U.S. Conference of Catholic Bishops' National Pastoral Initiative on Marriage,[8] to secular institutes and associations of lay faithful (Schoenstaat, Opus Dei, Community of the Beatitudes), to diocesan centers for marriage and family (e.g., Milwaukee's John Paul II Center), to the programs of each local parish, to marriage and family centers at various Catholic universities, and finally to the efforts of individual theologians.[9] Each of these efforts merits its own study; this analysis focuses on the efforts of contemporary Catholic theologians to articulate the crisis of marriage and its corresponding solutions.

Being honest about where the practice of Catholic marriage is today and where it ought to go requires affirming two points: (1) marriage is currently a status quo of Christian life entered for any number of reasons and for any number of goals apart from the ecclesial purposes and ends; and (2) marriage should be referred to as a vocation requiring as much discernment, training, and intentionality as the consecrated religious life. Marriage can no longer be something

---

8. The U.S. Council of Catholic Bishops (USCCB) created a number of pastoral initiatives not only for marriage preparation and formation (e.g., use of the FOCCUS [Facilitate Open Caring Communication, Understanding, and Study] inventory, mandatory marriage-prep classes, and the "For Your Marriage" website at http://www.foryourmarriage.org). In 1992 the USCCB put out a family-centered catechesis campaign called "Children and Families First," promoting "domestic church" language.

9. I cannot list here all the attempts at theologies of marriage since the Second Vatican Council, but I can distinguish among kinds of work by Catholics on marriage since the Council: feminist (e.g., Susan Ross, Christina Traina, and Rosemary Radford Ruether); personalist (John Paul II, Angelo Cardinal Scola, and Vincent J. Genovesi); neo-Augustinian (Jana M. Bennett and John Cavadini); neo-Thomist (Germain Grisez, Robert P. George, and Janet Smith), covenant-based (John F. Kippley, Walter Kasper), virtue-based (Patrick G. Riley, Elizabeth Anscombe), social-ethics based (Lisa Sowle Cahill and Julie Hanlon Rubio), trinitarian (Marc Cardinal Ouellet), pastoral (from the bishops' national conferences); and magisterial (papal writings from Paul VI, John Paul II, and Benedict XVI). Some of the effective lay ministry efforts at preparing, forming, and renewing Catholic marriage through the twentieth century have been the Cana Conference, the Worldwide Marriage Encounter program, Retrouvaille, Alexander House, and the Christian Family Movement.

Speaking of Marriage—Relationship or Practice?

people "fall into." Thomas Merton's thought represents the precarious position we find ourselves in today: "The ordinary way to holiness and to the fullness of Christian life is marriage. Most men and women will become saints in the married state."[10] This statement resonates with my own position, but it can just as easily perpetuate an attitude to be avoided—that marriage itself should be "ordinary." Merely by adverting to marriage as "ordinary" Merton subtly and unintentionally maintains the "clericalism" and dualism of Christian life of which contemporary theology so wishes to rid itself. Among my emphases throughout this book will be the idea that the practice of Christian marriage makes no small demand for virtue, being a Christomorphic practice in the Church.

Furthermore, in the twenty-first-century West, to order the married state explicitly toward the service of God and neighbor is to swim up a rapid stream. Little cultural or economic formation and support exist for successful performance of such a practice. While there are more married Christians than vowed religious, it is not to be assumed that the majority of married people are actually becoming saints in and through their marriage(s). So common are divorces and annulment proceedings in the Church that they constitute a scandal, raising serious questions about the Church's failure to prepare people well for marriage and protect people from attempting invalid marriages.[11] At the descriptive level marriage might as eas-

---

10. Thomas Merton, *No Man Is an Island* (New York: Sheed and Ward, 1965), 111.

11. This debate has the laudable pastoral intent of decreasing annulments and broken marriages. The most interesting pastoral solution is the introduction of a marital catechumenate in the Catholic Church. Two proposals for such a catechumenate have emerged in the Catholic Church (many already exist in the Episcopal Church). Michael Lawler's proposal is to invite couples to a formal betrothal rite that would initiate a period of cohabitation that would eventually be solemnized with the rite of matrimony; see Lawler, "A Marital Catechumenate: A Proposal," *INTAMS Review* 13 (2007): 161–77. A better, more developed proposal for a marriage catechumenate comes from Rev. Paul Holmes. Because he supports the Church's doctrine that marriage begins with the sacrament of matrimony rather than with betrothal (as Lawler argues), Holmes does not introduce cohabitation into the catechumenate; see

ily be construed and lived as a practice of self-fulfillment than as a sacrament of sacrifice and service. Too many couples enter and live marriage unaware of its theological, sacramental nature, uninformed of the virtues and internal goods sought by this ecclesial vocation and practice.[12]

What must happen, and what my present work attempts, is to provide Christians the language and paradigm to understand marriage as a consecrated way to holiness in the Church, a way that participates in the same principles of Christian householding as consecrated religious life and requires the same evangelical virtues as consecrated religious life.[13] This is why it is so important to understand marriage with consecrated life as a practice of householding with God. Living in God's household requires a complete gift of self: one's external goods (poverty), one's body (chastity), and one's will (obedience). A person makes these gifts to God by becoming

---

Holmes, "A Catechumenate for Marriage: Presacramental Preparation as Pilgrimage," *Journal of Ritual Studies* 6, no. 2 (1992): 93–113. The theory, as well as the rites necessary for the catechumenate, are developed and presented in his Ph.D. dissertation, "Betrothal: A Liturgical Rite of Passage; The Anthropological Perspective of Victor W. Turner as the Basis for the Development of a Catechumenate for the Betrothed" (Rome: Pontifical University of St. Thomas Aquinas, 1991).

12. There is debate over the sacramental status of marriage between baptized nonbelievers, see Lawler, *Marriage and the Catholic Church: Disputed Questions* (Collegeville, Minn.: Liturgical Press, 2002), 43–66; Walter Kasper, *Theology of Christian Marriage* (New York: Seabury, 1980), 78–84; Susan K. Wood, "The Marriage of Baptized Nonbelievers: Faith, Contract, and Sacrament," *Theological Studies* 48, no. 2 (1987): 279–301; and Bernard Cooke, "What God Has Joined Together ...," in *Perspectives on Marriage: A Reader*, edited by Kieran Scott and Michael Warren, 353–60 (New York: Oxford University Press, 1993). I agree with Susan Wood, who argues that marriages between baptized nonbelievers enjoy an assumption in favor of their validity and therefore their sacramental character—lest we return to a Pelagian or Donatist understanding of the sacraments.

13. By "common" I do not mean descriptive of the majority. Instead, I mean something to be shared. The terms "evangelical counsels" and "virtues" used throughout the book will always mean poverty, chastity, and obedience. I will use "counsel" when emphasizing the exceptional, vocational aspect of the three but will use "virtues" when emphasizing that these habits can subsist in people of distinct vocations (consecrated religious or married) on account of the universal vocation holiness in Christian perfection.

Speaking of Marriage—Relationship or Practice?

radically available and vulnerable to serve and love for the sanctification of another. In the case of religious life it is a universal availability that requires a permanent gift of possession, sexual intimacy, and self-reliance to Christ—that is, through a renunciation of the possibilities for possessing anything as one's own, for sharing sexual intimacy with any person at all, and for privileging one's own will over a superior's. These gifts are made to the one Christ for the sanctification of the universal Church, which constitutes the very body of Christ.[14] In the case of conjugal life spouses vow a particular availability that requires the permanent gift of possession, sexual intimacy, and self-reliance to a spouse—that is, through a renunciation of the possibilities for possessing anything as one's own, for sharing sexual intimacy with any other person, and for privileging one's own will over the spouse's. The gift is made to Christ through the spouse (and all community that may be engendered therefrom), for the sake of that community's salvation together, achieved by service to the other with each other.

The theological approach I have just described, however, has not been offered as a solution to the problems of marriage. In this chapter, therefore, I will consider the kind of language employed for speaking about the nature and ends of marriage in contemporary Catholic theology. The 1983 *Code of Canon Law*, no. 1055, uses the following terms to refer to the nature of marriage: "covenant," "partnership," "sacrament," and "contract." Whatever its nature, according to canon 1056, marriage's essential properties are "unity" and "indissolubility." As to its ends, canon 1055 identifies them as "the well-being of the spouses" and "the procreation and upbringing of children." Over the last decades of the twentieth century Cath-

---

14. This is not at all to say that the consecrated religious person has sexual intimacy with Christ, but rather that all possibility of that intimacy is given to Christ for the service of the whole Church.

olic theologians have labored to unpack and explore this language, which draws largely from the second Vatican Council's *Gaudium et spes*. Special attention, too, has been given to Pope Paul VI's description of conjugal love as "fully human," "total," "faithful," and "fruitful."[15] To accomplish this task theologians have employed larger linguistic paradigms of relationship and practice. I will look at each of these linguistic paradigms now and suggest how they point the way to my own linguistic paradigm of consecrated marriage.

Marriage as Relationship

Catholic scholars seeking to renew the theology of marriage note an emergence from the cold, even loveless and legal-sounding language of the marital "contract" found in canon law until 1983 to the warmer, person-centered, "relational" language found in the theologians of the 1940s (Herber Doms, Dietrich von Hildebrand), which made its way into the Second Vatican Council's Pastoral Constitution on the Church in the Modern World, *Gaudium et spes*. Within this linguistic paradigm one set of authors focuses on the relationship between the spouses and another set focuses on the relationship in terms of its social position and role.

Authors focusing on the marriage relationship between the spouses typically fall into one of two categories. On the one hand, authors such as Margaret Hogan, Michael Lawler, Lisa Sowle Cahill, and Susan Ross find the shift from contractual to relational language as suggesting the need for a change in the more controversial yet fundamental Catholic teachings on marriage (e.g., toward indissolubility as an ideal, in favor of same-sex marriage, and in favor of contraception). On the other hand, John Paul II, Peter Ryan, SJ, Germain Grisez, William May, Robert P. George, and Patrick Lee discover in the

---

15. Paul VI, *Humanae vitae* 9, http://www.vatican.va, accessed April 26, 2013.

shift to relationship language a further support for the Church's magisterial positions (e.g., they are in favor of ontological indissolubility, against same-sex marriages, and against contraception).[16]

I want to forward what is both common to all the authors using a relationship paradigm and consistent with Catholic doctrine. In general the group of authors focusing on "relationship" point out that, in *Gaudium et spes,* the Council calls marriage a divine institution, an intimate union, and a sacrament whereby God confers the grace necessary to perform the duties of marriage and strengthens its indissoluble character.[17] Emphasis particularly falls on the description of conjugal love in *Gaudium et spes* and the revision of Canon law to include the "covenant" and "partnership of the whole of life" (can. 1055.1). The notion of divine institution is carried over from the thought of Pius XI's *Casti connubii* and refers to the fact that God, not man, has authored marriage. As intimate union marriage is a particular kind of relationship: an "intimate partnership of married life and love."[18] In it the "spouses mutually bestow and accept each other" in a relationship that is so close as to be characterized by a *vinculum sacrum*.[19] The union is seen with greater emphasis on the love that resides at its center. It develops as "a man and a

---

16. Peter F. Ryan and Germain Grisez, "Indissoluble Marriage: A Reply to Kenneth Himes and James Coriden," *Theological Studies* 72 (2011): 369–415; and Patrick Lee and Robert P. George, "What Male-Female Complementarity Makes Possible: Marriage as a Two-in-One-Flesh Union," *Theological Studies* 69 (2008): 641–61.

17. Some scholars, though, background the canonical understanding of consummation and see the indissolubility of marriage as being actualized over time—as a goal to be reached rather than as a character given on account of marriage's ends; see, for example, Margaret Monahan Hogan, *Marriage as a Relationship: Real and Rational,* Marquette Studies in Philosophy 34 (Milwaukee: Marquette University Press, 2002), 53, 60. I reject Hogan's conclusion that marriage's procreative good requires only relative indissolubility. The conclusion makes a false assumption—parenthood ends when children reach legal adulthood—i.e., independence. Contrariwise, the parental task endures for the whole of the child's and the parent's lives, as does the child's dependence on the parent.

18. Pius XI, *Casti connubii* 24, 37; Paul VI, *Gaudium et spes* 48 (hereafter *GS*).

19. *GS* 48.

woman, by their compact *of conjugal love* 'are no longer two, but one flesh' (Mt 19:6)."[20] Further, the ends of marriage take a place beside one another, no longer hierarchically arranged. This is another of the changes to the canon law of 1983.[21]

In the relationship paradigm the essence of marriage is seen as a relationship of a particular kind rather than primarily an institution defined by an essential end. The marriage partners become forever ordered to and for the other, and their relationship emerges as a juridical being founded on love, consented to in marital vows, and consummated in the act of total personal self-gift.[22] Relying on Aquinas, scholars such as Margaret Hogan have identified marriage as a real relation existing in the objective order, the principles of which are the spouses, whose "to be" is permanently "for" the other upon consent and consummation.[23] John Paul II has continually attempted to raise the dignity of the marriage relationship itself, arguing that marital relation forms a "communion of persons." In fact, he identified the first task of families as precisely this: forming a communion of persons.[24] These unions, or communions, therefore, are to be sought as the primary, essential, necessary good, a good con-

---

20. GS 48; Hogan, *Marriage as a Relationship*, 52.

21. See *Codex Iuris Canonici* (hereafter CIC) 1917, can. 1013.1: "The primary end of matrimony is the procreation and education of offspring; the secondary end is mutual aid and the remedy of concupiscence"; my translation.

22. See Hogan, *Marriage as a Relationship*, 111–12, where she identifies the distinction between marriage relationship *in fieri* and *in facto esse*. Unlike Grisez and Peter Ryan, Hogan believes that an authentic development of Catholic marriage doctrine would see marriage as consummated over time rather than in a single act.

23. Ibid., 110. Here she relies on St. Thomas Aquinas, *Summa theologiae* (hereafter ST) I, q. 28, a. 1. Hogan offers a precise definition of the marital relationship: "(1) This relationship is the actual personal union of the partners, each of whom represents a partial manifestation of humanity to form a new being, the marriage; (2) within this union, the procreation and education of children are to be accomplished; and (3) within this union, the flourishing of the individual partners, as individuals, is to be accomplished as each helps and satisfies the other"; Hogan, *Marriage as Relationship*, 125–26.

24. John Paul II, *Familiaris consortio* (hereafter FC)15, 17.

Speaking of Marriage—Relationship or Practice?

tributing to the perfection of the spouses and existing as the matrix for the nurturing and procreation of children.[25]

Other theologians, though, focus on the marriage relationship as socially constituted rather than nuclear. Lisa Sowle Cahill, among the most well-known authors in Catholic marriage and sexual ethics debates, has articulated marriage and family from a social-ethics standpoint and thus merits attention.[26]

Cahill's story of the "family in crisis" is really two stories. Cahill is situated within the relational paradigm inasmuch as both of her stories resist (with Hauerwas) the absolute voluntarization of family relations, especially when it comes to the relationship of families to Church. The first story is a narrative about the relationships of spouses as mediated by economic and social realities. It has two parts. On the one hand, rising consumerism, individualism, and moral permissiveness have led to a breakdown in the durability of the marital institution. On the other hand, for the working class and the poor, marriage in many cases appears to be a non-option, as many of the poor are practically locked into life situations inimical to good marriage—marriage, for example, may simply not be viable given the crushing hours of work required just to get by at a menial salary, accompanied by the relative absence of marriageable (i.e., employed) men among the impoverished.[27] In other words, the typical story of the "conservative" "family values" ideal of marriage and family is only possible for the middle class, is actually destructive to

---

25. Hogan, *Marriage as a Relationship*, 53.

26. Lisa Sowle Cahill, *Family: A Christian Social Perspective* (Minneapolis: Fortress Press, 2000), intro and chap. 1.

27. Cahill, *Family*, 117. Cahill gets the second of these insights from the work of William J. Wilson; see Wilson, *When Work Disappears: The World of the New Urban Poor* (New York: Random House, 1996), 105, xiii–xiv, 20, and 87. Wilson writes, "From the point of view of day-to-day survival, single parenthood reduces the emotional burden and shields from the type of exploitation that often accompanies the sharing of both living arrangements and limited resources" (105).

Speaking of Marriage—Relationship or Practice?

the middle class, and propagates further disruption of marriage and family among the poor and working class.

At the same time Cahill notes a second narrative. Marriage has been challenged by the liberating force of feminism, which has diversified gender roles within the family and wider society. Unfortunately, while feminism has broken down oppressive structures, it has not offered better "ideals of kin-derived spousal and parental relationships or of how families serve the common good of society and are served by it."[28] Thus, what is left is the tendency to accept any family structure on account of the values of compassion, love, and inclusion. For Cahill the feminist freedom from oppressive structures and into voluntary choice of family form runs the risk of forgetting the importance of "body," of "kinship," the nonvoluntary nature of marriage and family.

Cahill proposes a solution to the destruction of marriage and family that includes an end and a method. First, she calls for a reimagination of marriage as the formation of a community that is fundamentally concerned with the common good rather than its own private good. Marriage, then, is a relationship of spouses for the world beyond themselves rather than simply a relationship entered to pursue each other's parallel goods. Second, the means for reordering marriage toward the common good is to reduce the gap between the family and the Church. In other words, marriage is a relationship between spouses that should have the characteristics of Church. As she argues, "identification of the Christian family with the Church is one way of transforming an important formative institution of civil society—family—to represent better and to educate for Christian values and practices."[29] Cahill is nonetheless careful to note that, although the family may be truly a symbol of God's reign

---

28. Cahill, *Family*, x.
29. Ibid., 4.

and may be conformed to the shape of his Church, there always remains the threat that patriarchal structures and power struggles will be reimported from the Church's hierarchy into the family or from the family's structure back into the Church.[30]

A Critique of Marriage as Relationship

Understanding marriage as a relationship is key, but for several reasons, "relationship" is not enough. First, though marriage is a person's ontologically being for-the-other until death, this relatedness requires enactment in a series of decidedly institutional, predefined practices. Becoming "spouse" fully is constituted by the conjugal act, an act that is the beginning of a practice of being sexually (and domestically and publicly) for-the-other freely, faithfully, and fruitfully. The "whatness" or essence of the relationship suggests the kinds of actions (from eating together, literally sleeping together, working on the house together, changing diapers together) that will coalesce into the practice of marriage, a practice of faithfully, freely, and fruitfully living. The marital relationship exists within and presupposes, as Cahill notes, a larger community. The relationship between the marriage and the ecclesial community is constituted by the practice of living as domestic church within the particular Church. My own linguistic paradigm of consecrated marriage locates and develops marriage as a relation constituted in a practice of conforming the partnership of life and love to Christ the poor, chaste, and obedient bridegroom.

Second, the relationship paradigm tends to be overly anthropological without an embedded Christological or soteriological element. Salvation and Christianity are often presented as layers on top of the basic human relationship rather than being its very founda-

---

30. For this reason, Cahill is less ambitious with the term "domestic church."

Speaking of Marriage—Relationship or Practice?

tion. If *Gaudium et spes* 22 is correct to say that Christ reveals what man is and what man is to become, then Christ ought to sit at the center of any account of the marital relationship. The relationship paradigm should be rooted in a description of how the relationship of spouses ever more conforms the spouses to the image of Christ the poor, chaste, and obedient bridegroom. Chapter 3 of this work offers such an account. Furthermore, the relationship paradigm should take firm root in the relationship between Christ and his spouse, the Church. Such will be the approach of St. Augustine taken in chapter 4.

Finally, not only does the relationship paradigm call for a deeper Christological foundation, it also demands a trinitarian foundation. The relation among spouses finds its foundation in the relation between the Persons of the Trinity, a subject addressed in chapter 3. The Father, Son, and Holy Spirit's being-for-each-other and their fundamentally genealogical orientation are the origin of all Christian life, whether consecrated religious or consecrated marriage, where the unconditional self-giving and reception of an other brings about fullness of life and superabundant fruitfulness.

Marriage as Practice

Readings of the tradition always vary, and theologians are ever attempting to understand the tradition authentically. Differences of emphasis, then, will always occur, even when theologians read the same text. For example, I begin this discussion of marriage as practice by noting that one document from the Second Vatican Council (*Gaudium et spes*) can be a central dramatic focus for both paradigms about the nature, ends, and crisis of marriage in the second half of the twentieth century. The two paradigms—marriage as relationship and marriage as practice—both revolve around this one text:

Speaking of Marriage—Relationship or Practice?

Marriage to be sure is not intended solely for procreation; rather, its very nature as an unbreakable compact between persons, and the welfare of children, both demand that mutual love of the spouses be embodied in a rightly ordered manner [*recto ordine*], that it grow and ripen. Therefore marriage persists as a whole manner and communion of life [*ut totius vitae consuetudo et communio*], and maintains its value and indissolubility, even when, despite the often intense desire of the couple, offspring are lacking.[31]

This passage can serve to demonstrate the central place for the ontological reality of the marital relationship among the nature and ends of marriage. The other goods are at the relationship's service because the relationship is the matrix of conditions in which the other goods (procreative and personalist) may develop.[32] According to this account the role of marital intercourse is first to serve the relationship, which is why retrievals of "relationship" as gravitational center of marriage, as the very definition of marriage, are good as far as they go, but unfortunately, they do not go far enough.

On the other hand, this same passage from *Gaudium et spes* could be read from a different vantage: the vantage of "practice." I think such an approach to marriage can work with the relational paradigm to create constructive possibilities for how to renew and reimagine marriage in the Church. In fact, Margaret Hogan's own reading of this passage begs for completion by a "practice" approach to the theology of marriage: "The actualization of the complete unity, the relationship itself, that 'intimate unity of persons and actions' [GS 48] is accomplished only in time."[33] Marriage is a relationship, yes—a matrix of conditions—but in that sense it is a potency that must be fulfilled in act, by order, by habits, by a practice.

Reading the same passage wherein is illustrated the centrality

---

31. GS 50.
32. Hogan, *Marriage as a Relationship*, 53.
33. Ibid., 53.

of the relationship, let me briefly point out the degree to which the language of practice enters the document of the Council. Marriage is identified in the passage quoted above from *Gaudium et spes* 50 as a "totius vitae consuetudo et communio," a practice or habitual manner and communion of *the whole of life*.[34] Now this practice of the whole of life, on account of the "unbreakable compact" and the "welfare of the children," must be a habitual manner of a particular kind. What kind? *Gaudium et spes* 50 suggests one in which the "spouses' mutual love be made present in right ordering [*recto ordine*]." Marriage does have an ontological unity through the gift of the sacrament, but at the same time it has a unity of order, as it is constituted by the right ordering of spousal love.[35] By what criteria is this "right ordering" determined, though? Notice that the two goods demanding this particular way of life, and thus owning a controlling stake in its shape, are chiefly theological and ecclesial. (1) The "unbreakable compact" is made as a Christian in virtue of baptism and guaranteed by the gift of grace. It is only possible ecclesially—that is, from within the Church—as a practice of the Church. A marriage between a Christian and the unbaptized is not a sacrament. (2) The welfare of the children too is finally theological; children belong in the household of God, the Church. Marriage, then, must be a particular, ecclesial, sacramental way of ordering a practice, manner, and communion of the whole of life—a life that is both temporal and eschatological. It is the Church, the household of God, the body of Christ that will offer to Christians the shape and

---

34. My translation of this phrase differs from the Vatican website's translation, which Hogan uses. The Vatican website's slightly misleading translation reads, "whole manner and communion of life," but a better translation is, "manner and communion of the whole of life." *Totius* is a singular genitive adjective (of the whole), so it does not modify "*communio*" or "*consuetudo.*" Instead, it takes on substantive quality and is translated with the other genitive word "*vitae*" (of life). The Vatican's German and French translations follow this better pattern.

35. See Patrick G. D. Riley, *Civilizing Sex: On Chastity and the Common Good* (Edinburgh: T. and T. Clark, 2000), 17, 18–23.

Speaking of Marriage—Relationship or Practice?

character of this practice of the entirety of life. Marriage, as a communion and practice of the entirety of life, is necessarily a communion and practice for the kingdom of God, which is after all the consummation of the entirety of life. The life of the Church, then, from the richness of its liturgical, transformational, and communal character and tradition, offers the resources for reimagining the way we enter marriage and what we are doing as married Christians.

The following section explores the work of more Catholic scholars narrating the crisis of marriage as a crisis of practice (or lack thereof). David Matzko McCarthy and Jana M. Bennett have contributed to the development of an approach to marriage as practice, specifically a practice *within* the Church. McCarthy's efforts will focus on the virtue of reciprocity in reproducing a different kind of domestic economy. Bennett's exploration, rooted (like my own) in Augustine, hopes to shift focus from the practices of "family" and onto practices shared by the household of God. A critique and description of the way forward will end the chapter.

Alasdair MacIntyre and "Practice"

A first inroad into the paradigm of marriage as practice comes from the work of Alasdair MacIntyre, into whose definition of "practice" I endeavor to fit marriage. MacIntyre defines "practice" thus:

> Any coherent and complex form of socially established cooperative human activity through which goods internal to that form of activity are realized in the course of trying to achieve those standards of excellence which are appropriate to, and partially definitive of, that form of activity, with the result that human powers to achieve excellence, and human conceptions of the ends and goods involved, are systematically extended.[36]

---

36. Alasdair MacIntyre, *After Virtue: A Study in Moral Theology*, 3rd ed. (Notre Dame, Ind.: University of Notre Dame Press, 2007), 189–91.

Speaking of Marriage—Relationship or Practice?

MacIntyre himself thinks "the range of practices is wide: arts, sciences, games, politics in the Aristotelian sense, the making and sustaining of family life, all fall under the concept."[37] Scholars employing the "practice" language assume that marriage fits MacIntyre's definition. What I will do here, though, is move beyond the assumption to demonstrate how marriage fulfills MacIntyre's criteria for a practice, particularly an ecclesial practice, the ultimate standard of excellence for which is Christ the poor, chaste, and obedient bridegroom.

MacIntyre's first criterion is coherence, which includes both descriptive and normative components. It might seem that, at least descriptively, marriage is not a practice. As Stephanie Coontz rightly points out, marriage has always produced a plurality of family forms.[38] In the twenty-first century that plurality exists to a greater degree and in different kinds. The fact of family plurality (descriptive incoherence) does not hinder, however, the argument that marriage is a practice with standards of excellence. Christian marriage does not demand a monolithic family form; in fact, if the conclusions I will make about the domestic character of all the Church's life are correct, then there are many ways married persons and their children might choose to organize living arrangements with single nonvowed persons, with elders, with vowed religious, or otherwise. The common domestic project of the entire Church suggests as much.

Descriptive coherence notwithstanding, MacIntyre seems to have more normative considerations of coherence in mind when he defines practice. Entering a practice means accepting the practice's and the community's preexisting "standards of excellence" and "the

---

37. Ibid., 188. Furthermore, "In the ancient and medieval worlds the creation and sustaining of human communities—of households, cities, nations—is generally taken to be a practice in the sense in which I have defined it" (188).

38. Stephanie Coontz, *Marriage, A History: From Obedience to Intimacy, or How Love Conquered Marriage* (New York: Basic Books, 2005); and Coontz, *The Way We Never Were: American Families and the Nostalgia Trap* (New York: Basic Books, 1992).

Speaking of Marriage—Relationship or Practice?

inadequacy of my own performance as judged by them."[39] Christian marriage does require certain moral forms (e.g., chaste permanent fidelity, responsible procreation and education without contraception, mutual love, and just distribution of work inside and outside the home). If the Christian standards of marital excellence are not met, the practitioner merely performs the practice poorly. As a result the spouses will achieve fewer of the goods internal to the practice and acquire fewer of the virtues that make the excellent performance easier. Furthermore, the goods themselves may no longer be perceived as good and thus may be even more unavailable. For Christians the social institution of the Church invites those wishing to marry into coherent, complex standards of excellence for their cooperative activity in conjugal life begun in and with ecclesial witness. For example, the Church initiates couples into the complex, coherent demands of the marital vows: to freely give oneself unconditionally to another, to receive, love, and honor the other as spouse for better, for worse, forever, and to receive and educate children lovingly from God and for God according to the law of Christ.[40] One of the most central socially established standards is indissolubility, though this standard has reached a point of scandal in the Church on account of annulment numbers.[41] This standard is set by the social reality that is the union between Christ and the Church, a union that is indissoluble—for Christ will never revoke the love

---

39. MacIntyre, *After Virtue*, 190. Furthermore, "In the realm of practices the authority of both goods and standards operates in such a way as to rule out all subjectivist and emotivist analyses of judgments. De gustibus *est* disputandum" (190, emphasis original).

40. *The Rites of the Catholic Church: As Revised by Decree of the Second Vatican Ecumenical Council and Published by Authority of Pope Paul VI*, trans. International Commission on English in the Liturgy (New York: Pueblo, 1978), 450–51.

41. Richard J. Jenks, *Divorce, Annulments, and the Catholic Church: Healing or Hurtful?* (New York: Haworth Press, 2002); Timothy Buckley, *What Binds Marriage? Roman Catholic Theology in Practice* (London: Continuum, 2002); and Edward N. Peters, *Annulments and the Catholic Church: Straight Answers to Tough Questions* (West Chester, Penn.: Ascension Press, 2004).

that caused him to be bound to the Church as a bridegroom to his bride. Another standard of excellence is chaste married sexuality and responsible parenthood, which the Church proposes should be expressed in forms of natural family planning. This standard too faces the specter of scandal, as a vast majority of spouses use contraception with the tacit approval of the lion's share of the ecclesial community.

While marriage fits MacIntyre's demand for normative skills (e.g., communication, fidelity, natural means of responsible parenthood, and Christian education of children) a practice "is never just a set of technical skills, even when directed towards some unified purpose and even if the exercise of those skills can on occasion be valued or enjoyed for their own sake," because practices have a history of determining and assessing internal goods, a history that is not merely the progress of technical skill.[42] For marriage to count as a practice, it must be also an activity "through which goods internal to that form of activity are realized in the course of trying to achieve those standards of excellence which are appropriate to, and partially definitive of, that form of activity." First, goods internal to a practice are those that can only be specified in terms of the practice or by means of examples from some other similar practice. Second, internal goods "can only be identified and recognized by the experience of participation in the practice in question."[43] Finally, internal goods are of two kinds: first, the excellent product and the excellent performance of the practice; and second, the entire form of life generated by the practice. For example, goods internal to the practice of painting are at least these: painting well, the excellent portrait, and living *as a painter*.[44]

In what follows I will illustrate examples wherein marriage con-

42. MacIntyre, *After Virtue*, 193.   43. Ibid., 189.
44. Ibid., 189–90.

tains internal goods of the kinds specified by MacIntyre. First, Christian marriage achieves the internal good of interpersonal communion, a unique kind of communion unattained in any other partnership.[45] Any two persons can achieve interpersonal communion, even a deep friendship and sharing of life, but spouses achieve a communion of the whole persons and the whole of their life. Marriage achieves a *communitas vitae et amoris coniugalis* (a communion of life and love, an interpersonal relationship that is specifically conjugal), a *"totius vitae consuetudo et communio,"* a manner and communion of the whole of life.[46] "Matrimonial consent is directed primarily and radically towards this relationship."[47] The *conjugal* aspect of this common life is what specifies it as unique to marriage. No other communion of persons has as its object the unity of whole persons expressed in domestic and sexual intimacy.

This good of the *consortium vitae* is at once the excellent product, the excellent performance, and the form of life. As the *excellent product*, it is that union initiated by the validly spoken vows and authentically consummated in the conjugal act and developed in the well-ordered, prayerful domestic life. It is a product that requires grace for its completion. As a sacrament, couples trust that in this practice God works his grace in and with them to create their *consortium vitae*. As the *excellent performance*, it is that generous sharing of life and love consented to in the wedding vows and lived out on a quotidian basis with cohabitation, co-ownership, co-parenting, common prayer, and co-responsibility for domestic and personal affairs. Again, as a sacrament, couples trust that this excellent performance is inspired and ennobled by grace, despite their failings. Finally, this

45. In *FC* 17, John Paul II calls this the first task of the family, to be a "communion of persons."
46. *GS* 48, 50.
47. Adolfo N. Dacanáy, *Canon Law on Marriage: Introductory Notes and Comments* (2000; repr. Loyola Heights, Manila: Loyola School of Theology, 2003), 114–15.

Speaking of Marriage—Relationship or Practice?

communion comes more into being as a *form of life* inasmuch as couples share ever more of their lives together with common property, shared education and care of children, shared work toward domestic maintenance and development, shared relaxation, shared sufferings, and shared joys.[48] The form of life and communion is initiated by the verbally spoken wedding vows and regular bodily consummation and restatement of those vows in the conjugal act. The good resulting from their marriage becomes their very living *as married people*.

A second internal good of Christian marriage is conjugal fecundity. This suggestion may give pause, since it would seem the child is not a good available only from the marital practice. Strictly speaking, conjugal fecundity would seem to be an external good relative to marriage. A child can be conceived, born, and raised outside the marital communion. This is true, of course, but the important fact is that the activities and skills required in achieving the good of conjugal fecundity are subject to the standards of excellence set by the ecclesial community; for Christians these actions and goods do not have meaning outside of that ecclesial context of marriage. According to the authoritative community in question, the actions that bring about a child (e.g., sexual intercourse, maintenance of a pregnancy, and parental education and nurture) are regulated and belong within the context of the marital practice. Apart from that context they are less intelligible. For example, in chess a player achieves the internal good of checkmate by trapping the opponent's king. Outside the game of chess taking a black chess piece, knocking over the white king, and declaring "checkmate" is meaningless. The good of "checkmate" has not really been achieved. Yes, the king is defeated, but only by ill performance of an activity that belongs properly

---

48. I will propose in chapter 6 that the practice of marriage more achieves the good of a "form of life" when lived according to a *regula matrimonii* that couples might create with spiritual direction.

Speaking of Marriage—Relationship or Practice?

to the practice of chess and is subject to the rules and standards of excellence established for that practice. Similarly, any two nonmarried Christian men and women could conceive a child without their being married, but they cannot do so without engaging in activities properly belonging to the practice of Christian marriage and subject to the rules and standards of excellence ecclesially established for that practice. Yes, a child can be born outside of marriage, but only by poor performance of what is properly a Christian marital practice—that is, activities socially situated within the practice of Christian marriage as determined by the primary authoritative community for this practice—the Church.

The final aspect of MacIntyre's definition that must apply to Christian marriage is related to the manner by which the goods of the practice and the capacity to achieve those goods are extended. A practice has "the result that human powers to achieve excellence, and human conceptions of the ends and goods involved, are systematically extended." In other words, practices generate and extend virtues, and virtues generate and extend the goods internal to a practice. Without virtues, writes MacIntyre, "the goods internal to practices are barred to us, but not just barred to us generally, barred in a very particular way."[49] Furthermore, "the possession of virtues—and not only of their semblance and simulacra—is necessary to achieve the latter [internal goods]; yet the possession of the virtues may perfectly well hinder us in achieving external goods."[50] Finally, "every practice requires a certain kind of relationship between those who participate in it. Now the virtues are those goods by reference to which, whether we like it or not, we define our relationships to those other people with whom we share the kind of purposes and standards which inform practices."[51]

49. MacIntyre, *After Virtue*, 191.   50. Ibid., 196.
51. Ibid., 191.

Speaking of Marriage—Relationship or Practice?

Marriage demonstrates well this relationship between virtue and the extension of internal goods, as well as the relationship between virtue and the kind of relationship required between the practitioners. Here I will briefly consider the virtues of poverty, chastity, and obedience. Chapter 3 argues that these virtues are at the center of both conjugal and consecrated religious life, as they are at the center of Christ's life. In marriage the internal good of *totius vitae consuetudo et communio* demands two habitually actualized potencies: the ability to share all that one has as if it were not one's own and the ability to put oneself in a position of real, vulnerable reliance on another for something necessary to life. In other words, sharing the whole of life demands the virtue of poverty and bids us to place ourselves in a state of poverty with respect to the spouse and even perhaps our neighbors. To lack this virtue is to reserve some area of life for and to oneself or to maintain a certain independence or safety net—in preparation or expectation of the relationship's demise. This kind of reservation explicitly excludes the central, excellent product of the marriage practice—namely, the interpersonal relationship as a *totius vitae consuetudo et communio*.

Second, chastity, the virtue of sexual self-possession and integration, goes hand in hand with another internal good of marriage: conjugal fecundity. This good is not only the responsible openness to children but the good of the child herself and her education and formation. Unchastity can lead to the irresponsible increase in family size; a couple might decide to continue being open to children because they do not want to or cannot abstain during a fertile period of the woman's cycle, for example. This lack of virtue does not bar them from the good that *is* the child, but bars them from the fuller sense of *the good of the child*, which would include provision for her material needs, education, and formation in the life of Christian discipleship. Furthermore, unchastity so unchecked that it leads to an extramarital affair hardly needs mention. Such actions threaten to destroy the entire practice by breaking the trust of the practitioners in community. Finally, chastity is a capital virtue for living the internal good of married life's form, which involves sexual intercourse as an expression of conjugal love. Unless each partner fully possesses himself or herself, he or she will struggle to make conjugal intercourse a gift of self to the other in the fullest sense.[52]

Obedience as a virtue represents the couple's realized capacity to give themselves over to the standards, common goods, and activities that constitute the practice of marriage as situated within the Church. By this virtue a couple put themselves in just relationship to the practicing community to learn from the community and contribute to the further development of the standards of excellence and goods of the practice. "Standards are not themselves immune from criticism, but nonetheless we cannot be initiated into a practice without accepting the authority of the best standards realized so far."[53] "For not to accept these" standards of excellence and virtues of a practice, says MacIntyre, "so far bars us from achieving the standards of excellence or the goods internal to the practice that it renders the practice pointless except as a device for achieving external goods."[54] For example, one of the standards for the practice of marriage in the Church is that the conception of a child must result from the conjugal act. In obedience to this standard, certain infertile couples may never achieve this good—namely, the child itself. They may still

---

52. The term "complete gift of self" is understood variously. I have borrowed the term from John Paul II's writings; see, e.g., John Paul II, *Man and Woman He Created Them: A Theology of the Body*, ed. and trans., introduction by Michael Waldstein (Boston: Pauline Books, 2006); at 68:2–3; 78:4; 90:5; 95b:2, 4; and 15, to name a few places the term "gift of self" appears. By "total gift of self" I mean a gift that imitates and has its source in the gift of self given in the Trinity and in Christ's own gift of self for the Church, a gift of self that freely, faithfully, and fruitfully enacts poverty (by giving all that one has—possessions), chastity (by giving all that one is—body and soul), and obedience (by giving all that one wills).

53. MacIntyre, *After Virtue*, 190.

54. Ibid., 191.

Speaking of Marriage—Relationship or Practice?

achieve the internal good of conjugal fecundity, though not biologically.[55] By disobedience to this standard, a couple can achieve this good at the biological level, but they would do so by stepping out of the practice. To do so would be to break faith and honesty with the other practitioners. In terms of the game of chess, for example, it would be like cheating, where the good of winning is now external to the practice because it is reached by disallowed moves. The good of "the child" would be external to their practice of marriage, a break with the practice and a rupture with the community of practitioners. In a certain sense the achievement of the good this way also presents a rupture in the relationship between the couple and the child, who has been conceived by activities external to the marriage practice. So, while a good is achieved, the achievement of this good by means excluded from the practice puts the rest of the internal goods of the practice in peril and alters the relationship between this couple and the rest of the practicing community for the worse. Conception apart from conjugal intercourse, for example, jeopardizes the foundational character of the interpersonal union. The good of the child is separated from this interpersonal union, not originating from it directly as it would if the child were conceived naturally.

On all the levels of MacIntyre's definition, then, marriage is aptly understood as a practice. First, it is a complex, (normatively) coherent set of cooperative human activity that is socially established. Second, it has certain internal goods (e.g., interpersonal union, conjugal fecundity) and standards of excellence and virtue (poverty, chastity, and obedience, as well as exclusivity and permanence) partially definitive of the practice. Finally, the virtues required for the practice extend the internal goods and the standards of excellence.

---

55. Conjugal fecundity, or the integral good of the child, extends beyond biological procreation. For example, conjugal fecundity for a Christian couple might involve adopting an HIV-positive child, spending significant time working in a missionary foster home or orphanage, or living and working at Boys Town and Girls Town.

Speaking of Marriage—Relationship or Practice?

David Matzko McCarthy and Jana Bennett

McCarthy and Bennett enter this discussion assuming marriage is a practice and setting it within two grammars: reproductive and eschatological. McCarthy offers a reproductive narrative.[56] His narrative suggests that marriage and family, as reproductive institutions, naturally reproduce not only human persons with certain virtues, vices, and desires, but an economy—that is, a way of ordering and transacting ourselves and our resources.

McCarthy argues that a dominant cause of the problem with marriage is economic, but not in the sense that Cahill points out. Cahill attends to the economic impact of poverty, while McCarthy emphasizes the economic impact of middle-class life. The Western world, he argues, operates on a market economy of *desire* wherein the principal participant is the autonomous individual and the central form of relationship is the contract—despite the glut of market and political rhetoric stating that the family is the source of society. As he concludes, "the family is steward to the state, and it will perform its function well if familial relations serve the dominant market economy. Children enter the public sphere primarily as consumers who dispose of their parents' income."[57] Being spouses and being family have become more an endeavor of what we consume together in the pursuit of making emotional connection in leisure than what we produce together in the pursuit of substantive connections and a common good.[58] The problem is that marriage and family are reproducing the wrong kind of economic social order. They

---

56. David Matzko McCarthy, *Sex and Love in the Home: A Theology of the Household* (London: SCM, 2001), 243–47.

57. Ibid., 69.

58. "Substantive connections" are those that dispose persons to act for each other's good apart from one's own immediate satisfaction. Persons will be connected substantially inasmuch as they work to achieve common goods. A substantive connection might be a virtue, a child, a home.

Speaking of Marriage—Relationship or Practice?

are acting as the stewards for the wrong institution. They are looking to reproduce the basic unit of the wrong kind of society—the autonomous individualist secular state.

Bennett's contribution likewise finds marriage and family in crisis because too much has been expected of them as affective centers of gravity.[59] "Browning, among others, has made these [largely feminist] concerns ultimate precisely by suggesting that the savior of the world, or at least of our broken American society, must be a good, functioning family."[60] Bennett rejects this narrative on the grounds that it is ecclesiologically wrong-headed and "leads to falsely eschatological ideals." Marriage and family are not first civil institutions standing *alongside* the Church. Instead, they are institutional realities given identity, shape, and accountability primarily by the Church as household of God—of which the family is a domestic instantiation—and only secondarily in civil society and the state.[61] Furthermore, rejecting the "false eschatology" that sees the salvation of human society in the human family based on biological kinship, Bennett argues that human society needs bonds thicker than blood—namely, the bonds created by the waters of baptism.[62] The problem, then, is not a lack of concern for the family. On the contrary, we have spent entirely too much thought, energy, and hopes on the family as primary locus of human belonging and capital hope for the creation of a better world.[63] Too many keyboard strokes at-

---

59. Jana M. Bennett, *Water Is Thicker Than Blood: An Augustinian Spirituality of Marriage and Singleness* (Oxford: Oxford University, 2008).
60. Ibid., 155.   61. Ibid., 141.
62. Ibid., 31.
63. Ironically, Bennett finds that John Paul II's "theology of the body" does not give marriage enough eschatological importance. Interpreting him primarily through the work of Angelo Cardinal Scola, *The Nuptial Mystery*, trans. Michelle K. Borras (Grand Rapids, Mich.: Eerdmans, 2005), Bennett finds that John Paul II's approach to marriage locates it on the mundane pole of the continuum between the world now and the eschaton, while isolating consecrated life on the eschatological end of the pole; Bennett, *Water Is Thicker Than Blood*, 16–19.

Speaking of Marriage—Relationship or Practice?

tend to how uniquely marriage will fix the world while too few focus on what common "domestic" practices are shared by married and nonmarried Catholics. Furthermore, theologies of the family tend to forget about the "domestic" concerns of the all states of life in the Church (whether married or consecrated religious). Therein lie McCarthy's and Bennett's solutions—theologies of the "household" rather than theologies of the family.[64]

For McCarthy, to end the crisis of marriage and family with a theology of the household, we must "set ourselves to cultivating a social landscape that reproduces love and passion of a different kind."[65] David Matzko McCarthy offers a narrative of married householding as the practice of reproducing the Church's story of God from generation to generation, in mission, worship, and pedagogy, reproducing Christ's presence in the world again and again. McCarthy attempts "to make sense of marriage as a sacrament, that is, marriage as a set of practices that do not stand in isolation, but are open to be transformed by God's gracious communion *as it is routinized in the social body of the Church.*"[66] The practice of marriage takes root in reciprocity and asymmetrical relationships of gratuitous giving, ultimately grounded in our asymmetrically gratuitous relationship of gratitude to God.

McCarthy argues that, instead of setting apart the couple as a nuclear unit, marriage enmeshes a couple within "a larger network of preferential loves," a specifically ecclesial network wherein "sexual practices have a grammar of belonging."[67] Rooted in ecclesial identity, marriage must be understood in terms of the task shared by all Christians. For McCarthy, "the common task of all Christians is to

---

64. Bennett, *Water Is Thicker Than Blood*, introduction and chap. 1.
65. Ibid., 64.
66. McCarthy, *Sex and Love in the Home*, 247 (emphasis mine).
67. Ibid., 246–47.

accept God's invitation to share Christ's body in the Eucharist, which means to have our bodies be formed by our call to discipleship and by our place in the one body of the Church. God's invitation is our call to live out God's hospitality as members of the body of Christ."[68]

In direct opposition to relational paradigm's conclusion that the unity chiefly sought in marriage is the conjugal union itself, McCarthy asserts that "indifference to private unions is not possible in the Church, for the *unity of Christ's* body is always the *central* concern.... Marriage and family conform to wider institutional practices and are called upon to support goods that *are not particular to marriage* or private family life."[69] McCarthy continues, relativizing the uniqueness and centrality of the marital relationship. The conjugal relationship is sacramentally set within the context of Christ's relationship to the Church. Furthermore, the relationship characterizes and contains a call "to live out practices of love and care that are definable apart from marriage (like fraternal correction and forgiveness). Marriage is only a particular instantiation of common practices of the Christian life."[70] Also countermanding the relationship paradigm, McCarthy argues "that that standard conception of interpersonal union offers an inadequate context for sexual practices" because it is dislocated from place and community, isolated in romantic moments and individual, voluntaristic, and contractual yet largely affective arrangements.[71] Set within the context of the liturgical, pastoral, and charitable practices of the Church, marriage should involve sexual and social practices of reciprocity, self-control, obedience, hospitality, and faithfulness. These practices are

---

68. Ibid., 221.
69. Ibid., 216 (emphasis mine).
70. Ibid., 216–17.
71. Ibid., 239. McCarthy considers this interpersonal union model to be too focused on the spouses themselves so that it results in their becoming lost in an I-Thou stare, and the spouses eventually become disenchanted when their relationship is not as fulfilling as it was hoped.

Speaking of Marriage—Relationship or Practice?

ultimately rooted in the asymmetric relations of grateful reciprocity between each person and the God who creates and redeems them.

For her part, Bennett prefers to call marriage a participation in the mystery of Christ and the Church rather than to call the Church a participation in the family. The household of God holds primacy of place in the life of the Christian, and the household of spouses ought to be worked out as part of this larger household. In Bennett's thinking, some of the domestic church activities that Catholic theologians Cahill and McGinnis advocate lack a strong, essential connection to or location within ecclesial life as Bennett understands it.[72] It is not enough to work for peace and justice; the Christian household must do so liturgically and sacramentally. Only the combination of peace-and-justice orientation along with rich liturgical and sacramental practices completely "reconfigures" the household ecclesially, making it a participation in Christ's and the Church's current eschatological orientation toward the household of God.[73] The power of Bennett's proposal is that by using the term "household," she can better integrate married, single nonvowed, and consecrated religious life as complementary ways of being household, each of which participates in one ecclesial reality seeking the goal of holiness—namely, life in the household of God. It is this insight that I will be developing in succeeding chapters.

A Critique of Marriage as Practice

Of course, the notion of marriage as practice carries its own costs. First, its resistance to the notion of marriage as relationship might

---

72. Bennett, *Water Is Thicker Than Blood*, 146. She goes on to fill out the claim with an exposition of Augustine's *City of God* (146–53). Bennett considers Cahill's and McGinnis's thoughts on domestic church to be focused on this-worldly justice and peace at the expense of eschatological beatitude, justice, and peace. Without the eschatological pole, which is essential to the Church's identity, it would be inappropriate to call the family "domestic church."
73. Ibid., 135.

Speaking of Marriage—Relationship or Practice?

seem to open the way for an assault on the sacramental indissolubility of marriage. If marriage is a practice, then it would seem that if the practice fails, then the marriage itself disappears. The marriage-as-relationship paradigm could answer this problem by postulating an ontological and indestructible bond between the spouses created as their marriage begins. A potential answer to such a critique from the perspective of practice would be to say that marriage is an ecclesially determined practice with its own ontological reality guaranteed by God, a reality to which the couple irrevocably consent and indissolubly enact by consummation. Whether or not they continue to excel in the practice, or even if they reject it entirely, the practice and their consent to it remain.[74] Furthermore, one might argue that marriage is a cruciform practice (often being placed on the cross by one's own spouse).[75] Were there no crosses to bear, no sin begging for forgiveness, there would be little Christian about the marriage. Marriage is a particular practice of telling the story of Christ's life, death, and resurrection. As such, it is a practice of requiring resources external to the spousal nucleus, especially the supernatural help of grace found explicitly in the sacraments of the Eucharist and reconciliation. In other words, if spouses stop living with each other and begin cohabiting with other people, their marriage is not gone; they are merely being unfaithful to its practice. In the absence of their doing the practice, the practice still exists, because they do not

---

74. Peter F. Ryan and Germain Grisez made a similar argument about the indissolubility of marriage from the perspective of relationship based on the difference between the act of consenting to marriage and the promises then made regarding how one will live out that institution consented to; see their "Indissoluble Marriage," 369–415.

75. In Lonergan's terms one could say that marriage witnesses to the way of the Cross: "This is why the Son of God became man, suffered, died, and was raised again: because divine wisdom has ordained and divine goodness has willed, not to do away with the evils of the human race through power, but to convert those evils into a supreme good according to the just and mysterious Law of the Cross"; Bernard Lonergan, *De Verbo Incarnato*, trans. Charles Hefling (Rome: Gregorian University, 1964), Thesis 17, 552; see Robert Doran, "The Nonviolent Cross: Lonergan and Girard on Redemption," *Theological Studies* 71 (2010): 46–61.

define it themselves. The practice predates the couple and is situated socially, ecclesially, rather than privately and individually. The practice endures even if the couple break faith with the virtues, activities, and goods internal to the practice.

Second, in suggesting a comparison between the practices of marriage and the practices of other ways to be Church (e.g., monastic life), this paradigm risks confusing Christian states of life or collapsing the various states of life into one another. The tradition of the Church has been to assert a unique character to a life modeled on the vows of the evangelical counsels, but viewing this way of life as of a kind with married and nonvowed single life may further deteriorate the already waning interest in and honor for a life consecrated to Christ through the evangelical counsels.

Finally, one might argue that all this practice language (just as all that relationship language) lacks a theological foundation in Christ and the Trinity.[76] We can say that marriage is a practice of the Church, but how do we justify using ecclesial language? To begin, MacIntyre's definition of the word "practice" lacks any explicit connection to theology at all, let alone the Church, Christ, and the Trinity. McCarthy's account of marital practice was rooted in the theological principle of God's gratuitous love in creation and redemption, but he does not flesh out the full Christological implications of this principle, and the inner communion of the Trinity only briefly factors into his account of the order of love. For her part, Bennett's account of marriage as a practice has a stronger connection to the Church. She prioritizes baptismal bonds between Christians over kinship and conjugal bonds. She even begins to look into

---

76. Julie Hanlon Rubio's recent, helpful monograph, *Family Ethics: Practices for Christian Families* (Washington, D.C.: Georgetown University Press, 2010), was organized around five practices: sex, eating, tithing, serving, and prayer. Not unsurprisingly, the explicitly ecclesial practices of poverty, chastity, and obedience found no place in her treatment.

the life of the Church for examples of Christian householding, suggesting that married and single people can participate in the same ecclesial goods. However, she does not go far enough in providing a rich theological account of these goods and how the lives of all who are in Christ can share in the one practice of Christian householding. The marriage-as-practice paradigm has not done enough to identify exactly what it is that the lives of the married and the consecrated religious share as their common practice. There has been work on principles of these two states of life as forms of Christian householding, but these practices remain ungrounded in Christology and the Trinity.

Conclusion

This chapter has provided a landscape on which to locate authors and narratives in the vast field of theology of marriage and family in terms of the paradigms of marriage as a relationship and as a practice. Each of these paradigms is helpful for talking about marriage, but each must be supplemented by the new language that I will offer: the language typically reserved for consecrated religious life, the language of the evangelical virtues, "regular" life, and long-term preparation and formation.

    I believe that the challenges facing marriage today are explicitly answered by renewing our awareness and understanding of the primary context and purpose of Christian marriage. Christian marriage is set principally within the Church, the household of God, the mystical body of Christ, the bride of Christ. The purpose of marriage is to bring about the sanctification of the spouses and all others in their household by the sharing of the whole of life and love (*consortium vitae et amoris*). This means that spouses must see their marriage as a relationship constituted in the domestic practice of being conformed to Christ the poor, chaste, and obedient bridegroom who is also the second Person of the trinitarian communion of Persons.

This goal and location of marriage is consonant with the goal and location of consecrated religious life, both of which are domestic practices of being consecrated and conformed to Christ. The practice of married life and the practice of consecrated religious life enact these ends distinctly, but, nonetheless, they share them equally. The language of the evangelical virtues of poverty, chastity, and obedience, the idea of a life lived according to a rule, and a robust preparation and continued formation along the lines of a novitiate may describe married life as properly as religious life.

In the proceeding chapters I will make a case for why the language typically reserved for consecrated religious life can be proper to marriage, and then I will explore marriage in light of that language. This language will fill in where relationship paradigm needs to be reminded that the relationship itself exists in and for the conformation of each spouse to Christ the poor, chaste, and obedient bridegroom. Furthermore, the relation of the spouses should also take as its image the communion of Persons in the Trinity. The practice paradigm needs to be reminded that the social setting of the practice is not the couple itself or the state but principally the Church, and so its standards of excellence are none other than Christ's own poverty, chastity, and obedience, and its model is none other than the trinitarian communion of Persons' love.

2

IS MARRIAGE MADE IN A MONASTERY?

Universal Vocation

Assuming that marriage is in crisis, and assuming the various ways of speaking about marriage (as relationship or as practice) do not give married couples all they need to live out their vocation, why hypothesize that language typically reserved for consecrated religious life also belongs to marriage and can help marriage? Three theological ideas serve as a heuristic for such a hypothesis: universal vocation, baptismal consecration, and vows. The most obvious connection between the two states of life is the common destiny and vocation of all the baptized to a life of Christian perfection[1] or holiness as expressed in the documents of the Second Vatican Council.[2] In *Lumen gentium*

---

1. "Perfection" typically requires an object. Perfection is the complete enactment of a potency. Therefore, the Council often pairs "perfection" with some other word. For example, the Council speaks of the "perfection of holiness" (*LG* 11) and the "perfection of charity" (*LG* 39, 40). Thus, even when we see the religious life referred to in the tradition as the life of "perfection," we should bear in mind what one is setting out to perfect—namely, Christ's own virtues of poverty, chastity, and obedience.

2. While the Second Vatican Council explicitly stated the universal call to Christian perfection or holiness, this teaching was not entirely new; see *Sacra virginitas* 46, http://www.vatican.va, accessed April 30, 2013. Dolores Leckey, in her popular monograph *The Ordinary Way: A Family Spirituality* (New York: Crossroad, 1989), 1–2, begins her work looking

the Council states, "The chosen People of God is one: 'one Lord, one faith, one baptism' [Eph 4:5]; sharing a common dignity as members from their regeneration in Christ, having the same filial grace and the same vocation to perfection; possessing in common one salvation, one hope, and one undivided charity."[3] Beginning chapter 5, on the Universal Call to Holiness, the Council affirms that each Christian "is called to holiness." Christ, they continue:

> the divine Teacher and Model of all *perfection,* preached holiness of life to each and every one of His disciples of every condition. He Himself stands as the author and consummator of this holiness of life: "Be you therefore *perfect,* even as your heavenly Father is *perfect* [Mt 5:48]." By the power of baptism, the faithful "truly become sons of God and sharers in the divine nature.... Then too, by God's gift, they must hold on to and *complete* in their lives this holiness they have received.[4]

"Thus it is evident to everyone," states *Lumen gentium:*

> that all the faithful of Christ of whatever rank or status, are called to the *fullness* of the Christian life and to the *perfection of charity*.... In order that the faithful may reach *this perfection,* they must use their strength accordingly as they have received it, as a gift from Christ. They must follow in His footsteps and conform themselves to *His image* seeking the will of the Father in all things.[5]

---

for practical insights for married people in monastic life with the call of the Second Vatican Council. She also invokes John Paul II's 1980 Synod on the Family; *Ordinary Way,* 5–6.

3. *LG* 32.

4. Ibid., 39 (emphasis mine). Here the Council begins by noting how Christ makes the entire Church perfect as his one bride by the power of the Holy Spirit. Within this one Church that will be finally perfected, each Christian is called to personal perfection in the imitation of Christ, who "is believed to be indefectibly holy."

5. Ibid., 39–40 (emphasis mine). To follow in Christ's footsteps would mean sharing his virtues of poverty, chastity, and obedience. In *Vita consecrata* 30 (hereafter *VC*), John Paul II explicitly states that the poverty, chastity, and obedience are in a certain sense evangelical imperatives: "In fact, all those reborn in Christ are called to live out with the strength which is the Spirit's gift the chastity appropriate to their state of life, obedience to God and to the Church, and a reasonable detachment from material possessions"; *VC* 30, http://www.vatican.va, accessed April 30, 2013.

Is Marriage Made in a Monastery?

As the Council has it, the call to complete, perfect holiness that is an imitation of Christ is not limited to some upper-crust of Christians (it never truly was) but is the vocation of all; "Fortified by so many and such helpful means of salvation, all the faithful, whatever their condition or state, are called by the Lord, each in his own way, to that [perfection of holiness] whereby the Father Himself is perfect."[6] This statement is particularly important for its location within the dogmatic constitution. This sentence serves as its own paragraph and as a conclusion to the first section on the universal priesthood of the people of God. It immediately follows a paragraph treating the power of the sacraments in the life of the Christian, and it specifically links the pursuit of holiness to marriage and religious life. The paragraph preceding this sentence contains the momentous identification of the family as the "domestic church,"[7] wherein the parents are the first teachers of the faith and the first to encourage their children toward their own proper vocation, with special attention to the religious vocation.

Post–Vatican II theology has made much of the insight that all are called to Christian perfection, but few have taken their egalitarian sentiment to its logical *telos*.[8] Rather than being seen as an invi-

---

6. LG 11: *"Tot ac tantis salutaribus mediis muniti, christifideles omnes, cuiusvis conditionis ac status, ad perfectionem sanctitatis qua Pater ipse perfectus est, sua quisque via, a Domino vocantur."* I have altered the translation here to emphasize what is being perfected.

7. The interesting history of the term "domestic church" at the Second Vatican Council has been well documented by Michael Fahey, "The Christian Family as Domestic Church at Vatican II," in *The Family*, edited by Lisa Sowle Cahill and Dietmar Mieth, 85–92 (Maryknoll, N.Y.: Orbis, 1995). Bishop Pietro Fiordelli's intervention at the 34th general congregation (December 5, 1962) was to argue that the Constitution on the Church required a substantial section on marriage. He argued that the smallest division of the Church was not the diocese but the Christian family. His evidence was patristic: John Chrysostom and Augustine. For both of these authors, the family shares in the evangelical, charitable, and educational ministries of the Church but not the ministry of the sacraments.

8. Authors vigorously take up the universal call to holiness, but in the call they hear the confirmation and sacralization of current practices of marrying and householding. Understood less as a call to alternative ways of living marriage and family life, it is heard too frequently as a mere blessing and renaming of practices that already exist. Florence Caffrey

tation to the rest of the laity to take up the greatest commandment and the evangelical counsels according to their own state of life, it has meant a virtual rejection of the evangelical counsels, especially celibacy, as helpful for Christian perfection.[9] In contrast to this tendency, the Council encourages the universality of the life of the evangelical counsels, a Christoform life. The Council states that the holiness manifested by those who live the evangelical counsels is the one holiness of the Church, the *sanctitas Ecclesiae*. This one holiness is not individual, but universal:

> This holiness of the Church is unceasingly manifested ... it is expressed in many ways in individuals, who in their walk of life, tend toward the perfection of charity, thus causing the edification of others; in a very special way this [holiness] appears in the practice of the counsels, customarily called "evangelical." This practice of the counsels, under the impulsion of the Holy Spirit, undertaken by many Christians, either privately or in a Church-approved condition or state of life, gives and must give in the world an outstanding witness and example of this same holiness.[10]

Bourg, in *Where Two or Three Are Gathered: Christian Families as Domestic Churches* (Notre Dame, Ind.: University of Notre Dame Press, 2004), 28, claims that it is only after the Second Vatican Council that the family is rediscovered as a context for living out the general Christian vocation. Moreover, Bourg identifies the crux of the problems surrounding theologies of "domestic church" after the Second Vatican Council: does the family model itself on the Church or does the Church model itself on the family? Unfortunately, answers to this question, as Bourg points out, have become embroiled in the same turf wars typically seen between "progressive" and "conservative" camps—where "progressives" see diverse families as informing and changing the nature of what it means to be Church and "conservatives" restrict and repress the move in this direction. Bourg's own tendency is to emphasize the family as a source for understanding what it means to be Church.

9. At the demographic level the number of men and women religious has dropped significantly since the Second Vatican Council; see Kenneth Jones, *Index of Leading Catholic Indicators: The Church Since Vatican II* (St. Louis, Mo.: Oriens, 2003). On the other hand, women now make up approximately 83 percent of all lay ministers; see John L. Allen Jr., "Lay Ecclesial Ministry and the Feminization of the Church," in *National Catholic Reporter*, June 29, 2007. He relies on 2005 census data.

10. *LG* 39.

Is Marriage Made in a Monastery?

The authors continue, briefly noting how each state in life can manifest the one holiness of the Church by living out in particular the general call to Christian perfection of charity:

> Married couples and Christian parents should follow their own proper path [to holiness] by faithful love. They should sustain one another in grace throughout the entire length of their lives. They should imbue their offspring, lovingly welcomed as God's gift, with Christian doctrine and the *evangelical virtues*.[11]

The Council even goes as far as to suggest that all Christians are obliged to strive for a life of the counsels:

> Therefore, all the faithful of Christ are invited [and held to pursuing] the holiness and perfection of their own proper state. Indeed they have an obligation to so strive.... Let neither the use of the things of this world nor attachment to riches, which is against the spirit of evangelical poverty, hinder them in their quest for perfect love.[12]

---

11. *LG* 41 (emphasis mine). "To holiness" is not in the Latin text, but the context clearly suggests its inclusion in the English. The English renders "*totius vitae decursu*" as "throughout the entire length of their lives," but "*totius vitae*" also carries the meaning of the entire content of life. "*Decursu*" should not limit the meaning to the duration of the fidelity. A total fidelity in all parts of life for the entire duration of life is intended. The desire to invite all Christians to the quest for Christian perfection of holiness as a response to God's grace is necessarily tied to the doctrine that there is one common origin and one common destiny of man. The universal call to holiness is also emphasized in John Paul II's attempt in *Veritatis splendor* to renew the moral theological method. "This vocation to perfect love is not restricted to a small group of individuals. *The invitation*, 'go, sell your possessions and give the money to the poor,' and the promise 'you will have treasure in heaven,' *are meant for everyone*, because they bring out the full meaning of the commandment of love of neighbor"; *Veritatis splendor* 18, http://www.vatican.va, accessed April 30, 2013; see also Servais Pinckaers, "An Encyclical for the Future: *Veritatis Splendor*," in *Veritatis Splendor and the Renewal of Moral Theology: Studies by Ten Outstanding Scholars*, edited by J. A. Di Noia and Romanus P. Cessario, 35 (Princeton, N.J.: Scepter, 1999).

12. *LG* 41, 42. The English translation on the Vatican website omits "*et tenentur*" from the translation; I have placed it back. Also, the English translation from the Vatican website renders "*Omnes igitur christifideles ad sanctitatem et proprii status perfectionem prosequendam invitantur et tenentur*" as "Therefore all of the Christian faithful are called to strive for *the* holiness and perfection of their own state of life." One might as easily render this passage "Therefore all of the Christian faithful are called and held to pursuing holiness and perfection of one's proper state of life." Note that this translation does not add the definite article "the" before "holiness and perfection." This second translation is to be preferred, since it is more flexible,

Is Marriage Made in a Monastery?

These exhortations to a life in the image of Christ and suffused with grace toward evangelical virtues come directly before the section on vowed religious life. They suggest that all the laity should strive toward the virtues (chastity, poverty, and obedience) expressed in the life of those who explicitly vow a life in the pattern of poverty, chastity, and obedience. If a theology of marriage and family is to take seriously the universal call to holiness in Christian perfection, then it ought to investigate the manners and practices of how married couples can strive toward that Christian perfection as an act of receiving God's grace worked out in a life of evangelical virtue. Taking the words of the Council to heart, then, one at least has reason to begin this study, to ask whether there is a further theological bond between the vowed religious and married ways of life.

Common Consecration and Vows

The thesis of this section is that marriage and religious life share the foundation of baptismal consecration to Christ and that both are called to perfect that consecration through their own set of vows. The purpose of making the argument is to further the consonance between the religious and conjugal states as vowed ways of life, to show that speaking of poverty, chastity, and obedience in marriage is not a "monasticization," but the particular conjugal specification of baptismal consecration. It is of little consequence that both states would involve vows *simpliciter*; the real upshot is that both are ecclesial vows—that is, they situate Christians more deeply within the life of the Church.

Church doctrine on both marriage and religious life shows that both of these states are rooted in and are specific intensifications

---

allowing for a distinction between "holiness" and "perfection of one's proper state of life" *or* a conjunction of the two.

of one common consecration to Christ.[13] First, the baptismal consecration is common to all, not just as individuals, but as the one household of God, the one body of Christ: "The baptized, by regeneration and the anointing of the Holy Spirit, are consecrated as a spiritual house and a holy priesthood." Second, baptismal consecration is primary, beyond any denominational commitments. All Christians "are consecrated by baptism, in which they are united with Christ."[14] Furthermore, the document on the renewal of religious life calls this life a special consecration, "which is deeply rooted in that [consecration] of baptism and expresses it more fully.[15] The religious consecration itself is characterized in continuity with the one baptismal consecration: "Indeed through Baptism a person dies to sin and is consecrated to God. However, in order that he may" pursue Christian perfection he vows to live the evangelical counsels whereby "he is more intimately consecrated to divine service."[16] Finally, conjugal consecration appears to be a similar reality. In celebrating and receiving the sacrament of marriage, Christian spouses "receive a kind of consecration in the duties and dignity of their state." This consecration allows them to "increasingly advance the perfection of their own personalities, as well as their mutual sanctification, and hence contribute jointly to the glory of God."[17] Furthermore, these words from the Rite of Christian Marriage reiterate the fact: Christ "has already consecrated you in baptism and now he enriches and strengthens you by a special sacrament so that you may assume the duties of marriage in mutual and lasting fidelity."[18] Marriage and religious life, then, share the fundamental theo-

---

13. See *LG* 10.   14. *LG* 15.
15. Second Vatican Council, *Perfectae caritatis* 1, 5, 11, 17 (hereafter *PC*), http://www.vatican.va, accessed April 30, 2013.
16. *LG* 44.   17. *GS* 48.
18. See 1969's *Ordo Celebrandi Matrimonium* (Rome: Typis Polyglottis Vaticanis, 1969 [hereafter *OCM*]), no. 23. References to the Latin of the rite will be from the revised version,

logical character of consecration as unique enactments of the one baptismal consecration.

Not only do married life and religious life share the concept of consecration, but both enter that consecrated state through vows. This fact is obvious when it comes to religious life, but contrary to popular understandings of marriage, neither the rite of marriage nor canon law refers to anything in the celebration of matrimony as a vow. Therefore, I will have to make a case that "vow" accurately describes what spouses do in the rite. The key words from the *Ordo Celebrandi Matrimonium* (hereafter, *OCM*) are *consensus, manifestastis,* and *promittere* (*OCM* 60–64),[19] and key words from the *Codex Iuris Canonici* are *foedus* (*CIC* 1055), *contractus* (*CIC* 1055.2), and *tradere* (*CIC* 1057.2). Words central to both are *consensus* and *accipere* (*OCM* 60–64 and *CIC* 1057.2; 1095–1107). The person assisting the marriage first asks about the *intentus* of the couple (*Interrogationes ante consensum*). The spouses then express (*exprimere*) and manifest (*manifestare*) their consent in the presence of God and Church (*coram Deo eiusque Ecclesia consensum vestrum exprimite*) by means of answers to questions or by recitation of promises (*promittere*).[20] The person assisting then formally receives the consent (*receptio consensus*) that the spouses just manifested in the presence of the Church (*coram Ecclesia manifestastis*).[21]

Let us now establish that the giving of intent and consent in the wedding rite fulfills the definition of public, solemn vow given in canon law as it refers particularly to the vows of religious life. Canon law defines "vow" as "a deliberate and free promise made to God

---

the *Ordo Celebrandi Matrimonium*, editio typica altera (Rome: Typis Polyglottis Vaticanis, 1991 [hereafter *OCM* 1991]), which has no official English translation publicly released. I will note wherever the Latin differs from the 1969 *OCM*. The English of the rite will come from the 1969 International Committee on English in the Liturgy translation.

19. See *OCM* (1991): 16–19.   20. *OCM* 61:17.
21. *OCM* (1991): 64:18.

Is Marriage Made in a Monastery?

about a possible and better good, [one that] must be fulfilled by reason of the virtue of religion."[22] First, is the marital consent (or vow) "deliberate" and "free"? The answer is yes. These facts are established three ways: (1) by the common practice in dioceses of the United States to require a six-month period of preparation before marriage can be solemnized in a Catholic parish; (2) by the priest's investigation of impediments (e.g., the banns); and (3) in the three questions of intent before the fiancés formally manifest their consent. The priest asks, "Have you come here freely and without reservation to give yourselves to each other in marriage? Will you love and honor each other as man and wife for the rest of your lives? Will you accept children lovingly from God, and bring them up according to the law of Christ and his Church?"[23] The first question requires the couple to declare their freedom to marry and their deliberate desire to marry. The second and third questions verify that they intend the same things about marriage that the Church intends—that is, it asks the couple to express their deliberate intent to contract a marriage as understood by the Church. That the consent be deliberate is clear also from rotal jurisprudence; ignorance can prevent a marriage from being valid.[24] The giving of marital consent, then, is necessarily free and deliberate.

Second, is marriage a "promise made to God"? Yes. Spouses say, "*Promitto me tibi fidem servaturum*" (I promise to preserve faithful-

---

22. CIC 1191.1; 1192.1–3: "More specifically, a vow is *public* if a legitimate superior accepts it in the name of the Church; otherwise, it is *private*. A vow is solemn if the Church has recognized it as such; otherwise, it is simple. A vow is *personal* if the person making the vow promises an action; *real* if the person making the vow promises some thing; *mixed* if it shares the nature of a personal and a real vow" (emphasis mine).

23. "*Venistisne huc sine coactione, sed libero et pleno corde ad Matrimonium contrahendum?*" OCM (1991): 60.

24. See Jerry M. Sherba, "Canon 1096: Ignorance as a Ground for Nullity," *Canon Law Society of America, Proceedings* 59 (1997): 282–99; Elissa Rinere, "Error Which Causes the Contract," *Studia Canonica* 38, no. 1 (2004): 65–84.

ness to you).²⁵ The other form avoids "promise" (*promitto*) entirely; instead, this second form (approved in the United States and without a Latin text) uses "take." "I, N., take you, N., for my lawful ..." (*OCM* 1969: 25, in *The Rites,* 542). Whether or not the word "promise" is used, couples bind themselves by word to certain actions on behalf of and to certain dispositions toward the spouse. The consent, therefore, involves making a promise regardless of the term's appearance in the rite. Furthermore, the Catechism of the Catholic Church states that "Baptism and Confirmation, Matrimony and Holy Orders always entail promises."²⁶

Third, is the giving of consent a promise made "*to God*"? Yes. The marriage rite is set up with the assumption that the consent is expressed in the presence of God and the Church (*coram Deo eisusque Ecclesia consensum vestrum exprimite*).²⁷ In addition, the situation of the marital consent within a liturgy characterizes the activity as an act of worship. The only legitimate object of worship is God. All liturgical actions, then, including the consent of marriage, are directed toward God. Thus we can say the promise is made to God. Finally, since the ministers of the sacrament are the spouses themselves, we could thus read the text as a promise to God mediated by the spouse, assisted by the priest or deacon, and witnessed by the body of the Church.

Fourth, is the giving of marital consent a "free and deliberate promise made to God *about a possible and better good*"? We cannot

---

25. The current English translation has the couple saying, "I promise to be true to you"; *OCM* (1969): 25. This official translation allows the suggestion that the spouses are actually making promises to God about their relationship to each other.

26. *Catechism of the Catholic Church* (hereafter *CCC*), 2101; see also Aquinas, ST II-II, q. 88, a. 1, s.c.: "It is written (Ecclesiastes 5:3): 'If thou hast vowed anything to God, defer not to pay it, for an unfaithful and foolish promise displeaseth Him.' Therefore to vow is to promise, and a vow is a promise." For Aquinas, three things are essential to a vow: "the first is deliberation. The second is a purpose of the will; and the third is a promise, wherein is completed the nature of a vow"; ST II-II, q. 88, a. 1, resp.

27. *OCM* (1991): 61.

Is Marriage Made in a Monastery?

answer "yes" or "no" to this question before asking another: vows concern promises about a good that is "possible and better" than what? Since the canonical definition of a vow follows Aquinas's definition, his clarification on the matter of a vow is instructive here:

> That which is not necessary, neither absolutely, nor on the supposition of an end, is altogether voluntary, and therefore is most properly the matter of a vow. And this is said to be a greater good in comparison with that which is universally necessary for salvation.[28]

It is not necessary for salvation that a person indissolubly, irrevocably bind herself to another as a partner in seeking sanctification through a *consortium vitae et amoris,* yet this is the substance of marital consent. Because it is voluntary, making a commitment to work for the salvation of at least one person (i.e., the spouse and any children that might arrive) can be considered a better good than making no commitment to seek any particular person's salvation. The marital consent promises a better good than a nonvowed celibate life because it takes on duties and obligations beyond those required of the Christian life in general—namely, the practices and duties of marriage as an ecclesial practice of Christian householding, a *consortium totius vitae et amoris.*

Finally, does the expression of marital consent establish duties that "must be fulfilled by reason of the virtue of religion"? The virtue of religion, according to Aquinas, belongs under the species of "justice," as religion is the virtue of giving to God what is God's due.[29] Understood thus, fulfilling the duties of marriage must be seen as acts of devotion to God, acts of worship. The liturgical and especially the suggested eucharistic setting of the marriage rite suggests that marital duties are fulfilled by virtue of religion. The spouses are encouraged to contextualize their own consent to love and honor one

---

28. Aquinas, ST II-II, q. 88, a. 2, resp.
29. Aquinas, ST II-II, q. 81, articles 1, 2.

Is Marriage Made in a Monastery?

another within the Lord's consent to love his Church and give himself to the Church in his life, death, and resurrection. The couple's marriage is situated within the prayer over the gifts, the eucharistic memorial, and the eucharistic preface. In this way the spouses are invited to see their own future self-sacrifice as participations in Christ's own paschal mystery made present in the celebration of the Eucharist.[30]

The case has been clearly made, now, that the action of consenting to the marital covenant can be characterized as a vow. The upshot of this fact is that marriage can be more fully understood as a participation in vowed ecclesial life, not because married people are borrowing some aspect of what is proper only to religious life, but because both are sharing in a common ecclesial practice of making vows about particular manners of living in God's household.

Marriage and Consecrated Life in Recent Scholarship: A Zero-Sum Game

The question of a consonance between vowed religious life and married life is not entirely untrodden ground. The common method for putting married life in direct conversation with vowed religious life has been to begin with a narrative. The now-standard narrative follows this pattern: the historical Jesus radically resisted the idolatry of Greco-Roman and Jewish first-century householding: its patriarchy and its tendency to close off the outsider.[31] Jesus him-

---

30. *OCM* (1991): 231–39:74–77; see *The Rites of the Catholic Church: As Revised by Decree of the Second Vatican Council and Published by Authority of Pope Paul VI*, trans. International Commission on English in the Liturgy (New York: Pueblo, 1978) [orig. pub. 1969], 543–45, 563–69.

31. John Howard Yoder, *The Politics of Jesus: Vicit Agnus Noster*, 2nd ed. (Grand Rapids, Mich.: Eerdmans, 1994), chap. 9. He considers the writers of Colossians, Ephesians, and 1 Peter to have called married people to "revolutionary subordination" that is more or less in continuity with Jesus' own insights on the participation in the family. The goal of the gospel is not to use righteous violence to change idolatrous social structures, but to witness to the fact

self lived a celibate life and called disciples to a kind of life that may have required a conflicted departure from the kinship household;[32] his practice and theory amounted to the support for what could be called a right to remain unmarried, a subordination of the earthly household to the spiritual household of believers. St. Paul, in his eschatological fervor, his desire to open Christians to broader love of neighbor, or simply out of his philosophical tendencies, preferred celibacy to marriage.[33] Some chose the path of celibacy and austerity as an attempt to follow Christ more closely, prepare for martyrdom, live a life of penance, or master their sin and do battle with the devil. Early treatises on chastity and virginity focus on the perfection of virtue and the offering of one's complete self, body and soul, exclusively to God, rather than imitation of Jesus.[34] The silent majority of Christians, though, married.[35] The early Church recog-

---

that Christ has already overcome and defeated them. They fall away, while Christ's kingdom remains and is fulfilled.

32. Wolfgang Stegemann, "The Contextual Ethics of Jesus," in *The Social Setting of Jesus and the Gospels,* edited by Wolfgang Stegemann, Bruce J. Malina, and Gerd Theissen, 45–61, at 55–59 (Minneapolis: Fortress Press, 2002) finds no evidence for a direct rejection of the patriarchal kinship model per se in any of the commonly cited passages. Instead, passages such as these reflect Jesus' claim that belonging with Jesus is prior to and in a sense involves "the dissolution of attachment to one's family." Following Jesus then, has a large social cost. It is a rejection of the priority of extending reciprocal relations of mutual service to those in one's kin group (however patriarchal or egalitarian it may be). At the same time, it is a requirement to extend reciprocal relations to social enemies—that is, to give without the hope of getting anything in return.

33. Readers need not reduce Paul's preference for celibate life to philosophical context or eschatological fervor as some authors do, nor do they have reason to argue that his position on this preference changed or would have changed; see Francis J. Moloney, *A Life of Promise: Poverty, Chastity, Obedience,* Consecrated Life Studies 1 (Wilmington, Del.: M. Glazier, 1984), 98–102; Richard B. Hays, *The Moral Vision of the New Testament: A Contemporary Introduction to New Testament Ethics* (San Francisco: HarperSanFrancisco, 1996), 51; and Will Demming's comprehensive treatment of the philosophical sources, in *Paul on Marriage and Celibacy: The Hellenistic Background of 1 Corinthians 7,* 2nd ed. (Grand Rapids, Mich.: Eerdmans, 2004), 1–46.

34. See, for example, Methodius of Olympus, *Symposium: A Treatise on Chastity,* trans. Herbert Musurillo (New York: Newman Press, 1958).

35. See Carol Harrison, "Silent Majority: The Family in Patristic Thought," in *Family in*

nized the good of marriage, but (as this narrative goes) troublesome philosophical tendencies (e.g., stoicism, a Platonic dualism, and gnostic dualism) invaded Christian thinking and resulted in a dubious, skeptical, even fearful stance toward sexuality and therefore marriage.[36] In the confusion, Augustine's theological preference for the virginal life, especially when lived in community, and his skeptical stance toward right use of sexuality in marriage take center stage through the medieval tradition up through the Council of Trent. During this time ecclesiastical institutions develop in light of the Augustinian doctrine, and the pinnacle of Christian life continues to be seen as a renunciation of marriage.[37] Married Christians could attain holiness, too, but only in the following ways: (1) in spite of their marital sexuality; (2) after one spouse dies, allowing the other to take up monastic life; or (3) by renouncing what is essential to marriage—if both spouses take on a celibate life of poverty and prayer—that is, a monastic life. The only way for married people to grow, it would seem, is to import the consecrated religious spirituality.[38] At the same time monastic spirituality apparently owes but a

---

Theological Perspective, edited by Stephen C. Barton, 87–105 (Edinburgh: T. and T. Clark, 1996).

36. See Kim Power, *Veiled Desire: Augustine on Women* (London: Darton, Longman, and Todd, 1995), and John Mahoney, *The Making of Moral Theology* (Oxford: Clarendon Press, 1987) for two typical (but not recommended) analyses of Augustine's thought on sexuality as negative, overly determined by his philosophical commitments, his own sexual obsession, and a latent Manichaeism. For a more historically accurate and complete understanding of Augustine's position on sexuality and the context within which Augustine addressed the issue, see David Hunter, *Marriage, Celibacy, and Heresy in Ancient Christianity: The Jovinianist Controversy*, Oxford Early Christian Studies (New York: Oxford University, 2007).

37. Jana M. Bennett's work too follows the first part of this common narrative: "Throughout Christian history the tendency has been to sharply define and separate marriage and celibacy from each other in ways that have not allowed the Church to draw on the gifts and opportunities of each state of life"; Bennett, "Mark 8: Support for Celibate Singles Alongside Monogamous Married Couples and Their Children," in *School(s) for Conversion: 12 Marks of a New Monasticism*, edited by Rutba House, 112–23, at 117 (Eugene, Ore.: Cascade, 2005).

38. The tendency to think this is not without cause. Augustine does suggest that the holier a couple is, the sooner they will begin abstaining from conjugal intercourse; see Augustine,

Is Marriage Made in a Monastery?

pittance to married life for contributions to the vowed religious pursuit of holiness.[39]

Furthermore, because of the "dark" Augustinian doctrine on sexuality—that it must be excused by various goods (as the means of procreation, or as a remedy for concupiscence, or as an act of mercy on behalf of the weaker spouse)—married people remain second-class Christians until the Second Vatican Council. Finally, we hear, the Church has officially declared two major points: (1) the universal call to holiness and Christian perfection; and (2) the goodness of sexuality in and of itself and the notion that sexuality in marriage is essential to how the married couple achieve holiness in and through

---

De bono coniugali 3, Corpus Scriptorum Ecclesiasticorum Latinorum (hereafter CSEL) (Vienna: 1866–), 41:190–91; translation in Augustine, "The Excellence of Marriage," in *Marriage and Virginity*, trans. Ray Kearney, intro. and notes by David G. Hunter, in part 1 of *The Works of St. Augustine: A Translation for the 21st Century* (Hyde Park, N.Y.: New City Press, 1999), 9:35: "the better persons they are, the earlier they begin by mutual consent to abstain from carnal union"; see also Augustine, *De Genesi adversus manichaeos* 2.19.29, CSEL 91, where Augustine interprets the punishment of Adam and Eve spiritually: "there is no restraint from carnal desire which does not have pain in the beginning, until habit has been bent toward the better part." Even in marriage the proper use of sexuality can be bent toward what is better—the gift of continence. For Augustine even chaste marriage would have included what would be unimaginable amounts of abstinence from intercourse by modern "sexually liberated" standards. He expected chaste married couples to abstain during pregnancy and after menopause entirely. Augustine does not take the position as a way of saying that married people must become monks. Rather, he understands the virtue of continence to be one all persons should seek, whether married or unmarried. Continence may lead to abstaining from conjugal intercourse at times, but it need not in all cases.

39. As Frederick J. Parrella has it, "a spirituality of the family, one that included the meaning of marriage and the raising of children, subsequently developed in a subordinate relationship to the spirituality of monasticism and a theology of virginity. The family was always understood in the context of a higher ideal—namely, the monastic life. This inevitably led to a hierarchy of holiness within the Church"; Parrella, "Towards a Spirituality of the Family," *Communio* 9 (1982): 128–41. In a standard work on the laity in the Church, Yves Congar, *Lay People in the Church* (Westminster, Md.: Newman Press, 1965), 12, cites a Bull of Pope Urban II from 1092 that stated, "From the beginning the Church has offered two kinds of life to her children: one to help the insufficiency of the weak, the other to perfect the goodness of the strong." In reality, this one-way directionality is a false characterization. As will be shown in the subsequent chapter, the life of religious orders has relied on domestic language of the family to make sense of and order their own project.

their marriage. In the marital act the couples give themselves to each other as an expression of a human love that is taken up into a divine love.[40] The marital act is the consummation of the marriage, seen as the pinnacle and clearest expression of sacramental love of the spouses. No longer to be excused, the conjugal act must be celebrated. The sexual desire (which is in part subject to *concupiscentia carnis*, one of many expressions of the basic concupiscence [*concupiscentia*] resulting from the fall)[41] was formerly viewed suspiciously for its idolatrous tendencies, but is now celebrated as each person's natural desire to be given entirely to another and receive the other entirely as gift.[42] With this development the door had been opened for a supposed authentic spirituality of marriage that can stand side by side with the spirituality of consecrated religious life (or perhaps above it).

As the story goes, it was only recently that marriage came back into view as a path to holiness on its own terms. Frederick J. Parrella, in a 1982 article in *Communio*, "Towards a Spirituality of the Family," applauds the early Church for the demand that even spouses had to be perfect (Clement of Alexandria), but he finds this insight to have been rather quickly lost and only recently recovered in any substantial way. He rejects, moreover, what he calls a context for thinking about marriage that "subsequently developed in a subordinate relationship to the spirituality of monasticism and a theology of virgini-

---

40. According to GS 48 and 51, "Authentic married love is caught up into divine love," and married couples "preserve the full sense of mutual self-giving and human procreation in the context of true love" when they consummate their marriage.

41. For an accurate description of the relationship between *concupiscentia* and sexuality in Augustine, see John C. Cavadini, "Feeling Right: Augustine on the Passions and Sexual Desire," *Augustinian Studies* 36 (2005): 195–217; David G. Hunter, "Augustinian Pessimism? A New Look at Augustine's Teaching on Sex, Marriage, and Celibacy," *Augustinian Studies* 25 (1994): 153–77.

42. See, for example, Peter Gardella, *Innocent Ecstasy: How Christianity Gave America an Ethic of Sexual Pleasure* (Oxford: Oxford University Press, 1985); and Christine Gudorf, *Body, Sex, and Pleasure: Reconstructing Christian Sexual Ethics* (Cleveland: Pilgrim Press, 1994).

ty."[43] Among the problematic constructs of this context Parrella lists the strict hierarchy of holiness, a notion of "duo genera Christianorum," and the idea that a virginal life was a sort of this-worldly "vita angelica." As clear evidence of this kind of adversarial stratification Parrella finds Pope Urban II (1092) stating that "from the beginning the Church has offered two kinds of life to her children: one to help the insufficiency of the weak, the other to perfect the goodness of the strong."[44] In light of this stratified relationship, Parrella laments that, throughout history, when spouses "aspired to deeper levels of holiness, however, their model of spirituality was primarily derived from monastic life, not from their immediate roles as husband, wife, lover, childbearer, craftsman, homemaker. Growth in the spirit did not take place directly through the procreative relation of the family."[45] As he tells the story, throughout history married spirituality was either (1) impossible; (2) accomplished only in spite of the realities of marriage—that is, not in and through those realities; or (3) accomplished only if one excised what was essential to married life.

The narrative I have outlined generally makes three moves: First, it villainizes a former hierarchical stratification of the religious and nonvowed states while praising a supposedly modern, level-playing-field approach to these ways of life assumed to be *novel*. Authors in the second half of the twentieth century write as if the Second Vatican Council finally introduced this kind of discourse into Catho-

---

43. Parrella, "Towards a Spirituality of the Family," 128–41, at 131. Despite the early insight of Clement of Alexandria, who wrote, "we must be holy in the whole manner of our lives ... the obligation to be perfect is incumbent on all, lay and religious alike," spirituality of marriage developed as subordinate and with nothing to contribute to the spirituality of the celibate life. "By the end of the fourth century, a strong dualism solidified in Christian spirituality so that *duo genera Christianorum* existed: the monk, the cleric, the virgin on the one hand and those left to life in the secular world on the other"; Parrella, "Towards a Spirituality of the Family," 131.

44. Ibid., 131.

45. Ibid., 131.

Is Marriage Made in a Monastery?

lic theology's mainstream, but in fact this method of argumentation was by no means a product of the Second Vatican Council or even the first half of the twentieth century. The attempt to equalize married and religious states is an ancient argumentative strategy, nearly as old as Antony of the Desert.[46] Second, the narrative attempts to move beyond a supposed dichotomization of the married life and the celibate life that paved the way for the hierarchical assessment of the states. Finally, the narrative has assumed a historical one-way street, seeing a unidirectional spiritual invasion from monastic life into marriage but little to no dependence on domestic life to inform the monastic spirituality.

Working within this narrative, some scholars (Frederick Parrella, Kenneth Russell, and Peter Phan) have considered the relationship between the two ways of life and developed new spiritualities of marriage around that relationship. Their work offers a "level-playing-field" approach to married and consecrated life that tries to put the two states of life beside one another (purportedly to free marriage from a "normative" monastic spirituality). Parrella wants a family spirituality authentically its own—that is, distinct from monastic spirituality. It must be trinitarian and sacramental.[47] This contribution is important because it makes a fundamental theological claim for the capacity of Christian marriage to be of its essence a path to Christian perfection. Russell proposes a contemplative marital spirituality based on spiritual friendship (via the thought of Aelred of Rievaulx) and a spousal love that avoids conflict with a love of God

---

46. In late fourth-century Rome, for example, Jovinian attempted to propose that marriage and virginity were of equal merit. The content of Jovinian's argument is known from the condemnations text of Pope Siricius, a letter from Ambrose to Siricius (*Epistola*. 42, *Rescriptum ad Siricium papam* 4) concerning Ambrose's condemnation of Jovinian through a council in Milan, Jerome's first response (*Adversus Iovinianum* 1.3, Patrologia Latina (hereafter PL) 23, col. 206–338), and a letter he sent when that response met with lack of enthusiasm (*Epistola*. 49, CSEL 54; and *Epistola*. 52).

47. Parrella, "Towards a Spirituality of the Family," 128–41.

Is Marriage Made in a Monastery?

(getting around the pesky 1 Cor 7).[48] Phan argues for a vision of marriage and monastic life on parallel spiritual tracks—separate but equal ways of attempting to love God with one's whole heart, mind, body, and soul.[49] Phan's own insight is closest to my own contribution, as it has room for describing both religious and conjugal life as consecration. These modern theologies are laudable, but they maintain four concerns that my own attempt at relating consecrated life to married life will have to address: (1) these modern spiritualities tend to maintain a dichotomy between the two states of life rather than seeing them as sharing in the same task; (2) these modern spiritualities perpetuate a competitive relationship between married and vowed religious life (albeit defanged); (3) the modern spiritualities of marriage (particularly Parrella's) inadvertently privilege marriage as an expression of God's life as Trinity; and (4) the modern complication of the ascetical hierarchy of merit is mistakenly identified as a new phenomenon, and, therefore, spiritualities assuming the novelty of complicating this hierarchy lack important material from the tradition. The most important missing link, though, in these accounts of the relationship between marriage and consecrated life is their Christology—they lack a recognition of Christ, son of man and Second Person of the Trinity, as the true nexus of religious and conjugal life inasmuch as he "fully reveals man to man himself and makes his supreme calling clear."[50] As will be argued in the next chapter, it is Christ the poor, chaste, and obedient Son of the Father and brother to humanity who draws these two states of life together into one body, one household. This theological foundation is

---

48. Kenneth Russell, "Marriage and the Contemplative Life," *Spiritual Life* 24, no. 7 (1978): 48–57; and Russell, "Loves in Conflict: Maritain on Marriage and Contemplation," *Église et Théologie* 7, no. 3 (1976): 333–40.

49. Peter C. Phan, "Possibility of a Lay Spirituality: A Re-Examination of Some Theological Presuppositions," *Communio* 10 (Winter 1983): 378–95.

50. *GS* 22.

so important that it must be dealt with before moving on to offer a counternarrative to the one we have just heard. The alternative for relating these two ways of consecration (marriage and religious life) emerges from the Eastern desert fathers and the thought of Augustine. It is a non-adversarial, complementary vision of the married and consecrated life that avoids a simple hierarchy of states and sees the two states as sharing in the same ecclesial goods, both domestic projects of being Church.

3

FOUNDATIONS FOR A CONSECRATED WAY

If married life is not merely borrowing from consecrated religious life, then these two consecrations to God must rest on the same theological foundation and share the same end. While the last chapter postulated their common consecration and end, "Christian perfection," this chapter fills out that end as a sharing in the life of Christ the poor, chaste, and obedient bridegroom through a specification of the one common consecration of all Christians in baptism. I will then harken back to their common origins in the trinitarian communion of persons.

The first part of the chapter shows that the vows of religion themselves (poverty, chastity, obedience) connect religious and matrimonial life because they lie at the heart of what it means to be a human person (anthropology) and what the human person is called to be (Christology). They sum up the state of the person *coram conjuge* and *coram Deo*—that is, they show us what a person can give to the spouse and God and what a person requires from God and spouse. The vows themselves are summed up in the person of Christ, the model and source of both conjugal and consecrated states of life. The evangelical virtues of poverty, chastity, and obedience disclose the truth about what we as Christians, as Church, as Christ's body, and as Christ's bride are invited to become and are in fact incorporated into with baptism.[1]

The second section links consecrated religious life and consecrated conjugal life in an even more fundamental theological locus—the Trinity. Not only is Christ the source of human fulfillment and flourishing and in a life of poverty, chastity, and obedience, but he is the source of our eternal beatitude as Second Person of the Trinity who invites us to share in his divine life as communions of persons. Specifically, trinitarian language has been used to describe both conjugal and consecrated states of life, but always in separate treatments. I intend to bring these descriptions together in one account. The connection between religious and married life, then, will not only be anthropological and Christological, but trinitarian as well.

Christ as Origin, Image, and End of Marriage and Religious Life

The evangelical counsels are first and foremost Christomorphic—that is, they fashion those who follow them into the shape of Christ's life, death, and resurrection. They belong, therefore, to all Christians, whose true human nature and destiny are revealed in Christ.[2] For the most part my exploration here will be more directly related to the life of the consecrated religious, and I will leave to chapter 6 a fuller demonstration of the evangelical counsels in the conjugal life. This section is most concerned to show how these counsels are firmly rooted in Christ and are therefore a proper goal of all practices of householding with Christ.

---

1. Christ is the revelation of God and man; see GS 22: "The truth is that only in the mystery of the incarnate Word does the mystery of man take on light.... He Who is 'the image of the invisible God' (Col. 1:15), is Himself the perfect man"; http://www.vatican.va, accessed May 8, 2013.

2. Ibid.

Foundations for a Consecrated Way

"Those called by God to the practice of the evangelical counsels," states *Perfectae caritatis,* "bind themselves to the Lord in a special way, following Christ, who chaste and poor (cf. Mt 8:20; Lk 9:58) redeemed and sanctified men through obedience even to death on the Cross (cf. Phil 2:8)." In the words of Columba Marmion, OSB, "Christ is 'the Religious' supereminently, and the character of the Rule is Christocentric."[3] As John Paul II puts it in *Vita consecrata,* those who live the evangelical counsels "make Christ the whole meaning of their lives," and they "reproduce the form of life that Jesus accepted and lived."[4] Consecrated life is a "living memorial of Jesus' way of living and acting."[5] Inasmuch as the counsels are lived, they conform the Christian to Christ. John Paul II imagines the life of the counsels as an icon of the transfigured Christ.[6] The life of the evangelical counsels is a gift from the Father to be like the son, joined to him in a special way by imitation, by a marriage of sorts, but through the Spirit by which the life of the evangelical counsels expresses the eschatological fulfillment the Church awaits.[7] Because all Christians are incorporated into Christ, all should be conformed to his virtues in a manner appropriate to their state. Furthermore, if the religious vows reveal a truth also found in marriage, then it follows that these vows have a role in conforming conjugal life as well as religious life to Christ's own life, death, and resurrection.

Therefore poverty, chastity, and obedience can be considered evangelical commands regarding Christ's own virtues, yet not in such a way that excludes the possibility of there being elective means of living out those evangelical commands. The evangelical counsels refer explicitly to those means identified in canon law for

---

3. Marmion Columba, *Christ the Ideal of the Monk: Spiritual Conferences on the Monastic and Religious Life,* trans. a nun of Tyburn Convent (London: Sands, 1926), 19.
4. *VC* 16.
5. Ibid., 22.
6. Ibid., 14.
7. Ibid., 16.

dedicating oneself to the undivided service of the Lord.[8] Expressed as the vows of consecrated religious life, they are particular, highly praised means of conforming oneself to Christ the poor (by owning no property), Christ the chaste (by forsaking all sexual pleasure), and Christ the obedient (by binding oneself in submission of one's own will to the will of a religious superior). We can also hypothesize that conjugal life, itself a vocation to follow the evangelical imperative to be conformed to Christ the poor, chaste, and obedient, might also be a venue for enacting elective evangelical imperative to be conformed to Christ the poor, chaste, and obedient. Within the Catholic tradition, married couples have done just that. What I will be setting the stage for here and developing in chapter 6, however, is practices whereby spouses fulfill imperative to be conformed by the Holy Spirit to Christ who reveals to us what our true humanity is. No person need take on either the married or the consecrated religious ways of life, but upon entering each vocation, a Christian accepts the unique instantiation of the requirement to be conformed to Christ's own virtues of poverty, chastity, and obedience.

Christ the Poor

Jesus Christ, son of Mary, son of God, is at once the richest and poorest man to ever live. The loci for developing the evangelical counsel of poverty are biblical and traditional. Mt 19:16–22 (rich young ruler; passage through the eye of a needle; reward in heaven), Lk 18:18–23 (rich young ruler; passage through eye of needle; reward now and in heaven), and Mk 10:17–22 (rich young ruler; passage through eye of needle; reward now and in heaven) are three gospel passages directly associated with the vow of poverty. Jesus called particular people to sell all and follow him. His closest fol-

---

8. CIC 573, 607, 654, http://www.vatican.va, accessed May 8, 2013.

Foundations for a Consecrated Way

lowers, the twelve, left all and followed him to great reward. Others took similar action without an explicit request from Jesus (Zacchaeus [Lk 19:1–10]; Matthew [Mt 9:9]). On yet other occasions, Jesus seems to make renunciation a requisite for *all* disciples ("So therefore, whoever of you does not renounce all that he has cannot be my disciple" [Lk 14:33]). At a broader level, Jesus' own itinerant lifestyle witnessed to a kind of poverty. Jesus claims that "foxes have holes, and birds of the air have nests; but the son of man has nowhere to lay his head" (Lk 9:58). When he sends out his disciples to preach he forbids them to carry anything beyond the most basic needs (Mt 10:5–15; Mk 6:7–13; Lk 9:1–6, 10:1–11). Even more extreme, Jesus seems to suggest that people throw planning and caution to the wind ([Mt 6:25–34] be as the birds and the lilies; care for today not tomorrow). Finally, Jesus even seems to reverse the proverbial wisdom of his forbears when he states in the Sermon on the Mount and the Sermon on the Plain, "blessed are the poor" (Mt 5:3–12; Lk 6:20–26). Finally, in light of their experience of Jesus, and after Jesus has risen and sent the Spirit, the Christian community in Acts 2:44–45 and 4:32–35 voluntarily shared possessions in common in order to provide for the needs of all.

The witness of Jesus' own life, the lives of those who followed him and supported him, and the life of the early Church suggests that poverty is as much about "giving everything" as it is about "having nothing."[9] Poverty is, in this sense, not a means to holiness but a reaction to what Christ has done for the Christian. Francis Moloney offers a corresponding exegesis of the "rich young man story" as it appears in the synoptic gospels. One interpretation of this passage is that there are two kinds of Christians, those called to attain the kingdom (by following the commandments) and those elites

---

9. See Francis J. Moloney, *A Life of Promise: Poverty, Chastity, and Obedience* (Wilmington, Del.: Michael Glazier, 1984), chap. 1.

called to radical renunciation. Moloney instead suggests that Jesus was not describing a higher path, but merely the one and only path: the path of "immediate, wordless obedience of the one called."[10] Moloney casts the entire passage as a drama of who should take the initiative in discipleship. Jesus issues the call, and we can merely give the response. Selling all, then, is a reordering of our material possessions for the common good in actions that proclaim, "All that I have I give to the community, and all that I need I receive from the community."[11] It is not only a state[12] but a virtue, a habitual disposition "which is one of the external consequences of our life in Christ, [and] is a part of the vocation to 'perfection' of all the baptized (see LG 40)."[13]

Reaching this state of perfect virtue requires that we set the conditions wherein the virtue of poverty is possible; conditions of real need are requisite for the practice of poverty as a virtue. Christ's life demonstrates as much.

Jesus was not only disposed to share all that was at his disposal for the good of all, but he actually disposed of all he had and all he was so that he might order it for the common good of the world he created and the humanity he would take up. "For you know the

---

10. Ibid., 55–61. A most common claim is that Jesus' teaching here is about having complete, total faith in him and his promise rather than in anything else—e.g., our material wealth. Commentators quickly point out the contextual link between piety and wealth in Jesus' day, but too often neglect such a link in the present context. For a typical interpretation of this pericope that emphasizes "justifying faith," see Alan P. Stanley, "The Rich Young Ruler and Salvation," *Bibliotheca Sacra* 163 (January–March 2006): 46–62.

11. Moloney, *Life of Promise*, 70.

12. In the previous section I spoke of the "states of life," while here I am speaking of each of the evangelical counsels itself as a state. These counsels are also virtues and practices. On the one hand, "state of life" refers to a person's official status within the Church. Here "state" refers more generally to a person's status before all other people (or specific persons) and before God. For example, we exist in a state of poverty before each other because the world's goods have a "universal destination" (*GS* 69) and before God because we are radically contingent beings dependent on him for origin, continued existence, and final end.

13. Ibid., 64–65.

Foundations for a Consecrated Way

grace of our Lord Jesus Christ," writes Paul, "that though he was rich, yet for your sake he became poor, so that by his poverty you might become rich" (2 Cor 8:9). As John Paul II puts it in *Vita consecrata*, Christ "gave up all to come to earth, receives all from and gives all back to the Father." Because Jesus renounced his divinity as something to be grasped at, he made possible our own divinization (Phil 2:6–10; Eph 3:14–21; 2 Pt 1:3–4).[14] Because Jesus renounces his own inheritance by becoming a curse (Gal 3:13), he shares it with all those he makes his brothers and sisters and thus co-heirs (Jn 1:1–9; Rom 8:10–17; Gal 3:29; Eph 3:6; Ti 3:7; Jas 2:5; 1 Pt 3:7).

Jesus entered the world as we all do, in the position of radical dependence—namely, infancy. His mother, for her part, depended on the mercy of Joseph, who could have easily rejected her. In John 5:19 Jesus conveys his radical dependence on the father for everything, even all that he does: "Truly, truly, I say to you, the Son can do nothing of his own accord, but only what he sees the Father doing." Further, when Jesus says, "Foxes have holes, and birds of the air have nests; but the Son of man has nowhere to lay his head" (Mt 8:20; Lk 9:58), he is not merely stating his radical "otherness," but a simple fact about his own life. Just as he lives a life of dependence, Jesus puts his disciples in situations of radical dependence. He sent his disciples to preach carrying no extra food, water, or supplies (Lk 10:1–11); their dependence on hospitality becomes a matter of life and death.

Jesus, through whom all creation is made, enters that creation only to be rejected by it. How great a poverty this is. It can only be heightened by the poverty of Holy Saturday, when Christ, as von Balthasar has proposed, experienced the true suffering of hell as no

---

14. Theosis (divinization) has a long history in Christianity from both the Greek and the Latin traditions; see Michael J. Christensen and Jeffrey A. Witung, eds., *Partakers of the Divine Nature: The History and Development of Deification in the Christian Traditions* (Grand Rapids, Mich.: Baker Academic, 2007).

Foundations for a Consecrated Way

human could experience it. He suffered the greatest poverty imaginable, the loss of God from Godself. Only one who had experienced the beatific vision and complete union with God could understand, let alone experience, complete separation from God. Christ, and no one else, has experienced the deepest poverty possible.[15] Jesus did not help us "from above" but joined us in the dust to remake humanity again. Poverty, then, is ultimately not a virtue isolated in an individual piety; rather, poverty is a definition of our solidary relationships in community. Christian, religious poverty is a commitment to solidarity with our coinhabitors in God's household.[16]

The virtue of evangelical poverty, then, even as a disposition to make all our possessions available for the common good and to receive our personal good from the community, is reduced wherever there is an attempt to insulate people from the fact that we actually need each other. The American dream of married suburban self-sufficiency and independence has created a class of people for whom the conditions necessary to learn the virtue of poverty are all but completely nonexistent.[17] The American dream is that I will never have to depend on anyone except myself. If I will need to rely on someone else, then I should not undertake the task. Over against this notion is the evangelical notion of poverty. Not only must we seek dependence on others, but we must realize the unavoidability of such dependence.

---

15. Hans Urs von Balthasar, *Mysterium Paschale: The Mystery of Easter*, trans. Aidan Nichols (San Francisco: Ignatius Press, 1981), 49–52, 168–76.

16. John Paul II's *Solicitudo rei socialis* 38 defines solidarity as "not a feeling of vague compassion or shallow distress at the misfortunes of so many people, both near and far. On the contrary, it is a firm and persevering determination to commit oneself to the common good; that is to say, to the good of all and of each individual, because we are all really responsible for all."

17. David Matzko McCarthy, *Sex and Love in the Home: A Theology of the Household* (London: SCM, 2001), 2–3, 66, 80, 88–89, 93, 96, 155, 171–72, 174, and 243, describes this kind of situation. He describes the virtue of reciprocity, which develops in conditions of real dependence and need.

Foundations for a Consecrated Way

This interdependence reminds us of the essentially communal aspect of poverty as a principle of Christian life together. Certainly poverty is the individual person's renunciation of possessions as her own, but no less is poverty the formation of a communion of goods—whether among celibates or spouses or a mix of both. This social aspect of poverty is most clear in the early Church's example of poverty in the Jerusalem community (Acts 2:44–45 and 4:32–35). The early Jerusalem community, the desert fathers, and the vowed religious who came after them ordered their renunciation to the goal of reaching the kingdom of God. This meant their poverty was entered for the sake of those in need, in solidarity with those who do not choose poverty, and as a commitment to creating the kind of community that prepares for and attempts to participate now in the coming kingdom—a social reality. Our modern Western communities must be intentionally ordered around creating the conditions to develop the virtue of poverty. I will hypothesize ways of doing just this in the final chapter.

Christ the Chaste

As with poverty, chastity finds its exemplar in Christ. Conciliar and synodal documents call Jesus "the exemplar of chastity."[18] Moreover, the evangelical virtues lived by consecrated religious are a participation in and an effort to make present to the whole world "Christ who is chaste, poor, obedient, prayerful, and missionary."[19] These documents understand Christ's chastity in a twofold sense. First, it is the means by which Jesus, and now vowed religious, can "dedicate themselves with undivided heart to the service of God."[20] In a sense there is a logic of effectiveness at work in this claim—that celibacy makes a person more radically available for the service

---

18. PC 25; VC 16, 21.   19. VC 77.
20. PC 12; VC 14.

of God in ministry (a claim that one may or may not find convincing). As *Perfectae caritatis* has it, chastity for the sake of the kingdom is "the most suitable means" for this devotion.[21] Jesus was of pure and singular devotion in his love, and the religious, it is argued, imitate that devotion by making themselves radically available for prayer and ministry. Second, chastity, as expressed in consecrated celibacy, is a sign of and witness to the eschatological goods we all share as members of the one Church, the one body of and bride of Christ. It is an eschatological maximalism that anticipates the fulfillment toward which the Church is moving.[22] Christ's pure love for the Church is the model for consecrated celibacy, a pure and complete gift of love that unfailingly bears fruit.

Theologians since the Second Vatican Council have reacted against the logic of availability for ministerial effectiveness and any claim that celibacy is lived by Jesus because it somehow makes persons more available than the conjugal life. For instance, Moloney's 1984 work *A Life of Promise* and Sandra Schneiders's 2004 monograph *Selling All: Consecrated Celibacy* both resist the argument that the Christ chose the life of chastity because it allowed for greatest ministerial availability. Both of these authors ultimately rely on nuptial language to explain how Christ's life is the root of celibacy.[23] For Moloney Christ has "fallen for" God's reign in the romantic sense and can do none other than be wholly committed to it.[24]

While I sympathize with Moloney's and Schneiders's attempt to avoid reducing Christ's celibacy to a means chosen for effectiveness,

---

21. *PC* 12. 22. *VC* 14.
23. Sandra M. Schneiders, *Selling All: Commitment, Consecrated Celibacy, and Community in Catholic Religious Life*, Religious Life in a New Millennium 2 (New York: Paulist Press, 2002), 2:137–59. She considers ministerial effectiveness a possible explanation for why a person might consecrate her life in celibacy, but she is wary of its power to endure trials. Instead, she suggests that the nuptial imagery to understand celibacy provides the strongest and richest symbolism.
24. Moloney, *Life of Promise*, 108.

I am wary of Moloney's overly romantic language, which attempts to put marriage and consecrated life on a level playing field of affective love. "Celibacy," Moloney argues, "is nothing else but the existential consequence which flows out of the prior experience of the urgent presence of the kingdom of God."[25] "Just as, in an authentic situation of sexual love, the couple can do no other than marry and consecrate themselves to each other and their families through a life of consecrated chastity, so also the celibate, in an authentic situation of celibate love, can do no other than be a 'eunuch because of' the kingdom of love in his or her life in a different but parallel form of consecrated chastity."[26] I would suggest that persons who plan to marry because "they can do no other than" should wait for a moment. This kind of intoxicating, overtaking love is not permanent but effervescent and momentary. People who marry or choose celibate life because they have, in Moloney's words, "fallen" and "can do no other," will quickly find that they very easily can and may very soon want to do something other. Unfortunately, the reasons for marriage cited by Moloney are normal, but they ought not be normative. The kind of irreplaceability and definitive love Moloney wants to see at the center of celibate and conjugal love in Christ develops over time through struggle. It is at the same time received as gift, as Christ's love. Christ's witness to this love comes at the dark moment of Gethsemane, when he was tempted to do something other than live out his love of complete devotion to God. In the same way, for example, true married love is found in the challenge of saying "yes" to marital chastity when it is so easy to do other than live out the love of sexual self-possession and self-gift.

Hans Urs Von Balthasar, in his meditations on consecrated celibacy, has offered perhaps the best way to understand the union of

25. Ibid., 110.
26. Ibid.

ministerial effectiveness and the essence of a kenotic love that "can do no other." For von Balthasar virginity is "a participation in the bodily mystery of the Cross and Resurrection." "The Lord's surrendered flesh and blood," he continues, "is the origin of all Christian fruitfulness through the ages; it is the archetype and source of the consecration of life in the 'vowed state.' This bodily midpoint (where the spirit takes on bodily form and where eternal goods become a man's very essence) makes it possible to understand the form that structures the life of those who follow the Lord."[27] For von Balthasar the Lord Jesus' motivation to give up his body is not principally his knowledge that it will be the best way to bring the kingdom, but rather that it is the *only* way. Christ's redemptive love for all of creation, as expressed in the incarnation, *requires* the sacrifice of his entire person, body and soul, for whatever God's plans may have in bringing about that redemption. He would be unavailable for this kind of gift if he were married to one person. Christ's own body, given entirely to God on the cross and offered entirely for the Church in the Eucharist, is at once the font and result of the gift of self in virginity.[28] Furthermore, Christ the chaste, as font and first fruit of consecrated virginity, is witnessed in the life of Mary. Mary is both mother and virgin; even more, she is mother because she is virgin, and she could respond to God with pure, complete love because the grace of Christ was already at work within her by the Immaculate Conception.[29]

Christ the Obedient

The obedience of Christ is perhaps the most well-attested of the evangelical counsels from the New Testament sources.[30] According to the

---

27. Von Balthasar, *The Laity and the Life of the Counsels: The Church's Mission in the World*, trans. Brian McNeil, with D. C. Schindler (1993; San Francisco: Ignatius Press, 2003), 197.
28. Ibid.   29. Ibid., 194–96.
30. "There is no easy proof-text for obedience because this is the one that is most biblical"; Moloney, *Life of Promise*, 121; see PC 25: "The sacred synod highly esteems their way of

Foundations for a Consecrated Way

witness of Paul, "by one man's disobedience many were made sinners, so by one man's obedience many will be made righteous" (Rom 5:19). Christ's obedience is a recapitulation of Adam's failure, an obedience that makes possible our rebirth in baptism by which we have a share in Christ's filial obedience to God. In the Letter to the Philippians Paul holds out Christ's own humility and obedience for the community, saying Christ removed from himself the glory of his godhead and "humbled himself and became obedient unto death, even death on a cross" (Phil 2:8). The author of Hebrews also invokes Christ's obedience as an encouragement for Christians suffering for their faith. "Although he was a Son, he learned obedience through what he suffered" (Heb 5:8). For his own part Jesus is reported in the gospels speaking about his own obedience. It is a complete obedience that puts him in harmony of action and word with the Father. As to his miraculous signs, particularly those relating to the Sabbath, Jesus says, "Truly, truly, I say to you, the Son can do nothing of his own accord, but only what he sees the Father doing; for whatever he does, that the Son does likewise" (Jn 5:19). As to his teaching, Jesus makes clear, "My teaching is not mine, but his who sent me; if any man's will is to do His will, he shall know whether the teaching is from God or whether I am speaking on my own authority" (Jn 7:16–17).

Christ's obedience comes from his close connection to the Father's will; in fact, the connection between the two wills is so close that they are identical. It is because Jesus' will is at once God's will that obedience and poverty are so connected in Christ. In this obedience is his freedom. The son's attitude discloses the mystery of human freedom—that we as a communion of persons are together

---

life in poverty, chastity, and obedience, of which Christ the Lord is Himself the exemplar"; see VC 22: "Jesus is the exemplar of obedience, who came down not to do his own will be the will of the One who sent him [see Jn 6:38; Heb 10:5, 7]. He places his way of living and acting in the hands of the Father [see Lk 2:49]."

destined for a path of obedience to the Father's will, a path that will demand our response in practices of Christian householding made free by grace.[31] Christ does and teaches nothing of his own, but only what he sees the Father doing (Jn 5:19; Jn 7:28–29).

Hans Urs von Balthasar explains the relationship well, using the concept of "permission." The Son's existential act is "permitting himself to be sent from the Father ... to behave in all situations of his human life as the one *sent* by the Father, the one *made available* to the Spirit and *led* by him on his mission. The fundamental act of his existence is that he does, not his own will, but the *will of the Father*."[32] In the practices of Christian householding those incorporated into Christ through baptism share in this fundamental act of being made available for the will of God in the service of the community, whether it is composed of consecrated religious, a conjugal family, or a combination of both.

Christ's obedience offers again the same the tension we saw with poverty: a tension between "virtue" and "state." The documents of Vatican II offer both kinds of language. In *Perfectae caritatis* we find that, "in professing obedience, religious offer the full surrender of their own will as a sacrifice of themselves to God and so are united more firmly and securely to God's salvific will."[33] *Lumen gentium* echoes this account of renunciation. It is done to "become subject of their own accord to another man on account of God, in the matters of perfection. This is beyond the measure of the commandments, but is done in order to conform oneself to the obedient Christ."[34] The synod on religious life that produced *Vita consecrata*

---

31. *VC* 91–92. John Paul II takes up the challenge of modern notions of freedom as "license" as opposed to freedom as the capacity to do the good.

32. Von Balthasar, *Laity and Life of the Counsels*, 211 (emphasis in the original).

33. *PC* 14, my own translation from the Latin, because the Vatican's English translation dismisses the comparative form of the modifiers here (*constantius, securius*).

34. *LG* 42.

develops this language of sacrifice; consecrated religious "sacrifice their own freedom to accept the mystery of Christ's filial obedience and thus profess that Jesus Christ is infinitely beloved and loving as the one who delights only in the will of the Father."[35] The obedience of the religious, then, does not merely parrot Christ's obedience, but *participates* in the *mystery* of Christ's filial obedience and his all-consuming delight in the will of the Father. This kind of participatory language helps allay the fears of some theologians and psychologists: that obedience can be destructive to the human person, especially those for whom it remains a means to continue in emotional, spiritual, and psychological immaturity. The motive and goal of obedience is to come to a union of will with the Father as close as possible to what Christ Jesus experienced—a union that joins our will to the Father's without obliterating our own personal will and identity.

Christ's example of obedience is of special importance in that it demonstrates the essentially social character of obedience as a virtue. Even Christ, whose obedience to his Father was as unmediated as possible, experienced obedience not as an autonomous individual but in a social context. Christ learned, practiced, and knew obedience at the very least as mediated by his mother Mary and father Joseph. Luke's Gospel (Jesus "lost" at the temple) and John's Gospel (Jn 2:1–11, wedding at Cana) give examples of Christ practicing obedience in domestic settings. Christ's example must demonstrate for us that obedience is not the task of an individual but a practice of life together. If even Christ's obedience to the Father was mediated in a social, domestic context, then certainly we must understand obedience of the vowed religious as a practice situated in the context of Christian householding, as well. This fact was not lost on the spiritual masters who first organized desert ascetics into communi-

---

35. *VC* 16.

ties. One of the central reasons for the development of cenobitic life was the discovery of this insight. Monks attempting to live in unmediated obedience to the will of God more often than not ended up being ruled by self-will rather than divine will. Benedict, for his part, emphasizes the need for mediated obedience—that is, obedience as a domestic practice, as a key reason for making religious life a domestic project rather than an individual endeavor.[36] Benedict would not abide those seeking the way of the Lord who could not submit themselves to a rule other than their own.

The simple fact in Benedict's preference for cenobitic over anchoritic life is that life in community demands a virtue that often slips away in solitary life—humility. Living in community means living according to a rule other than one's own, and if that community is to be a means of salvation, it means finding, loving, and obeying Christ in each member of that community.[37] Benedict's own desire to replace pride with humility is so strong that his rule constructs a step-wise approach to the virtue that can only take place within a situation of mediated obedience. "The first step of humility," he writes, "is *unhesitating obedience, which comes naturally* to those who cherish Christ above all."[38] Benedict's twelve-step ladder seems to be an attempt to work from the outside in as much as from the inside out. "Now the ladder erected is our life on earth, and if we humble our hearts the Lord will raise it to heaven."[39] As Paul Evdo-

---

36. Adalbert de Vogüé, ed., *The Rule of Saint Benedict: A Doctrinal and Spiritual Commentary*, by St. Benedict (Kalamazoo, Mich.: Cicstercian, 1983), chap. 1.10 (hereafter *RB*); and Timothy Fry, ed., *RB 1980: The Rule of St. Benedict in Latin and English with Notes* (Collegeville, Minn.: Liturgical Press, 1981), 171 (hereafter *RB 1980*).

37. Michael Banner, "Who Are My Mother and My Brothers? Marx, Bonhoeffer and Benedict and the Redemption of the Family," *Studies in Christian Ethics* 9 (1996): 1–22, makes a study of the way Benedict maximizes the amount of communal time and space as a way to force the issue of humility and giving way.

38. *RB* 5.1–2; *RB 1980* 187 (emphasis mine).

39. *RB*, 7.7–8; *RB 1980* 193.

kimov writes of the vowed life of holiness, we sweat, but God does the work. The spiritual life is "no question of reward or merit, but of man working within the divine action."[40] It is the monk's task to practice obedience and God's to grow humility within him.

In summary, Benedict's insight and the insight of the practice of obedience and humility in vowed religious life in community are that, for humans, obedience to God must be mediated personally, communally, dialogically. Even for the first Christian disciples, even for Mary the *theotokos,* God's will was not immediate. As von Balthasar aptly puts it, "the disciple's obedience to the Master is in the first place unambiguously obedience to a human being."[41] "The disciples' paradigmatic, archetypal obedience to the Lord," he continues, "is and remains obedience from man to man in the clearest possible way; it remains a genuinely dialogical and genuinely incarnate obedience, which through the juxtaposition of two wills and two freedoms always keeps the person from believing he is obeying God when in fact he is ultimately obeying only his own self."[42] Obedience, then, is not essentially the sacrifice of one's will to an arbitrary other's will, even the will of a spiritually superior director. Rather, it is a state and virtue of coming to know God's will in humility through accepting the way another shows us how our own will is hardly identical to God's. In this way we finally participate in Christ's obedience to the Father by doing what Jesus does—namely, putting ourselves at the service of others, even our enemies.

---

40. Paul Evdokimov, *The Sacrament of Love: The Nuptial Mystery in Light of the Orthodox Tradition,* trans. Anthony P. Gythiel and Victoria Steadman (Crestwood, N.Y.: St. Vladimir's Seminary Press, 1985), 79.

41. Von Balthasar, *Laity and the Life of the Counsels,* 198–99. He continues, "It is an obedience based on an acknowledgment of the spiritual superiority of the Master and his prestige but, at the same time, also his selflessness and humility vis-à-vis God. Accordingly, this obedience is understood implicitly from the beginning as obedience to God."

42. Ibid., 199–200.

Christ the Poor, Chaste, and Obedient Bridegroom

Not only is Christ a poor, chaste, and obedient son, he is a poor, chaste, and obedient spouse. These virtues belong to Christ fully in both of these paradigmatic roles. Christomorphic virtues are as fundamental to marriage as they are to religious life because Christ discloses truth about marriage in the heart of his identity and mission. "Bridegroom" is among the Lord's frequently chosen images for speaking of himself and proclaiming the kingdom.[43] Christ the groom is poor because he has shared his inheritance with the Church, counting the spiritual treasure of his merit not as his own but to be shared with his spouse. Christ is chaste because his love for the Church is complete and exclusive, an eternal act of the will rather than a flight of the passion (Rom 8:31–38; nothing can separate us from the love of God). This pure love bears fruit in the coming of the Spirit and its gifts in the life of the Church (Gal 5:22). Christ the bridegroom is obedient because he weds as a completion of the Father's will to bring the blessing of Abraham's covenant to all nations, to make a holy people for himself, a pure and spotless bride (2 Cor 11:2; Eph 5:25–32; Rv 19:7; 21:2, 9; 22:17). It is this obedient, chaste, and poor Christ who reveals the essence of marriage to us, the indissoluble and redeeming love that serves and purifies by an authentic gift of self, often in and through suffering. Christ's marriage, after all is begun, or ratified, with Mary's words of consent at the annunciation (Lk 1:38; "let it be done to me according to your word"); it is brought to completion on the cross, when Christ declares, "it is finished" (*consummatum est*) (Jn 19:30); and it is renewed when Christ's obedient gift of self is made present again

---

43. Mt 9:14–17, Mk 2:19–20, and Lk 5:34–36 (the impossibility of fasting when the bridegroom is present); Mt 25:1–13 (the wise and foolish virgins waiting for the bridegroom; Jn 3:29 (John the Baptist's reference to Christ as bridegroom).

in the worshipping community and the bread and wine at each Eucharist.[44]

Trinity as Origin, Image, and End of Marriage and Religious Life

While Christ is and reveals humanity to us, he simultaneously reveals to us the Trinity as its Second Person. If consecrated and married persons are called to be conformed to Christ, then it follows that they are also invited into Christ's life in the Trinity (*LG* 2; *Ad gentes* 2). The central mystery of Christianity, the Trinity itself, orchestrates the most profound consonance between these states of life. While authors have considered the relationship between consecrated life and the Trinity (principally John Paul II in *Vita consecrata*), as well as the connection between the Trinity and marriage (chiefly Marc Cardinal Ouellet in *Divine Likeness: A Trinitarian Anthropology of the Family*), neither has seen this as an opportunity for dialogue. In what follows, I will outline the fundamentally trinitarian grounding in both states of life and demonstrate how that foundation both draws together and distinguishes marriage and vowed religious life. Three points of common ground will be spied in the Trinity's landscape: the Trinity is (1) the origin of both consecrated and married life; (2) the model of unity within marriage and consecrated life in community; (3) and the source of the fruitfulness in both states.

---

44. The moments of consent and consummation are, in canon law, the moments when the marriage becomes valid (*ratum*) and radically indissoluble as (*consummatum*). This doctrine was developed through the Scholastic period when controversy abounded as to whether consummation or consent made the marriage. Canonically the Church has opted for a both/and approach, but one that puts more weight on consent. In juridical situations challenging consent, consummation is assumed unless challenged and proven otherwise; see *CIC* 1141, 1142; see also John P. Beal, James A. Coriden, and Thomas J. Green, eds., *New Commentary on the Code of Canon Law* (New York: Paulist Press, 2000).

Consecrated Life and the Trinity

The Second Vatican Council has made clear the trinitarian grounding of the Church in general. The Church finds its origin in the Trinity, "proceeding from the love of the eternal Father ... founded by Christ in time and gathered into one by the Holy Spirit."[45] Originating in the Trinity, the Church also finds there its model:[46] "The highest exemplar and source of this mystery is the unity, in the Trinity of Persons, of one God, the Father and the Son in the Holy Spirit."[47] It is precisely the trinitarian nature of religious life as a specification of ecclesial life, though, that we seek. Reflections and studies of the nature of vowed religious life (especially historical studies) abound, but only infrequently does "Trinity" appear in these studies. One recent monograph and a journal that dedicated an entire issue to this relationship have worked to fill this void.[48]

The Trinity as the origin and exemplar of all ecclesial communion is also the exemplar of unity in vowed religious life. *Perfectae*

---

45. *LG* 40.

46. Here the Council uses "exemplar" to describe the relationship of the Church to the Trinity. An exemplar is an object of imitation. It is a model for fashioning a re-presentation. The Church's unity *is not* the Trinity's unity in a univocal way, since the intersubjective and intrasubjective unity of the Church is created and accidental rather than uncreated and essential. The Church's unity finds its "source" in the mystery of the Trinity inasmuch as the Church's unity is fashioned after the Trinity's unity as revealed in Christ and his relationship to the Father and the Spirit. Also, the Trinity is the source of the Church's unity, because the Trinity has inspired and enlivened that unity since the Pentecost with the gifts and fruits of the Spirit.

47. *Unitatis redintegratio* 2; see also Fabio Ciardi, *Koinonia: Spiritual and Theological Growth of the Religious Community* (Hyde Park, N.Y.: New City Press, 2001), 220–22, for an analysis of this trinitarian ecclesiology.

48. Ciardi, *Koinonia*, 220–22; Alberto Ablondi, "Dalla Trinità alla comunità," *Consacrazione e Servizio* 28, no. 10 (1979): 7–17; Giordano Cabra, *Breve meditazione sui voti*, Introduzioni e trattati 22 (1978; Brescia: Queriniana, 1983); Xabier Pikaza, "Trinidad," in *Diccionario Teológico de la Vida Consagrada* (Madrid: Publicaciones Claretianas, 1992), 1758–77; Pikaza, "En communidad: Como la familia del Dios-Trinidad," *Vida Religiosa* 66 (1989) 57–66; Nereo Silanes,"Trinidad y vida consagrada," *Comunidades* 17, no. 66–67 (1989): 47–65 (this issue is dedicated to a bibliography of "Trinity and consecrated life").

caritatis summarizes the Trinity's role in religious life: "After the example of *Jesus Christ* who came to do the will of the *Father* (cf. Jn 4:34; 5:30; Heb 10:7; Ps 39:9) and, 'assuming the nature of a slave' (Phil 2:7), learned obedience in the school of suffering (cf. Heb 5:8), religious under the motion of the *Holy Spirit,* subject themselves in faith to their superiors who hold the place of God."[49] To enter religious life, then, is to step into the narrative of the Trinity's own life: the life of the Son who does the will of the Father in the power of the Spirit. In other words, it is to follow or imitate the drama of the Trinity's life as it is revealed to us in Christ.

    John Paul II continues and expands this narrative line of thought when saying that those entering religious life state with their lives: "*confessio Trinitas.*"[50] Those professing the vows of religion are responding to a gift that draws them to the giver. As the Son responds eternally in kenotic love (as he is eternally begotten of the Father), so the religious too are "*a patre ad patrem*" (from the Father and to the Father).[51] They receive their charism and vocation from the Father, but that vocation is a grace that allows nothing else but a return to the Father. This *reditus* to the Father is worked "*per filium,*" in the footsteps of Christ, who is himself the way and in whom every virtue comes to perfection. With the counsels the religious embarks on "a divine way of living embraced by Christ as an expression of his relationship as the Only Begotten Son with the Father and the Holy Spirit."[52] Finally, the consecrated life is lived "*in Spiritu*"—that is, as a reliving of James, Peter, and John's experience on Tabor.[53] It is their experience of being enveloped in the cloud wherein Christ is transfigured and to remain on the mountain, sharing Peter's overwhelming desire to abide with the one he now sees as God (Mt 17:1–

---

49. PC 14.
51. Ibid., 17.
53. Ibid., 23, 40.

50. VC 16.
52. Ibid., 18.

13; Mk 9:2–13: "Master, it is well that we are here; let us make three booths, one for you and one for Moses and one for Elijah").

This Tabor experience, this falling in love that tends toward a desire to abide in the presence of the beloved, can authentically lead to and be part of the complete gift of self to God in consecrated religious life. Nonetheless, I would not want to romanticize the decision. This love is a love for the whole Trinity: (1) for the Son, which leads to closeness to him; (2) for the Holy Spirit, which opens hearts to his inspiration; and (3) for the Father, the origin and supreme goal of the consecrated life.[54] Furthermore, the counsels themselves witness to the Trinity. Chastity proclaims the infinite love that links the three Divine Persons indissolubly and unconditionally, even spousally.[55] Poverty, by proclaiming that God is man's only treasure and portion, becomes an expression of dependence and gift that participates by grace in the self-gift and interdependence among the three Divine Persons. Obedience reflects the filial rather than the servile relationship between the Son and the Father, which is so fruitful that from it the Spirit proceeds.

Not only does the life of the individual religious confess the Trinity, but the common life of the religious community attempts to imitate the shared life of the three-in-one God, as well. As the Second Vatican Council so well expressed in *Lumen gentium,* God the Father desires to make of humanity one family. Religious orders witness to this fact in their life of fraternal love, giving form to the Lord's saying, "call no man your father on earth, for you have one Father, who is in heaven" (Mt 23:9). Only the abbot or abbess is called by a name oth-

---

54. Ibid., 21.
55. See John Paul II, *Man and Woman He Created Them: A Theology of the Body,* trans. and introduction by Michael Waldstein (Boston: Pauline Books, 2006), 412–57, esp. at 437–41, where John Paul II regards the spousal meaning of the body as the foundation of Christ's call to continence for the sake of the kingdom of God. Consecrated religious live out the spousal meaning of the body eschatologically, whereas the married live out that meaning historically.

Foundations for a Consecrated Way

er than "brother" or "sister," and this title is highly qualified, having nothing to do with the particular person holding the office. Instead, the term refers to the One whose will and paternal love are represented in the abbot's or abbess's direction.[56] This life together, according to the medieval rule of St. Francis, is nothing other than the living of the gospel[57]—that is, a conformity to the life, death, and resurrection of the Son, "who gathers the redeemed into a unity, pointing the way by his example, prayer, words, and above all his death."[58] Christ the Son recapitulates humanity in the incarnation, providing both the example and the capacity for us to live as communion of persons in love. Finally, it is the Holy Spirit that enlivens this communion of love. Imagine the initial gathering of frightened disciples in the upper room. They had come together in their love for the Father and their desire to imitate his Son, yet their community bore no fruit, for it was deadened by confusion and fear of death and failure. When the Spirit descends on Pentecost, the confidence and first fruits of the Church are born and continue to be reproduced.[59] As the early disciples did not embody life of the Trinity as a communion of love that overflowed beyond its own borders until the flame of the Spirit rested on their heads, so too a religious community is dead without the Spirit enlivening their mission and aiding their authentic development of and reliance on their original charism.[60]

---

56. See Ciardi, *Koinonia*, 223–24; and *RB* 2.1–3; *RB 1980*, 173.

57. "The rule and life of the lesser brothers is this: To observe the holy gospel of our Lord Jesus Christ, living in obedience without anything of our own, and in chastity"; *Rule of 1223*, at "Medieval Sourcebook: The Rule of the Franciscan Order," http://www.fordham.edu/halsall/source/stfran-rule.html, accessed May 8, 2013.

58. *VC* 21.

59. Aquinas, *In Johannem* 17, 26, quoted in Ciardi, *Koinonia*, 227.

60. See *PC* 2, where principles of renewal for religious life are outlined. The second principle emphasizes the founder's "spirit and special aims." "The adaptation and renewal of the religious life include both the constant return to the sources of all Christian life *and to the original spirit of the institutes*" (emphasis mine). Since the Church is founded in the Holy Spirit, it must be vivified by special attention to that Spirit's "special aims."

Foundations for a Consecrated Way

Conjugal Family and the Trinity

Theological reflection on the relationship between the family and the Trinity sets any author or reader before a theological minefield. On the one hand, creedal statements about God as "Father" and Jesus as "begotten" "Son" explicitly draw a link between God's trinitarian life and the life of the human, conjugal family. The image of Church as born from Jesus' side on the cross[61] and the picture of Jesus as the new Adam with Mary as the New Eve also seem to invite trinitarian ideas for the conjugal family.[62] The history of the Church is full of passionate debate about the family's capacity to be an analogy of the Trinity. While the Cappadocians found little problem with the idea of Adam, Eve, and Seth as Trinity,[63] Augustine balked for many reasons: first, the first family inadequately represents the sameness of all subjects within the Trinity; and second, the relationships between Adam, Eve, and Seth confused the relationships among the three persons of the Trinity.[64] Augustine's social image of

---

61. Augustine, *Tractates on John* 10.4, trans. John W. Rettig (Washington, D.C.: The Catholic University of America Press, 1988); and Augustine, *Homilies on the Gospel According to St. John, and His First Epistle by Saint Augustine, Bishop of Hippo*, trans. with notes and indices, 2 vol. (Oxford: J. H. Parker, 1848).

62. By "conjugal family" I mean that family created by the sacrament of matrimony in the Catholic Church. I am not ruling out other kinds of families altogether, but I prescind from treating those families here.

63. As Lionel Gendron writes, "For these fathers [Gregory of Nazianzen and other Cappadocians] it was relatively easy to show the consubstantial unity of the Trinity thanks to the image of the human family, and particularly thanks to the first family"; Gendron, "La famille: reflet de la communion trinitaire," in *La famille chrétienne dans le monde d'aujourd'hui* (Montreal: Bellarmin, 1995), 127–48, at 133; translation in *Divine Likeness: Toward a Trinitarian Anthropology of the Family*, by Marc Cardinal Ouellet, trans. Philip Milligan and Linda M. Cicone (Grand Rapids, Mich.: Eerdmans, 2006); see also Gregory of Nazianzen, *Oratio XXXI (Theol. V)*, Patrologia Graeca (hereafter PG) 36, 144.

64. Augustine, *De Trinitate* xii.5, 8; *On the Trinity*, ed. John Rotelle, intro., trans., and notes by Edmund Hill (Brooklyn, N.Y.: New City Press, 1991), 324, 326; and Maurice Nédoncelle, "L'Intersubjectivité humaine est-elle pour saint Augustin une image de la Trinité?" International Augustinian Conference, in *Augustinus Magister* (Paris: Études Augustiniennes, 1954), 1:586. Augustine preferred the psychological analogy that finds the image of the Trinity in

Foundations for a Consecrated Way

the Trinity was the Church itself, the common "nature" therein being charity.[65] Richard of St. Victor and Bonaventure found and developed this idea, which has made its way back into the modern theology of the family in genealogical terms—in other words, wherever we hear language of man and wife whose self-giving love becomes a third person in the child.[66] John Paul II, following St. John of the Cross, has promoted the idea that the spousal gift of self and reception of other (made by those who marry and by the consecrated religious) in this world is a most clear manifestation of the love of the Trinity.[67]

Risks abound, though, in any attempt to relate the Trinity to human family—or any social body, for that matter. Whose family? Which relationships? There is a temptation to use the conjugal family (or any family) as an expansive analogy for the Trinity—that is, as a means to discover the nature of and relationships among the Trinity. This analogical method is a bottom-up approach. If conjugal family (or any family) is the source of information on the Trinity, then there is a chance that destructive relationships and practices of family life may erroneously be mistaken for revelations of the nature of trinitarian life. Furthermore, a strictly analogical approach does not

---

each person; Augustine, *De Genesi ad litteram* 3.19–20, 22; *On Genesis*, ed. John E. Rotelle, intro., trans., and notes Edmund Hill, part 1 of *The Works of St. Augustine: A Translation for the 21st Century* (Hyde Park, N.Y.: New City Press, 2002), 13:237–38 see also *De Trinitate* xii.2.5–9; *On the Trinity*, 324–27.

65. Ouellet expands on this idea in *Divine Likeness*, 24, when he writes, "In his *Tractatus XXXIX*, while describing Church unity founded on the charity between the community members, Augustine states that therein lies an analogy of the unity which exists between the divine Persons. He observes, in fact, that love possesses the capacity to create a common soul and a common heart among those who love one another. He perceives this capacity especially in God, in whom the Holy Spirit appears as the bond and the fruit of the mutual love of Father and Son. However, he also sees it in ecclesial love, which the Holy Spirit brings to life and consecrates within the community."

66. Ouellet, *Divine Likeness*, 25, here relying on Gendron, *La famille*, 140; Hemmerle, "Matrimonio e Famiglia in una antropologia trinitaria," *Nuova Umanità* 6 (1984): 3–31, at 31.

67. See Michael Waldestein's introduction to John Paul II, *Man and Woman He Created Them*, 23–34.

comprehend the great rift between the divine, uncreated, eternal nature of the Trinity and the created, temporary nature of the universe. After all, the Church officially holds that "all resemblance between the Creator and his creature is limited by an always-greater dissimilarity."[68]

The immanent Trinity remains mystery unbeheld until the beatific vision, yet God has made known his relation to creation through the revelation of the economic Trinity. God has revealed himself as Father and source of all being, as Son who is Word and truth of the Father become flesh, and Spirit who proceeds from both to sanctify. As relation *ad alium*, the Trinity is most definitively seen in Christ Jesus. We learn that the Trinity is *per se* self-donative and generative. In salvation history, the Trinity is God for us. God for us is the Father who creates a universe for fellowship with himself. He walks in the garden with Adam and Eve. God for us is the Father who sends his Son, Jesus in perfect filial obedience to return us to his friendship. In Christ Jesus, God reveals himself as God for us, who empties himself to bring us into communion with himself and sends his Spirit to vivify that communion.

To show just how difficult it is to avoid problems with Trinity and the family, let me explore one modern example of a trinitarian theology of the family that has much to recommend it.[69] Frederick J. Parrella, whose work was introduced in chapter 2, is clear in noting that God has revealed himself as three relations *ad alium*, yet the "other" to which each Person of the Trinity is related is also itself. He then goes on to talk about human relatedness by means of an

---

68. See the doctrine of analogy; Henrico Denzinger, *Enchiridion Symbolorum Definitiorum et Declarationum de Rebus Fidei et Morum*, no. 432 (Freiburg: Herder, 1911), 192. John Paul II makes note of it in *Mulieris dignitatem* 8.

69. Also see Bertrand de Margerie, "L'analogie familiale de la Trinité," *Science et Esprit* 24 (1972): 77–92; and Gérard Rémy, "L'analogie et l'image: de leur bon usage en théologie," *Recherches de science religieuse* 92 (2004): 383–427.

Foundations for a Consecrated Way

implicit analogy wherein the relation *ad alium* of each person of the Trinity to the other is analogical to the relation *ad alium* of each human person to the other, especially within the family. Human persons are constituted in their relationships to others and for others. "*We are God's image only insofar as* we stand in relation to others."[70] For Parrella the primary occasion and location for these relationships of persons "ad alium" is the family. "The family," he writes, "allows us an insight into the very heart of God":[71]

> *No other commitment* is as absolute in its intensity nor as eternal in its duration as marriage.... In uttering Thou, he stands in relation, existing *ad alium* with his whole being. In this process he becomes himself, *in se,* a person. Sexuality in marriage is the unique language that expresses the all-encompassing power of the relationship. Through this language, two persons are so intensely *ad alium* in body and soul that the spirit of love between them becomes incarnate as a free and independent third person, the child. *No other formal relationship allows a human being to reveal God as Trinity so perfectly.*[72]

Marriage, then, especially in its genital expression of integrated sexuality, is the privileged means of expressing the Trinity in the world.

I would issue two caveats with Parrella's point of entry to the family as analogy for the Trinity. First, the Bible and the Christian tradition have often referred to the human person "in" or "to" the image of God (Gen 1:26–27), but only Christ "*is* the image of the invisible God" (Col 1:15). Thus we must be more reserved than Parrella with respect to the ability of the human person to reveal the nature of the Trinity.

Second, we must recognize that Parrella's move to privilege married sexuality risks absolutizing the revelatory power of marriage, and especially the sexual act within marriage, potentially making sex

---

70. Parrella, "Towards a Spirituality of the Family," *Communio* 9 (1982): 136.
71. Ibid., 137.
72. Ibid. Drawing a one-to-one analogy is always dangerous; emphasis of "No other commitment" is mine.

an idol. Despite his best efforts, Parrella has fallen prey to the chief danger of using trinitarian analogy; it would appear that married people have the market cornered on expressing God's own nature. When Parrella states that marriage is the superlative form of eternal commitment, he would seem to be forgetting Jesus' own words in response to the Sadducees, "In the resurrection they neither marry nor are given in marriage, but are like angels in heaven" (Mt 22:30). If the marriage commitment were eternal, then widows or widowers would be theoretically incapable of remarriage. Of course, Parrella may be referring to the fact that the marriage commitment is ordered toward the eternal reality of the child born of the spouses, a child destined for eternal beatitude. If this is the case, he is forgetful of the tradition regarding the true fruitfulness of the consecrated celibate spousally given to Christ. Further, when Parrella argues for the superlatively eternal commitment of marriage, he erroneously privileges genital, orgasmic expression of human sexuality. What of chaste celibacy? Is it not a complete gift of self? Does not the religious give over herself as sexual person? Is this gift not an expression of an intense desire to be wholly and completely *ad alium*, where the other is the Trinity itself, or the entire human family? Cannot this self-donative love of the religious be equally as intense as the love of spouses, even though it is not expressed in orgasm? Is the self-donative love of the consecrated celibate person not as fruitful as that of the married person, even though it results only in spiritual offspring? Unfortunately, in his effort to resist the subordination of marriage to monastic spirituality, Parrella has perhaps unwittingly subordinated consecrated religious life to sacramental marriage.

Parrella's desire to understand the family's relationship to the Trinity is helpful and needed. My critique is not that using the term "image" is wrong or misguided. Quite the opposite. My critique is that the image of the Trinity is so powerful that it can enlighten our understanding of all examples of true human community. The family generated by Christian marriage does not have sole claim to being in the image of the Trinity. Vowed religious life in community has the same domestic characteristics that make the home a space and time for relatedness *ad alium*. For example, married sexuality—conjugal intercourse and marital chastity in general—may be part of the unique way that the spouses attempt to conform their lives to the image of the self-donative love of the Trinity, but vowed religious sexuality expresses the same self-donative, fruitful love in its chaste celibacy. Again, just as children and parents have claims on each other without regard to each other's wants or even feelings, the members of the religious congregation have a claim on each other beyond the individual religious's own willing. The claim is based on the permanence of the community formed and the *telos* of the community to become the kind of persons who seek first God's kingdom. Take, as another example, the vow of poverty. Poverty canonically requires each to provide for and rely on the other. Vowed religious, then, participate with married Christians in the same task of existing as beings *in relation,* beings directed toward another. Therefore, both married and religious must live in the image of the same divine reality, the Trinity, but in distinct ways. The Trinity unifies married and religious life more powerfully than it sunders them.

In light of these difficulties with analogy, I agree with John Paul II's suggestion that "the original model of the family must be sought in God himself, in the trinitarian mystery of his life."[73] Note John Paul II's use of "model" here. The family is to make itself like what has been revealed about the Trinity. For John Paul II the actual connection between the Trinity and the conjugal family is not strictly a correspondence between the persons themselves (as man or woman)

---

73. John Paul II, *Letter to Families (Gratissimam sane)* (Rome: Libreria Editrice Vaticana, 1994), no. 6.

but between the "*communio personarum.*" In other words, the family should attempt to imitate the communion of persons that God has revealed the Trinity to be—to provide a kind of image of that communion for and in the world:

> In the words of the [Second Vatican] Council, the "communion" of persons is drawn in a certain sense from the mystery of the trinitarian "we," and therefore "conjugal communion" also refers to this mystery. The family, which originates in the love of man and woman, ultimately derives from the mystery of God.[74]

Furthermore, "this conforms to the innermost being of man and woman, to their innate and authentic dignity as persons" with the capacity and need to live in truth and love.[75] Inasmuch as the conjugal family is a true communion of persons, it is made to the image of the Trinity.

Following John Paul II's thought, we can also say that the family, inasmuch as it participates in the fruitfulness of the trinitarian communion of persons, conforms itself to Trinity. The Trinity is a communion of love that eternally engenders, maintains, and gives the Divine Persons to, from, and for each other; the Trinity contains a genealogy of Persons that is the source of the genealogy of persons in the conjugal family. When spouses consent to be "willing to accept children from God," they are taking up a mission that is revealed by the life of the Trinity, whose love is so personal as to actually *be* a person. The married couple are choosing to be conformed to this model as a communion of persons whose love is a personal reception of the other as person and a gift of one's own person; this love becomes a person in the child welcomed into the home as

---

74. Ibid., 8. Earl Muller has developed a "communitarian analogy" of the Trinity from Pauline sources; see Muller, *Trinity and Marriage in Paul: The Establishment of a Communitarian Analogy of the Trinity Grounded in the Theological Shape of Pauline Thought* (Frankfurt: Lang, 1990).

75. John Paul II, *Letter to Families*, no. 8.

Foundations for a Consecrated Way

gift, as stranger, as Christ, as good in herself or himself.[76] This openness to life is at once biological and spiritual. John Paul II writes, "God himself is present in human fatherhood and motherhood quite differently than he is present in all other instances of begetting 'on earth.'"[77] Creation is an act of the Trinity, and spousal love is a willingness to participate by receptivity in that act of creation at the spiritual and biological levels.

A family's biological procreation participates in God's spiritual act of creation, but a family's share in the Trinity's genealogical power goes beyond procreation of children. John Chrysostom commanded the families of his diocese to "make your home into a Church."[78] He was speaking of the practices required for a trinitarian communion of persons: "domestic concord, openness to strangers and the poor, welcome and hospitality as essential virtues."[79] Paul

---

76. Stratford Caldecott, in "The Drama of the Home: Marriage, the Common Good, and Public Policy," in *Marriage and the Common Good: Proceedings from the Twenty-Second Annual Convention of the Fellowship of Catholic Scholars*, edited by Kenneth D. Whitehead 1–26, at 19–21 (South Bend, Ind.: St. Augustine's, 2001), reflects on the idea of the child as the "embodiment" of the common good of the marriage. He is relying on John Paul II, *Letter to Families*, 10–11. John Paul II writes, "*In the newborn child is realized the common good of the family.* Just as the common good of the spouses is fulfilled in conjugal love, ever ready to give and receive new life, so too the common good of the family is fulfilled through that same spousal love, as embodied in the newborn child. Part of the genealogy of the person is the genealogy of the family, preserved for posterity by the annotations in the Church's baptismal registers, even though these are merely the social consequences of the fact that 'a man has been born into the world' (see Jn 16:21)"; *Letter to Families*, 11, emphasis original.

77. John Paul II, *Letter to Families*, 9 (emphasis original).

78. John Chrysostom, *Homilies on Genesis* 6.2, PG 54, 607; and Chrysostom, *Expo. In Ps* 41:12, PG 55, 158.

79. John Chrysostom, *Homily 20 on Ephesians, On Marriage and Family Life*, trans. Catharine P. Roth and David Anderson (1986; repr. Crestwood, N.Y.: St. Vladimir's Seminary Press, 2003), 57: "If we regulate our households in this way, we will also be fit to oversee the Church, for indeed the household is a little Church. Therefore, it is possible for us to surpass all others in virtue by becoming good husbands and wives"; see also John Chrysostom, *Homily 26 on Acts*, ed. Philip Schaff, trans. J. Walker et al., in *Nicene and Post-Nicene Fathers*, vol. 11 (Buffalo, N.Y.: Christian Literature Publishing, 1889), at http://newadvent.org/fathers/210126.htm, accessed February 9, 2011. From these quotes it is apparent that, for Chrysostom, the household is a Church because it shares in the *practices* of the Church and because it benefits from Christ's promise of presence to the gathered Christians.

VI, developing on the Second Vatican Council's renewal of the term "domestic church," emphasized in *Evangelii nuntiandi* that the family's criteria of ecclesiality was evangelization. The home is a legitimate source of evangelization. John Paul II, in *Familiaris consortio*, makes three kinds of references to the family as "domestic church." One is to affirm that the family is such an ecclesial reality, sharing by word, sacrament, and unity in the life and mystery of the Church.[80] Second, with Paul VI he restates the family's evangelical mission.[81] Finally, he sees the family as a sanctuary (as a Church building has a sanctuary) wherein prayer and worship are offered.[82] For John Paul II, because the conjugal family's proper identity and role is to share in the Trinity's (and thus the wider Church's) genealogy and function, "the family is more than a field for implementation of Church pastoral policy, but is an authentic manifestation of the Church."[83]

To the Trinity ... and Beyond!

There are two immediate implications of my conclusion that consecrated and conjugal life meet in Christ the second Person of the Trinity, the poor, chaste, and obedient bridegroom. My conclusion should fairly put to rest worries of those who fear a "monasticization of marriage." I have reframed the question of how the two states relate to and influence one another. Rather than seeing marriage and consecrated life as *parallel* tracks, I have offered a picture that imagines conjugal and religious life as intertwined practices of being conformed to Christ the poor, chaste, and obedient bridegroom. Poverty, chastity, and obedience constitute the fiber of both threads of this one twine inasmuch as both are a participation in Christ. We

---

80. See *FC* 21, 38, 48, 49, cited in Ouellet, *Divine Likeness*, 41.
81. See *FC* 51, 52, 53, cited in ibid.
82. See *FC* 55, 59, 61, cited in ibid.
83. See Ouellet, *Divine Likeness*, 41; Normand Provencher, "Vers une théologie de la famille: L'Église domestique," *Église et théologie* 12 (1981): 9–34.

have now reached a point where we can speak of poverty, chastity, and obedience not as "things the religious life can offer married people," but as practices *inherently,* though distinctly expressed in both states of life. On the one hand, this conclusion is a "thing new," but on the other hand, as the proceeding chapters will show, it is rooted in a way of relating married and religious life that comes from the traditional treasures of "things old."

4

SOMETHING NEW FROM SOMEONE OLD— AUGUSTINE

According to the narrative of theological development given by modern scholars relating marriage and religious life, a dichotomization and hierarchy of religious and married life began early in the Church and persisted until the second half of the twentieth century, when the Church and many theologians finally rejected the preference of the consecrated life over married life. While Parrella, Russell, and Phan may be correct to note that a tide seems swelling against the claim that the life of vowed religious life is objectively superior to marriage, this chapter demonstrates that the pot of popular and theological fervor on this question has been boiled and bubbled, toiled and troubled throughout most of Christian history.

My argument will proceed as follows. First, I will show that Eastern monastic fathers had a more complicated view of personal holiness than was given credit in the standard narrative. Second, I will show in the theology of Augustine an alternative to both the competitive spirit of ascetical hierarchy and its egalitarian challenge. He recognizes distinction in personal merit, but emphasizes its elusiveness and moves beyond the question to develop our common and primarily ecclesial identity as Christians, which relies on spousal language that relates to both the consecrated and the married life. Over the course of his life he develops three "nuptial goods" (*proles, fides,* and *sacramentum*) shared by both consecrated virgins and married persons. These "nuptial goods" are properly and primarily ecclesial goods shared by all those baptized into Christ.

Patristic Evidence Against a Simple Ascetical Hierarchy in Eastern Desert Tradition

First, there is evidence from the Eastern monastic fathers to suggest a complication of the simple hierarchy of merit assumed by the common narrative. Kalistos Ware's study "The Monk and the Married Christian: Some Comparisons in Early Monastic Sources" offers telling examples of monks finding themselves inferior to married men and women.[1] Some might argue that examples of monks comparing themselves negatively to married persons are the exceptions that prove the rule of a simple ascetic hierarchy. After all, there would be little rhetorical power to the comparisons if they did not in some way surprise the reader. Such an argument might be convincing if the examples really constituted a miniscule sample. In fact, it appears that the debate was more evenly split. St. Isaac the Syrian and St. Theodore the Studite doubted that the grace of contemplation and vision of God could be given to the married.[2] On the other hand, St. Gregory the Great thought the *lumen contemplationis* was available to all.[3] Furthermore, Ware finds that "St. Maxi-

---

1. Kalistos Ware, "The Monk and the Married Christian: Some Comparisons in Early Monastic Sources," *Eastern Churches Review* 6, no. 1 (1974): 72–83.

2. Isaac of Nineveh, *Mystic Treatises by Isaac of Nineveh,* trans. A. J. Wensinck (Amsterdam: Koninklijke Akademie van Wtenschappen, 1923), 102; and Theodore the Studite, *Epistle* ii, 43, *Patrologiae Cursus Completus,* Series Graeca (hereafeter PG), ed. Jacques-Paul Migne (Paris: 1857–66), xcix, col. 1245AB, cited in Ware, "Monk and the Married Christian," 74.

3. St. Gregory the Great, *Homilies in Ezekiel* 2, 5, 19, in *Patrologiae Cursus Completus,* Se-

mus the Confessor, embodied some of his deepest teaching about *theosis* and union with God in his Second Letter, addressed to a layman, a civil servant; St. Gregory Palamas considered that continual prayer is for lay people as well as monks, and that full purity of heart can be attained by the married Christian, 'although with the greatest difficulty.'"[4]

A second kind of evidence suggesting that holiness could be achieved in marriage comes from a genre of literature popular in the Byzantine Empire, the *vitae* of the saints, or hagiographical literature. These *vitae* were the popular medium of the day and every bit as exciting for the audience. The earliest versions of some of these *vitae*—that is, those of St. Symeon the Stylite and Melaniae—emphasize the monastic aversion to marriage and the superlative value of physical virginity. The lives of some married saints are related, but they either do not consummate the marriage or they eventually lead a life of celibacy. Take Melania the Younger, for example. The earliest versions of her *vita* claim that "After the death of her two sons she felt an aversion to marriage (*misos tou gamon*) and told her husband that she would stay with him 'as her lord and master' only if he agreed to lead a life of chastity; if not, she would give him all her belongings and 'liberate her body.' In the later *Vita* of Melania, the sharpness of this anti-marital tendency was reduced, the 'aversion' disappeared, and only the call for chastity (*agneia*) remained."[5] For example, revised versions of Melania's and Symeon's *vitae* include the praise of marriage as "honorable," and the aversion to marriage

---

ries Latina (hereafter PL), ed. Jacques-Paul Migne (Paris: 1844–91), lxxvi, col. 996A, cited in Ware, "Monk and the Married Christian," 74.

4. Ware, "Monk and the Married Christian," 74. Ware cites St. Maximus the Confessor from PG xci, col. 391–408; Ware cites St. Gregory Palamas from *Encomium S. Gregorii Thessalonicensis*, PG cli, col. 573a–574a, and from *De passionibus et virtutibus*, PG cl, col. 1056A.

5. Alexander Kazhdan, "Byzantine Hagiography and Sex in the Fifth to Twelfth Centuries," *Dumbarton Oaks Papers* 44 (1990): 131–43, at 133.

is muted. From this trend, Alexander Kazhdan has made the following observation that over three centuries "the concept was developed that sanctity could be achieved not only in the desert or in the monastery but in family life. Maria the Younger and Thomais of Lesbos ... were married women who deserved the reward of holiness; Nicholas Kataskepenos, in the *Vita* of Cyril Phileotes, conjured up the image of a saint who, after the birth of his child, limited his sexual intercourse with his wife but did not accept consistent celibacy."[6] Even more surprising, Eustathios of Thessalonike judges the lay saint of greater honor than lonely anchorites living in isolation.[7]

A third kind of evidence for a more nuanced view of the ascetical hierarchy comes from a genre of literature known as *Streitnovellen* or "stories of rivalry" found in the *Apophthegmata Patrum*. In each of these stories, a monk is told in a dream or by an angel about a person (man or woman) whose holiness exceeds his own. The monk investigates and discovers his own weakness, which is usually pride or a lack of charity. When the married person is judged holier than the monk, it is on one of four grounds: (1) on account of holy, ascetic practices; (2) on account of virtuous deeds; (3) on account of holy disposition, such as the virtue of humility or simplicity; and (4) on account of an intention to live a life of renunciation, even if such a life is impossible. In the first case, a villager named Eucharistus is holier than a certain monk. This shepherd and married man divides his money in thirds, giving one third to the poor, one third for hospitality, and one third for his own needs. He lives an ascetic life, is married, and practices celibacy within his marriage. In this story it is Eucharistus's ascetic practices that impress. There is a sug-

---

6. Ibid., 133.

7. Ibid. For more on the development of a positive theology of marriage in comparison to monasticism in Byzantine tradition, see Kazhdan, "Hermitic, Cenobitic, and Secular Ideals in Byzantine Hagiography of the Ninth [to Twelfth] Centuries," *Greek Orthodox Theological Review* 30 (1985): 484–87.

gestion that his life conforms to the monastic already, since he practices celibacy. Regarding the second case, a monk is told he is not as holy as a local flute player and known sinner. This flute player, though, saved a woman in distress on two occasions, and for this is counted holier than the ascetic monk. The emphasis here is on his deeds of compassion. In the third case, a monk is compared to Emperor Theodosius. Here Theodosius's superiority to the monk is not his asceticism or his charitable deeds but his true humility, simplicity of heart, and detachment from the world, the chief expression of which is his ability to copy religious manuscripts while in attendance at the hippodrome.[8] It is of special interest that the author does not suggest Theodosius would be holier as a monk, whereas in the first two models becoming a monk would perfect the holiness of the nonvowed persons.

Finally, Macarius of Egypt is compared to two women. These women married brothers and had children by them. The two couples live together, but despite their wives' request the husbands have refused to live in celibacy. These two women, out of a desire for holiness, vow to never speak a word of quarrel or conflict between them. Seeing the holy intention of these two women and "marveling at their ability to live so long together without quarreling, Macarius exclaims, "In truth there is neither virgin nor married, neither monk nor secular, but God gives his Holy Spirit to all, according to the intention of each."[9] Here the emphasis falls on the strong intention to a life of renunciation, despite the fact that it could not be realized in full.

In the final analysis these "rivalry stories" are ill-named. Any reader is confronted with the fact that the very desire and attempt to rank

---

8. Ware, "Monk and the Married Christian," 75–76; he relies on Patrologia Orientalis viii, ed. F. Nau, Johannes Rufus, Severus Antiochenus, et al., *Patrologia Orientalis* (Paris: Firmin-Didot, 1912), 171–74.

9. Ware, "Monk and the Married Christian," 79.

oneself with respect to another person is already a symptom of pride and already betrays an incomplete renunciation of and detachment from the world and its temptations toward renown. Ware concludes that, in the world imagined by these anecdotes, "inward purity is always possible, whatever the outward circumstances." The flight from sin is more spiritual than geographical. The "rivalry stories" reveal an embryonic layman's spirituality. "The Emperor enthroned in the hippodrome, hearing the acclamations of the crowd yet never lifting his eyes from his manuscript; the greengrocer sitting in his room at night hearing the songs of the drunkards yet thinking only of their salvation—these are two of the most striking figures in the *Apophthegmata*. It is not easy to forget them."[10]

Augustine and Equality of Merit: A Radical Alternative to the Zero-Sum Game

The debates and hortatory literature relating the personal holiness of the vowed religious and the married Christian were not limited by any means to the Eastern tradition. Augustine and his Latin-speaking contemporaries hotly disputed the same questions, though their audiences and genres differed. First I will present the context for Augustine's involvement in three ecclesial controversies as they relate to marriage: Manicheism, Jovinianism, and Pelagianism. I will also address their relationship to the modern construals of the problems and solutions to the "crisis" of marriage as well as their relationship to the modern zero-sum understanding of the relationship between consecrated and conjugal life. The second part attempts to develop what Augustine called the "*medium veritatis*,"[11] the middle way of truth between two extreme stories about the relationship between re-

---

10. Ibid., 82–83.
11. Augustine, *De sancta virginitate* 19, CSEL 41, 252–53. Ironically, this passage is not cited when authors describe Augustine as staking a middle ground on marriage.

ligious life and married life (Jerome's hierarchy of merit and Jovinian's equality of the states). In so doing I will explore the three major accomplishments of Augustine's re-narration of this relationship: (1) prioritizing ecclesial belonging over individual merit; (2) complicating but not rejecting differentiation of merit; and (3) creating a threefold *bonum nuptiarum*. Augustine makes a unique proposal that moves beyond concern for individual merit and picks up a social, ecclesial, co-participative understanding of the *bonum nuptiarum*. The *bonum nuptiarum*, in other words, is principally *bonum ecclesiae* that people of different states share. These accomplishments ground and shape the Augustinian counternarrative wherein consecrated and conjugal life mutually inform one another.

Augustine's Context

Just as the Eastern fathers experienced and reflected on the tension between married and religious life, especially with respect to how persons might locate themselves on a hierarchy of holiness, so too did the Western fathers. At the end of the fourth and the beginning of the fifth century, Augustine himself was embroiled in debates over the relative merit of virginity over married life. Whereas the Eastern fathers offered anecdotal stories to challenge individual monastics in their own life with Christ, Augustine dealt with three major controversies and opponents in his thinking on marriage: the Manichaeans, the Jovinian controversy, and the Pelagians. Augustine's genius in his defense of marriage and virginity, a genius that makes him relevant to my claim for consonance between the two, is Augustine's "making them both magnificently social."[12] As social they must constitute part of a larger association; this larger association is first and foremost the Church, the mystical body of Christ.

---

12. See Peter Brown, *The Body and Society: Men, Women, and Sexual Renunciation in Early Christianity* (New York: Columbia University Press, 1988), 402.

Something New from Someone Old—Augustine

Augustine understands this mystical body to be one with and composed of Christ's bride the Church. Christ is head of his body, which is also his own bride in realistic and analogical ways.[13]

Before I tackle Augustine's constructive task itself, I must fill in the polemical background of the two theologies Augustine takes on in *De bono coniugali*—Manichaeism and Jovinianism—and the final heresy that will dominate the late portion of his career—Pelagianism as propounded by Julian of Aeclanum. A Manichaean for ten years himself, Augustine vigorously fought against Manichaean teachings after his conversion to Christianity, especially regarding marriage.[14] In works predating *De bono coniugali* against Manicheans, Augustine resists Manichean arguments against marriage,[15] and he does not leave that polemic behind in *De bono coniugali*, especially given that he is still trying to complete his *literal* commentary

---

13. See Stanislaus J. Grabowski, *The Church: An Introduction to the Theology of St. Augustine* (St. Louis: Herder, 1957). Augustine's ecclesiology is chiefly that of the mystical body. The Church is the body of Christ. Augustine nonetheless includes Church as bride and Christ as bridegroom. We see this in two ways, first explicitly; for example, see *Ennarrationes in Psalmos* 44.3, CSEL 38, 495, 515, where Augustine refers to Christ as the bridegroom in this wedding feast of the King and the Church as the virgin to be wed. Second, whenever Christ refers to the Church as the mystical body of Christ, the Church as bride is also included therein implicitly on account of scriptural warrant (e.g., Eph 5:23–32). Augustine holds to a more than merely metaphorical understanding of the bond between Christ and his Church as bridegroom and bride. The bride becomes one body with Christ analogously (though not sexually) to the way husband and wife are one body; see Pius Schelkens, "De Ecclesia Sponsa Christi," *Augustiniana* 3 (1953): 145–64; Tarsisius van Bavel, *Recherches sur la christologie de saint Augustin: L'humain et le divin dans le Christ d'apres saint Augustin* (Fribourg: Editions universitaires, 1954), 79–85, at 83; and Denis Faul, "Ecclesia, Sponsa Christi: Origenes y Augustín ante la exegesis de Eph. 5, 27," *Augustinus* 15 (1970): 263–80.

14. See Augustine, *Confessions*, bk 4. The classic biography is Peter Brown, *Augustine of Hippo: A Biography*, 2nd ed. (1967; repr. London: Faber and Faber, 2000), 35–49; a newer biography that challenges Brown's for comprehensiveness is Serge Lancel, *Augustine*, trans. Antonia Nevill (London: SCM, 2002), 37–42.

15. Augustine wrote many works against the Manichaeans, among them *De moribus ecclesiae catholicae et de moribus Manicheorum, Acta contra fortunatum manicheum, De genesi ad litteram liber unus imperfectus, Contra faustum manicheum*, and *De genesi adversus manichaeos* 1.19, as well as *De genesi ad litteram*, written at the same time as *De bono coniugali*. For a wider treatment of Augustine and the Manicheans, see Kam-Lun Lee, *Augustine, Manichaeism, and the Good*, Patristic Studies 2 (New York: Peter Lang, 1999).

on Genesis (a crucial peg in an argument against Manicheans).[16] Manicheans often ridiculed Christian reading of the Old Testament, especially Genesis. The Manicheans taught that the material world was evil, having been created by a god who rivals the true god. In this material world the rival god has trapped pieces of the true god. Human souls are these trapped pieces. The goal of life, then, is to escape material reality, a process completed by certain dietary and ascetical practices, accompanied by gaining secret knowledge. Their teachings on marriage follow logically from their understanding of the origin and purpose of the material world—that is, the origin and nature of evil. As procreation traps more spirit in the prison of matter, the Manicheans naturally treat procreation with abhorrence. Therefore they conclude that marriage is the invention of the rival to the true god of spirit. The spiritual elite must be celibate on account of the evil, material world. While sexual intercourse is allowed for those outside the Manichaean inner circle (as Augustine was), contraception was mandated. Augustine pulled no rhetorical punches when attacking this position, claiming that the Manicheans made a wife "no longer a wife but a prostitute, who in return for certain compensation is given to the man to satisfy his lust.... But it is not matrimony when the effort is made that she not become a mother."[17] The translation to English unfortunately loses Augus-

---

16. See Augustine, *Retractationes* 1.10, on *De genesi ad litteram;* Augustine, *On Genesis*, ed. John E. Rotelle, intro., trans., and notes Edmund Hill, part 1 of *The Works of St. Augustine: A Translation for the 21st Century* (Hyde Park, N.Y.: New City Press, 2002), 13:36–37). A "literal" interpretation of Genesis is important because the Manicheans rejected the goodness of procreation, which keeps the "light" trapped in matter. In *Confessions* 5.23–24, chap. 13, *Corpus Christianorum*, Series Latina (hereafter *CCL*) (Paris: 1953–), 27:70–71, Augustine reports that learning to read scripture spiritually had a great deal to do with his ability to read the Old Testament in the face of Manichean criticism.

17. See in particular Augustine, *De moribus* 2.65, CSEL 90: 147: "Si enim uxor est, matrimonium est. Non autem matrimonium est ubi datur opera ne sit mater"; see Augustine, *The Manichean Debate*, ed. Boniface Ramsey, trans. and notes Roland Teske, part 1 of *The Works of St. Augustine* (Hyde Park, N.Y.: New City Press, 2006), 19:98. Marriage is entered for the

tine's rhetorical skill. He links the word *mater* to *matrimonium* in this sentence, claiming that there is no *matrimonio* absent the intent to become *mater*.

As a second point of attack, the Manicheans assailed the moral character of the Old Testament patriarchs. For one, these men had multiple wives, an obvious contradiction to Christian practice. In *De bono coniugali* Augustine defends the patriarchs by seeing in their multiplicity of wives a sign or prophetic character (multiple churches subject to the one man Christ), as well as the expression of the virtue of obedience (the patriarchs would have preferred celibacy but married out of obedience).[18] According to this account, the patriarchs, then, are not only morally sound, but they are more virtuous than the vast majority of married people today, even though they had multiple wives.

While the Manichaean issue perhaps most closely affected his own life, Augustine also had to deal with polemics brought his way by concerned Christian friends; among these we find the Jovinian controversy. In his *Retractationes* Augustine writes that the two works *De bono coniugali* and *De sancta virginitate* respond to Jovinian's heresy.[19] Jovinian taught four contentious doctrines: "(1) Virgins, widows, and spouses, having been washed once in Christ, if

---

mutual, honorable purpose of *liberorum procreandorum causa*, not for the sake of satisfying lust; see Augustine, *Sermon III. 51.22; Sermons* [51 94] *on the New Testament*, ed. John E. Rotelle, trans. and notes Edmund Hill, part 3 of *The Works of St. Augustine* (Brooklyn, N.Y.: New City Press, 1992), 4:33–34.

18. Augustine, *De bono coniugali* 15, CSEL 41, 207–8; see Augustine, *Marriage and Virginity: Holy Virginity; The Excellence of Marriage; The Excellence of Widowhood; Continence*, trans. Ray Kearney, introduction and notes David G. Hunter, part 1 of *The Works of St. Augustine* (Hyde Park, N.Y.: New City Press, 1999), 9:44–45.

19. The content of Jovinian's argument is known from the condemnations text of Pope Siricius, a letter from Ambrose to Siricius (*Epistola. 42, Rescriptum ad Siricium papam* 4) concerning Ambrose's condemnation of Jovinian through a council in Milan, Jerome's first response (*Adversus Iovinianum* 1.3; PL 23, col. 206–338) and a letter he sent when that response met with lack of enthusiasm (*Epistola. 49*, CSEL 54; *Epistola. 52*). In *Adv. Iovinianum* Jerome lays out four Jovinian theses.

they do not differ in other works, are commended as of the same merit; (2) whoever in full faith is born again in baptism cannot be overthrown by the devil; (3) there is no distinction between abstinence from food and receiving it with acts of thanksgiving; (4) for all who will preserve their baptism, there is one reward in the kingdom of heaven."[20] Pope Siricius had condemned Jovinian in Rome, as had Bishop Ambrose in Milan. He was sentenced to exile and flogging. At the theological level Jerome attempted a vitriolic rebuttal of Jovinian's teachings, which only further fanned the flames.[21] This heresy continued to grow despite efforts to stop it, and Jovinian had even inveigled some consecrated virgins to precipitate marriage.

Most importantly, Augustine had to answer the charge that Jovinian could only be refuted by denigrating marriage—that is, by taking a Manichaean position. Augustine, therefore, sets out to prove that a praise of marriage is possible that refutes Jovinian's heresy.[22] The challenge was to succeed where Jerome and Ambrose had failed. Jerome had refuted Jovinian but at what seemed to be the cost of marriage's inherent good. Augustine's challenge, then, in refuting Jovinian, was not merely to construct a positive account of marriage. Jovinian could easily do as much. What Augustine needed was to offer an optimistic theology of marriage while maintaining the basic doctrine that persons can differ in virtue and that difference in virtue has eternal consequence. Augustine would have to argue that, despite their both being Christian, the married Christian can contrast in merit from the celibate Christian, and the difference

---

20. Jerome's *Adversus Iovinianum* 1, lines 41–50, report the four errors of Jovinian. Cetedoc Library of Christian Latin Texts (CLCLT) published electronically through Brepols at http://www.corpuschristianorum.org/series/clclt.html (translation mine).

21. Jerome's friends in Rome were not receptive to his rebuttal of Jovinian, and even his second, rhetorically softer attempt (*Epistola* 49) leaves unstated the positive marital good. Defining this good of marriage is the unique, creative task of Augustine.

22. See *Retractationes* 2.22, CCSL 57, 107–08.

will be rewarded differently in the kingdom of God. Augustine's answer measures merit based more upon the virtues operative in the person than on his or her state in life.

David Hunter, in a series of articles that culminate in his recent book *Marriage, Celibacy, and Heresy in Ancient Christianity: The Jovinianist Controversy*, has significantly expanded the understanding of what is at stake in the polemical context of *De bono coniugali* and *De sancta virginitate*.[23] He sees the debate occurring on three fronts: (1) the concern among all the authors (Jovinian, Ambrose, Jerome, and Augustine) to fight Manichaean tendencies in any theology of marriage; (2) the competition among theologians to garner favor and to proliferate their theological positions among the Roman, aristocratic elite; and (3) the clerical and lay resistance to or embrace of an ascetic hierarchy in the late fourth and early fifth centuries.

While the first two points are interesting, most relevant is Hunter's third point; Hunter actually aligns Augustine with Jovinian *against* Jerome and Ambrose, claiming that Augustine intended to subvert the clear ascetic hierarchy of celibates over married persons.[24] In a concluding paragraph of that section, Hunter writes, "Augustine undermined the ascetic hierarchy in a form that mirrored the intentions, if not all the arguments, of Jovinian."[25]

Hunter has expanded the polemical context and squarely located Augustine's position as a "middle way" that retains some of Jovinian's, Ambrose's, and Jerome's conclusions, but where Hunter leaves off is on the question of Augustine's particular, *constructive* project for marriage. Can we identify what Augustine calls the "middle way

---

23. I will not list all the articles here, since much of their work is folded into the book; see David G. Hunter, *Marriage, Celibacy, and Heresy in Ancient Christianity: The Jovinianist Controversy*, Oxford Early Christian Studies (Oxford: Oxford University Press, 2007).
24. Ibid., 269–84.
25. Ibid., 284.

Something New from Someone Old—Augustine

of truth" (*medium veritatis*)? What are its payoffs in this debate? It is here, then, that I must pick up. I hope to show what Augustine built up in place of facile ascetical hierarchy. For now, though, I must finish contextualizing Augustine's theological soundings as they relate to marriage with the third, most taxing debate of Augustine's late life—Pelagianism.

There were a host of fundamental theological points at stake in Augustine's debates with the Pelagians, especially Julian of Aeclanum (perhaps Augustine's most worthy opponent). Among the most important points was the Pelagians' eerily reminiscent doctrine of one holiness, which all *"Integri Christiani"* (authentic Christians, as Pelagius called them) must live.[26] In other words, Christianity demanded one rigorous moral standard for inclusion in the community. The tendency toward forming a "Church within the Church" had sprung up before in the heresies of Montanism[27] and Donatism,[28] and here again it was visible in the efforts of Pelagius and Julian.[29] Both Montanism and Donatism required extraordi-

---

26. Peter Brown, "Pelagius and His Supporters: Environment and Aims," *Journal of Theological Studies* 19 (1968): 101. This theory of one holiness sounds familiar because theology after Vatican II has so emphasized *Lumen gentium*'s universal call to holiness.

27. See William Tabbernee, *Fake Prophecy and Polluted Sacraments: Ecclesiastical and Imperial Reactions to Montanism*, Supplements to Vigiliae Christianae 84 (Boston: Brill, 2007); Daniel H. Williams, "The Origins of the Montanist Movement: A Sociological Analysis," *Religion* 19, no. 4 (October 1989): 331–51; and John G. Davies, "Tertullian, *De Resurrectione Carnis* 63: A Note on the Origins of Montanism," *Journal of Theological Studies*, new series 6, no. 1 (April 1955): 90–94. Interestingly, Montanism developed a rigorous teaching on marriage in the works of Tertullian, e.g., *Ad uxorem*. Tertullian and other Montanists did not allow remarriage of widows.

28. Peter Iver Kaufman, "Augustine, Evil, and Donatism: Sin and Sanctity before the Pelagian Controversy," *Theological Studies* 51 (1990): 115–26; Carol Scheppard, "The Transmission of Sin in the Seed: A Debate Between Augustine of Hippo and Julian of Eclanum," in *Doctrinal Diversity: Varieties of Early Christianity*, edited by Everett Ferguson, 233–42 (New York: Garland, 1999).

29. A later example of this kind of theological tendency, though in many ways from the opposite approach, appears in Jansenism; see Ronald Arbuthnott Knox, *Enthusiasm: A Chapter in the History of Religion, with Special Reference to the XVII and XVIII Centuries* (New York: Oxford University, 1950); and Nigel Abercrombie, *The Origins of Jansenism* (Oxford: Clarendon

nary witness of holiness for ecclesial membership (and certainly for ministry). For the Montanists this took the form of ecstatic prophecy and for the Donatists heroic faithfulness in the face of persecution. Peter I. Kaufman points out that the Donatist claim to be a Church of the pure, authentic Christians was part of Augustine's impetus for developing the doctrines of sin and grace that become even more pronounced in his later debates with the Pelagians. These understandings of sin and grace have an important role in how Augustine conceptualizes the relationship between consecrated and conjugal life (which I will explore later in this chapter).

These groups were, in a sense, theologically "conservative." The Montanists wanted to conserve the early tradition of prophecy and the Donatists the early tradition of radical *martyros* (witness) and ecclesial exclusion of sinners. For the Donatists the Church was the Church of the holy, the pure, not a Church of sinners.[30] In a similar way, the Pelagians (Julian of Aeclanum and Pelagius himself) too could be construed as the "conservatives" of their day, hoping to preserve Christianity as a religion requiring a practice of existing in severe tension with the surrounding societal mores.[31] Augustine, on the other hand, could have been cast as a sort of "liberal," allowing lukewarm Christians in the Church with his "ontological" rather

---

Press, 1936). The "Church within the Church" tendency based on moral or liturgical rigorism is still alive and well in the contemporary Church.

30. See Kaufman, "Augustine, Evil, and Donatism," 115, 117–18, 122–23. For Augustine, baptism cleans the soul of guilt and frees the will, but it does not completely repair the wound of original sin; Augustine, *Contra Iulianum* 6.18; *Saint Augustine: Against Julian*, trans. Matthew A. Schumacher, Fathers of the Church 16 (New York: Fathers of the Church, 1957), 364–66: "Christian baptism gives us perfect newness and perfect health from those evils by which we were guilty, not from those evils we must still combat lest we become guilty. These, too, are in us and they are not another's, but our own." English translations of *Contra Iulianum*, unless otherwise noted, come from *Saint Augustine: Against Julian*. *Contra Iulianum* is not in the *CCL* or the *CSEL*. The best Latin edition is *Corpus Augustinianum Gessense 2*, ed. Cornelius Mayer (Basel: Scwabe, 2004). Citations of *Contra Iulianum* will appear in this way: *Contra Iulianum* book.chapter; *Against Julian*, page number.

31. Peter Brown, "Pelagius and His Supporters," 93–123.

than "expressive" understanding of baptismal effectiveness and his emphasis on our slow limp toward the kingdom.[32]

I will lay out here Julian of Aeclanum's theological accusations against Augustine, as well as his positive theological assertions, which will help clarify Augustine's response and Augustine's counternarrative for the relationship between conjugal and consecrated life.[33] It will become apparent that much of Julian's theology has survived and even gained popularity in the late twentieth- and early twenty-first centuries.[34] First and foremost Julian called Augustine a Manichaean, a charge not uncommon even to this day.[35]

---

32. Augustine notes the more-than-voluntary character of salvation in *Contra Iulianum* 4.8; *Against Julian*, 204, when he states that baptism's effect is real when undesired and even when contradesired—e.g., when an infant resists reception of the sacrament: "Actually, even while they are being baptized they sometimes scream, spit, and struggle against it—yet they receive and find it is opened to them, and they enter into the kingdom of God where they have eternal salvation and the knowledge of the truth." Furthermore, in *Contra Iulianum* 6.3; *Against Julian*, 312, Augustine states, "we hold that infants believe in Christ through the hearts and voices of those who carry them."

33. Julian of Aeclanum's theology survives in the lengthy quotations by Augustine in his polemical responses to Julian.

34. The problem preventing a clearer vision of this fact is that there is a general assumption that Augustine "won" his argument against the Pelagians (especially Julian of Aeclanum). The immediate reception of Augustine with respect to this debate was moderate, and theologians (including Cassian) more or less loudly disagreed with Augustine until the Council of Orange 529. Josef Lössl, Peter Brown, and B. R. Rees have made the argument that the Pelagian theological tendency is a matter deeply rooted in our notions of sin and Christian identity vis-à-vis the world and our interpretations of Paul. Furthermore, the Pelagian theological tendency continues to exist (validly) today; see Lössl, "Augustine, Pelagianism, Julian of Aeclanum, and Modern Scholarship," *Zeitschrift für antikes Christentum* 11, no. 1 (2007): 129–50; Peter Brown, *Body and Society*, 408–27; and Rees, *Pelagius: Life and Letters* (Rochester, N.Y.: Boydell, 1998). William E. Phipps has claimed, even more forcefully, that Augustine, not Pelagius, is the great heresiarch; Phipps, "The Heresiarch; Pelagius or Augustine?" *Anglican Theological Review* 62, no. 2 (1980): 124–33.

35. See *Contra Iulianum*, book 1, where Augustine explicitly defends himself and all other theologians Julian lumps with the Manicheans; see Mathijs Lamberigts, "Was Augustine a Manichean? The Assessment of Julian of Aeclanum," in *Augustine in the Latin West* (Ithaca, N.Y.: Snow Lion, 2002), 113–36. The most common modern claim is that Augustine never left behind his Manichean tendencies; see Elizabeth Clark, "Vitiated Seeds and Holy Vessels: Augustine's Manichean Past," in *Ascetic Piety and Women's Faith: Essays on Late Ancient Christianity*, Studies in Women and Religion 20 (Lewiston, N.Y.: Edwin Mellen, 1986).

Something New from Someone Old—Augustine

Second, Julian belittled Augustine's grasp of philosophy as inept and confused.[36] Third, Julian called Augustine's Christology docetic, or Apollinarian.[37] Augustine is also supposed to have taught the following: the devil is the creator of man and his marriage is the devil's instrument;[38] Augustine makes God unjust for damning infants;[39] Augustine denies the forgiveness of all sins in baptism;[40] and Augustine says sin is inevitable, which encourages moral laxity and despair.[41] As for his positive assertions, Julian claimed first that only Adam was harmed by original sin.[42] As a correlative, Julian taught that people learn sin by imitation, not propagation. Only personal (not original) sin sends people to hell. Another corollary is that sin cannot be passed to the child of baptized spouses, since sin is gone from them.[43] Furthermore, concupiscence (here limited to the unwilled desire for sex and the nonrational arousal of the sexual organs) is a natural, biological force and gift that is only evil when used in excess.[44] Finally, Mary and Joseph did

---

36. Augustine quotes Julian's attacks in various places. Julian says that because Augustine is unsophisticated in philosophy, he "will probably assert we should use the testimony of Scripture, *not syllogisms,* to prove that offspring born of the union of bodies must be ascribed to the divine work"; *Contra Iulianum* 3.10; *Against Julian*, 124. Julian takes Augustine to task on the philosophical impossibility of passing on guilt: "That which inheres in a subject cannot exist without the thing which is the subject of its inherence"; *Contra Iulianum* 5.14; *Against Julian*, 291. Furthermore, he uses philosophical categories to detheologize sexual desire by philosophical dissection of its genus, species, mode, excess, and origin; *Contra Iulianum* 3.13.

37. *Contra Iulianum* 5.15, where Augustine defends himself against the Apollinarian charge; see also Mathijs Lamberigts, "Was Augustine a Manichean?" 113–36, at 130. He is citing Julian's letter, *Ad Florum* IV.47, PL 45, col. 1365.

38. *Contra Iulianum* 2.1, 10; 3.18, 24; 5.7; 6.23.

39. Ibid., 2.1, 3.5., 19.   40. Ibid., 2.1.
41. Ibid., 2.8.   42. Ibid., 1.5; 2.9.
43. Ibid., 2.9.

44. "Their genus is vital fire. Their species is genital action, their mode is the conjugal act, and their excess is intemperance of fornication"; ibid., 3.13; and Elizabeth Clark, "Vitiated Seeds and Holy Vessels," 291–349. Clark makes a good analysis of the Manichean roots in the background of Augustine's debate with Julian and how Augustine's thought changed over time. She gives too much credence, though, to the distinction between "biological" and "theological" understandings of human sexuality and origins. The strictly "biological"

not have a true marriage, as they never had conjugal intercourse.[45]

The stark contrast between Augustine and Julian on these topics has many implications for the relationship between consecrated and religious life. If Julian is correct, then biological reproduction would be equivalent to ecclesial, spiritual reproduction. If children are born just (that is, in right relationship to themselves, the community, and God) then they are born in the Church. Procreation *is* evangelization. Furthermore, if sexual desire is not somehow disordered and therefore need not be fought against, then it is certainly no more honorable to abstain entirely from sexual congress than to make good use of the same. The same virtue is required for both, since what is being restrained is a good rather than something broken that we might still put to good use anyway. Julian and Jovinian, then, are early representatives of the theologians we saw in chapter 2. They all attempt to find a way to level out the Christian life—that is, work against easy hierarchical judgments about the holiness available to members of certain states of life. The result is an account of conjugal and consecrated life where the two states have little to teach each other. If Augustine is correct, though, then there is a distinction between consecrated life and conjugal life, and these two states of life will have reason to speak to one another. If the process

---

understanding she attributes to Julian is not value-free. By calling it "biological," an attempt is made to locate it in the realm of the good, as if the "theological" nature of Augustine's account is what prevents him from seeing carnal concupiscence as good. For Augustine, "biology" has an explicit theological meaning and significance. Julian assumes the theological positive meaning of biology while pretending it is theologically neutral. Human physiology and genetics have theological meaning; it is ultimately a question of whether the theologian attributes to them the correct meaning. Are they broken or properly functioning? If they are broken, is that brokenness transmittable materially?

45. *Contra Iulianum* 5.12; Augustine, *De nuptiis et concupiscentia* 1.11–1.13; *Answer to the Pelagians II*, ed. Jon E. Rotelle, trans. Roland J. Teske, part 1 of *The Works of St. Augustine* (Hyde Park, N.Y.: New City Press, 1998), 24:35–37. Augustine defends the reality of Mary and Joseph's marriage on the grounds that, more than any other marriage, they achieved the three goods of marriage: *proles, fides, sacramentum.*

of biological procreation is somehow malfunctional as a result of sin, then even the best use of this capacity (for the procreation of children to be regenerated in Christ) will be less virtuous than the complete abstinence from that capacity (for the sake of the kingdom of God). At the same time, as we will see in Augustine's thought, even the most continent, temperate consecrated virgin will have much to learn from the conjugal life of an obedient, humble, chaste, and faithful spouse. It only makes sense to talk about a consonance between conjugal and consecrated life if in fact they are distinct. Augustine maintains this distinction, while much of the modern scholarship moves dangerously close to losing the distinction on the altar of an egalitarian approach to Christian spirituality.

We have just walked through Augustine's polemical context with respect to his doctrine on marriage. Let me take a moment now to review the connection between this section on Augustine's context and a concern of the whole chapter—to demonstrate that modern attempts to equalize marriage and monasticism are not new. Julian's and Jovinian's teachings have a certain post–Vatican II sensibility to them—that is, they have affinities with theological conclusions of post-conciliar attempts to put consecrated and conjugal life in dialogue. Julian's theology sounds hopeful in the face of Augustine's apparent pessimism; it is inviting rather than condemning. In baptism, according to Julian, we are cleansed from all the guilt of our personal sins, and all that is required is for us to unlearn our bad habits and replace them with virtue by the Holy Spirit's help.[46] Julian and Jovinian both seem to echo the Second Vatican Council's invitation to the one universal holiness available to all.[47] Certainly Jovinian, in his

---

46. Julian has a hard time affirming the need for infant baptism. According to Julian, in baptism, what is made good by creation "God makes better by renovation and adoption"; *Contra Iulianum* 3.3; *Against Julian*, 112.

47. See *LG* 5 on the universal call to holiness.

forceful claim that there is no difference in merit between celibate and married life, per se, would garner popularity today. The same is true for Jovinian's decidedly social understanding of Christian identity as expressed by modern, communion ecclesiology;[48] he emphasizes the unity of the Church as the primary place of belonging over against a tide of individualistic ascetical competitiveness: "be not proud: you and your married sisters are members of the same Church."[49] This mantra would find many an adherent in contemporary theology.

Just as Jovinian's theology has remained popular, so Julian's theological commitments remain throughout history and in current theology as well. Julian's doctrine that sin is taught anticipates the enlightenment's "noble savage" and twentieth-century lamentation of "structural sin." Most relevant is Julian's understanding of concupiscence. For Julian, the concupiscence required for the conjugal act is considered chiefly in its biological (thus natural, given) character; therefore, it is a "gift" from God. This approach to sexual desire as natural and gift seems to resonate well even with magisterial statements on sexuality from the Second Vatican Council onward,[50] and has gained place in the Catechism of the Catholic Church.[51]

It is true that there is much beneficial in the thought of Jovinian and Julian and that many of their insights were carried through history as part of the authentic development of doctrine. My goal here is not to villainize these theologians and holy men,[52] but to point

---

48. Communion ecclesiology has grown in popularity since the Second Vatican Council and is well expressed in Henri de Lubac's *Catholicism: Christ and the Common Destiny of Man*, trans. Lancelot C. Sheppard and Elizabeth Englund (San Francisco: Ignatius Press, 1988), as well as the overview by Dennis Doyle, *Communion Ecclesiology: Vision and Versions* (Maryknoll, N.Y.: Orbis, 2000).
49. Jerome, *Adversus Iovinianum* 1.5.
50. See, for example, GS 51.
51. *Catechism of the Catholic Church* (Boston: Pauline Books, 1994), no. 2337.
52. Augustine made note of the Pelagians' particular piety and irreproachability and

out that their theological tendencies tend toward the same conclusions made by the theologians mentioned in chapters 2 and 3 (Parella, Russell, and Phan). Jovinian's and Julian's attempts to valorize married life exemplify the same zero-sum game played by theologians in the latter half of the twentieth century. The zero-sum game makes conjugal life and consecrated religious life separate but equal. The apparent tension between consecrated and married life, as well as the desire to relieve that tension, is (like most ideas and trends) both *nova et vetera*.

It is this tension that Augustine must cut. He is aware of the issues at stake and the insights of Jovinian and Julian. His solution incorporates some of those insights but uses them to fashion a counternarrative for the relationship between celibate and conjugal life. In the following section I will lay out the Augustinian counternarrative and revision of the simple, antagonistic account (whether zero-sum or not) of the consonance between consecrated and conjugal life. I intend to show how this saint and theologian met the challenge of ranking holiness with a far more creative and liberating alternative than had been offered by his contemporaries or by the modern authors treated in the preceding chapters.

Augustine's Accomplishment: The "Medium Veritatis"

I can now focus on the three major accomplishments of Augustine's lifelong constructive project for marriage and family: (1) while leaving intact a version of ascetical hierarchy, he rejects general attempts to evaluate the merit of an individual in any particular state of life; (2) he prioritizes the social nature of Christian life over a more individual approach easily co-opted by competition and pride; and (3) he creates an account of the good of marriage and virginity that

---

treated them cordially; Gerald Bonner, "Pelagianism and Augustine," in *Doctrinal Diversity: Varieties of Early Christianity*, ed. and intro. Everett Ferguson (New York: Garland, 1999), 198–99.

allows the two a participative share in the same goods. The combination of these three outcomes is an enduring reformulation of the place of marriage and virginity within Christian life, wherein it could neither be said that all people were of equal virtue or that all virgins are of greater virtue than all married persons.

First, if Augustine's constructive project is to leave an ascetic hierarchy in place while resisting arguments over personal merit, he must subvert *the way people position themselves* within that hierarchy rather than subvert the hierarchy itself.[53] The first step to combating evaluations of individual merit is to relativize the virtue of continence in the conversation by introducing a virtue accessible to all Christians, married or virgin—obedience. Both Jovinian and Augustine share a theological tendency—namely, militating against the vice of pride and placing the virtues of humility and obedience above continence. Both worry more about pride in the virgin than incontinence in the married. Jovinian declares to all virgins, "Be not proud! You belong to the same Church as married women."[54] For his part Augustine says in *De bono coniugali*, "the matron who is more obedient is to be preferred to the virgin who is less so."[55] In *De sancta virginitate,* Augustine continues, "For we must not only preach virginity ... we must instruct [admonish] it, so that it does not become puffed up."[56] As he states in *De bono coniugali,* the one

---

53. See *De sancta virginitate* 24, CSEL 41, 259–60, where Augustine asks who would "maintain that those who with devoted resolve remain continent, disciplining their bodies to the point of spurning marriage, castrating themselves not physically but at the very root of concupiscence, pondering the life of heaven and of angels in their mortal life on earth, are merely equal to the merits of married people?" The best critical edition is *De bono coniugali; De sancta virginitate* [*The Good of Marriage; On Holy Virginity*], trans., ed. P. G. Walsh (Oxford: Clarendon Press, 2001), 95–96. I will generally reference *De bono coniugali* and *De sancta virginitate* from the CSEL (unless Walsh's critical edition differs) and follow the CSEL reference with a reference to my preferred English translation of that passage.

54. Jerome, *Adversus Iovinianum* 1.5.

55. *De bono coniugali* 30, CSEL 41, 225; *Good of Marriage*, 55.

56. *De sancta virginitate* 1, CSEL 41, 236; *On Holy Virginity*, 68.

Something New from Someone Old—Augustine

who forgoes the goods of marriage is only holier, "provided, however, that individuals exploit that freedom to ponder, in Scripture's words, 'the things of the Lord, how to please God,' which means pondering constantly that obedience should not take second place to continence."[57]

The second step in combating the competitive spirit over individual merit is to show the near impossibility of proving (outside of revelation) the moral character of any individual. To this end Augustine reflects on Jovinian's favorite question: "Are you better than Sara, Susana?" In *De bono coniugali* Augustine deals with the complex answer: the virgin could respond "yes, insofar as I have the practice of continence," but "no, inasmuch as I do not possess the virtue any more than Sara did," and "no, insofar as I would not have lived the married life with as much obedience as Sara did."[58] For his part, Jovinian asks the same question: "are you [a celibate] better than Sara?" as if the assumed answer "no" will prove that the married state cannot be worse than the celibate state. Augustine asks as if the assumed answer simply means that judging our own virtue, let alone that of others, is well neigh impossible. Both seek to embattle the Jeromian and Ambrosian notions of ascetical hierarchy: Jovinian by attempting to destroy it entirely, Augustine by destabilizing the link between a given virtue and one's state in life.[59]

Augustine also offers the case of the apostles John and Peter. Who is more virtuous? John the virgin or Peter, married? Jerome argued that even Peter's martyrdom could not wash away the grime of his married state; thus he was inferior to John.[60] Augustine, however, insists that John's equal holiness to Peter comes not primarily

---

57. *De bono coniugali* 32, CSEL 41, 228; *Good of Marriage*, 57.
58. *De bono coniugali* 27, CSEL 41, 223; *Good of Marriage*, 51.
59. See Hunter, *Marriage, Celibacy, and Heresy in Ancient Christianity*, chap. 6, esp. 281–84.
60. Jerome, *Adversus Iovinianum* 1.26.

from the continence he expressed, but from the virtue necessary for martyrdom—namely, patience, which he possessed "solely in disposition"—that is, *in habitu*. John's virtue of patience is comparable to Abraham's virtue of continence; both were maintained "solely in disposition," *in habitu*, hidden from view.[61] The virtues given to any individual, then, may be hidden or expressed, making judgments of merit exceedingly complicated.

The second major accomplishment of Augustine's constructive task is to prioritize membership in the Church through baptism over individual merit. The most important piece of evidence supporting this claim is that, for Augustine, the bride of Christ is first and foremost the one Church instead of the individual Christian.[62] In his sermon on Psalm 45, thought to have been preached on September 2, 403, in Hippo, Augustine develops just this sort of social account of Christian life with nuptial imagery. Augustine refers to the bride of Christ as the Church first; our common identity as members of one bride precedes any analogy of the individual virgin as bride. "These invited to the wedding are themselves the bride, for the Church is the bride, and Christ the Bridegroom."[63] Furthermore, "the whole Church, of which they are members, is itself his spouse, because by the integrity of her faith, hope, and love she is a virgin, *not only in holy virgins but in widows and the married faithful too*. The apostle says *to the whole Church*, of which they are all mem-

---

61. *De bono coniugali* 26, CSEL 41, 221.

62. Hunter, "The Virgin, the Bride, and the Church: Reading Psalm 45 in Ambrose, Jerome, and Augustine," *Church History* 69, no. 2 (2000): 296–302; Émile Schmitt, *Le mariage chrétien dans l'oeuvre de saint Augustin: Une théologie baptismale de la vie conjugale* (Paris: Études Augustiniennes, 1983).

63. *Ennarrationes in Psalmos* 44.3, CSEL 38, 495. In the wedding procession, after the bride of Christ, the virgins follow into the wedding banquet. "To what extent do virgins now seek favor with the King? How are they moved to do so? Because the Church has preceded them. 'Behind her the virgins shall be brought to the King, her companions shall follow her'"; *Ennarrationes in Psalmos* 44, 30, CSEL 38, 515; see Hunter, "Virgin, the Bride, and the Church," 298–99.

bers, *I have prepared you to present you to the one husband, Christ, as a chaste virgin* (2 Cor 11:2)."[64] Augustine also emphasizes this richly social nature of Christian life in *De bono coniugali,* written at the same time or during the next year. "The one city," says Augustine, "will be composed of many souls who have 'one soul and one heart' in God, and after this earthly pilgrimage it will be the perfection of our unity ... for this reason the sacrament of marriage has in our time been reduced to one husband and one wife."[65] This approach to the meaning of Christian life mitigates claims to personal merit, as a consecrated virgin can identify as the bride of Christ primarily in a participative way—that is, as a constitutive part of the one bride that is gathered up from the Church.[66]

So strong is Augustine's sense that all Christians (married or celibate) belong first to one ecclesial, bridal body that he refuses to approach his theological rivals as "an individual." Augustine's first argumentative strategy against Julian is, in fact, not to defend himself but to bring to bear the cloud of witnesses that Julian also of necessity accuses—that is, the Church itself.[67] Augustine does not construe the debate the way Julian does, as some kind of single combat, mind against mind. Augustine makes a social argument. He argues with, for, and from the Church. "God forbid," he writes, "that

---

64. Augustine, *De bono viduitatis* 10; "Excellence of Widowhood," in *Marriage and Virginity,* 118–19.

65. *De bono coniugali* 21; CSEL 41, 2142–15; *Good of Marriage,* 27.

66. *De bono coniugali* 32; CSEL 41, 227–28: "Nec prolem autem carnalem iam hoc tempore quaerere ac per hoc ab omni tali opere immunitatem quamdam perpetuam retinere atque uni viro Christo spiritaliter subdi melius est utique et sanctius." Notice that here Augustine says "uni viro Christo"—"to only one man, Christ." Augustine's image of marriage as a sacred sign requires that we prioritize the social aspect. Also, this marriage is one all Christians can and must take part in, but the continent may take part in it while avoiding all participation in the carnal "opera" of marriage in this world in favor of the spiritual "opera" of the one marriage between Christ and Church.

67. *Contra Iulianum* 1.3; *Against Julian,* 6–7. The list Augustine provides includes Irenaeus of Lyon, Bishop Cyprian, Bishop Reticius of Autun, Bishop Olympius from Spain, the Gallic bishop Hilary, and many more.

Something New from Someone Old—Augustine

I among Catholics should arrogate to myself the role you are not ashamed to assume among Pelagians.... Before I was born to this world and before I was reborn to God, many Catholic teachers had already refuted your future errors."[68] Alone we are lost, but with the Church we are saved and find the truth.

Augustine's social, ecclesial approach to "the bride of Christ" is significant for its divergence from the position of his contemporaries Ambrose, Jerome, Jovinian, and Julian of Aeclanum. Unlike Ambrose and Jerome, Augustine offered a positive account of marriage. Unlike Jovinian, Augustine's vision of social belonging in the Church did not lead to a concept of one reward in heaven shared by all, a situation risking the loss of the person's individuality in the ecclesial whole. Unlike Julian, Augustine did not want to have his cake and eat it, too; he refused to treat concupiscence as something at once good and yet needing to be dominated and overcome. Unlike Julian, Augustine refused a privatized Christian ethic that put all the weight of holiness on the shoulders of the individual. Augustine saw in Julian the Donatist problem all over again—the problem of the Church within the Church, the problem of putting the weight of God's righteousness squarely on an individual's shoulders.[69] Augustine, therefore, needed the concept of *concupiscentia carnis* as the great leveler, not because he was overly dark and pessimistic, but because he was attentive to experience. Augustine's account of sin, sexuality, marriage, and virginity helps Christians understand their experience of just how hard it is to live the way Jesus did. For Augustine there is no elitism in the Church; instead, the Church is the community of the convalescent limping and being carried home. There is little room for superstars on this journey.

It was these two extremes (Jovinian's over-social and Julian's

---

68. *Contra Iulianum* 6.8; *Against Julian*, 332.
69. See Scheppard, "Transmission of Sin," 241.

over-individualistic) that make these theologies extraordinarily apropos to the modern crisis of marriage addressed in chapter 1. As we saw, the modern crisis of marriage can be construed in terms of social ethics (the family underparticipating in society or overparticipating in the wrong social structures—the state instead of the Church) or individual ethics (the family breaks down due to lack of individual moral commitment). Correspondingly, authors offered "social" or "individualistic" solutions: better state and social policy or holier individuals can save marriage.

Augustine's conception of all Christian belonging (both consecrated and conjugal) in the bride of Christ avoids both of these problems through the way he conceives of salvation and virtue. While Jovinian and Julian are arguing about what an individual is capable of or not capable of, Augustine proposes the solution that each person is saved by incorporation into a new body, free from the *concupiscentia carnis* that limits *our own* ability and freedom. We are incorporated into the *corpus Christi* itself.[70] As Christ's body is free from this concupiscence, so too will be the members of that body, the Church. While each Christian will share the benefit and reward of one who is without concupiscence (delivery from death and eternal life), each must war against it until the redemption of the body is completed in God's kingdom. Each Christian differs in virtue, in holiness, but the Christian's incorporation into the ecclesial body means that he is at once sharing in the one identity and the one reward of the Church—union with God—while at the same time developing personal, unique virtues. In the one body of the pure bride of Christ, a consecrated virgin may have a more noble position than a married woman who shares equally in all other virtues, but that noble position would be meaningless if disconnected from the

---

70. Mathijs Lamberigts points up this fact in his article "Was Augustine a Manichaean?" 132.

body. For example, even if married people are the toe of the bride and the virgin is her eye, an eye severed from the body is grotesque in comparison to the toe united with its body. As Augustine puts it, a virgin who has continence but not obedience loses what should be common among all Christians—namely, obedience, which is a command rather than a counsel.[71] Said boldly, for Augustine, virtues are no virtues at all unless they are Christian. "God forbid," writes Augustine, that "there be true virtues in anyone unless he is just [here this means baptized], and God forbid he be truly just unless he lives by faith, for he who is just lives by faith."[72]

In Augustine's thought there is no true virtue in the non-Christian.[73] Therefore, the non-Christian marriage, be it ever so chaste, does not possess conjugal chastity. Likewise, the secular virgin, be she ever so humble and modest, has no true modesty.[74] These lack virtue by their disconnection from the body of Christ because their actions and dispositions have not been ordered to a Christian end. "Whatever good is done by man, yet not done for the purpose for which true wisdom commands it be done, may seem good from its function, but because the end is not right, it is sin."[75] It is the fact of our membership in the ecclesial body that makes any holiness whatsoever possible for either the virgin or the married. This belonging is prior to anything else they might hope for or hold out. It is this belonging that brings these states of life together.

---

71. *De bono coniugali* 30–31, CSEL 41, 225–26; *Good of Marriage*, 55–57.
72. *Contra Iulianum* 4.3; *Against Julian*, 181.
73. Ibid., 4.3. Augustine even goes as far as to say that a gentile clothing a naked man as an act of mercy would be committing sin. Clothing the man is not sin per se, but not honoring God in such a work is sin. "In itself, mercy out of natural compassion is a good work ... and he who does this good thing unbelievingly does it in an evil way; but whoever does something in an evil way sins." The unbeliever is not yet a "good tree" and cannot bear good fruit.
74. *Contra Iulianum* 4.3.
75. Ibid.; *Against Julian*, 196.

Something New from Someone Old—Augustine

A Threefold Integrating Bonum Nuptiarum, Bonum Ecclesiae

It is to this third accomplishment, Augustine's threefold construction of the *bonum nuptiarum*, that we now turn. In *De bono coniugali* Augustine identifies two *universal* goods of marriage: *proles* and *fides castitatis*.[76] There is a third integrating and *particularly Christian* good: *sacramentum*.[77] First I will treat the way ecclesial belonging transforms the meaning of *proles* (procreation) and *fides castitatis* (chaste faithfulness) to allow both married and virginal participation in their good. Then I will treat the most central Christian meaning of marriage in Augustine's thought, *sacramentum*. Augustine's account of this good of marriage provides the basis and shape of the Augustinian counter-narrative for the relationship between conjugal and consecrated life.

Let us treat first the good of procreation. In the earliest years of the fifth century (ca. 403–4), Augustine had not decided how Adam and Eve would have reproduced in the garden, but he believed they would have procreated somehow, as an act of obedience.[78] After the

---

76. *De bono coniugali* 6: "The sealing of the marriage compact is so clearly governed by a kind of sacrament that it is not made void even by the act of separation"; *Good of Marriage*, 17. In the next section, Augustine continues, though: "However, it is only 'in the city of our God, upon his holy mountain' that this situation with a wife applies"; *Good of Marriage*, 19.

77. There is a wealth of literature on Augustine's understanding of "sacrament." Four important strains of thought to follow are these: (1) the relation between the Latin term "sacramentum" and the Greek term "mysterion" (mystery or secret revealed by God); (2) Augustine's understanding of "sacramentum" as a character of the marriage between two Christians that demands it be monogamous and confers on its bond indissolubility; (3) Augustine's use of the term "sacramentum" to describe what marriage symbolized during different ages of salvation history; and (4) to what extent Augustine had or paved the way for what would become a Scholastic understanding of the marital sacrament as sign and instrument of grace. Among many sources, see Theodore Mackin, *The Marital Sacrament* (New York: Paulist Press, 1989), 129, 215–19; John C. Cavadini, "The Sacramentality of Marriage in the Fathers," paper given for the USCCB Committee on Marriage and Family's 2006 Theological Colloquium on the Sacramentality of Marriage at Notre Dame, at http://www.usccb.org/laity/marriage/Cavadini.pdf, accessed July 8, 2009; and Schmitt, *Le mariage chrétien*.

78. In the years shortly following *De bono coniugali*, Augustine concludes that the sexual

Something New from Someone Old—Augustine

fall, and as part of salvation history, the patriarchs participated in the good of *proles*, again by obedience, so as to prepare for the coming of Christ.[79] Finally, after the coming of Christ, the duty to perform this good physically has gone away.[80] It would not be until later, in the anti-Pelagian writings, that Augustine will fully develop the notion (beyond its incipient form in *De bono coniugali*) that the good of procreation too is only intelligible within the Church. Marriages are honorable, but "not because they produce children." Instead, they are honorable for producing children "honorably," "lawfully," "chastely," and "in a social role."[81] That social role is not principally for the world but for the kingdom of God. Rather, what lends value to procreation at all (after the incarnation) is that the child may become a member of the Church and thus a potential member of God's eschatological kingdom.[82] Consequently, "children should be generated ... by good use of the evil of lust, with the intention of reigning with them in eternity."[83]

In stark contrast to this praise of procreation in Christian marriage is the shocking character Augustine attributes to procreative activity among non-Christians: "By using the good of marriage without faith, unbelievers turn it to evil and to sin; likewise the mar-

---

organs would have been used in procreation in paradise. He concludes that they would have operated as one's arm operates; *De genesi ad litteram* 9.3, CSEL 28, 1:271. Later, in his debates with Julian of Aeclanum, Augustine admits that there could have been a kind of concupiscence in paradise that would have moved the sexual organs, a concupiscence of marriage. This concupiscence would not have preceded nor exceeded the will, though; see *Contra Iulianum* 4.35.

79. Jana M. Bennett, *Water Is Thicker Than Blood: An Augustinian Theology of Marriage and Singleness* (Oxford: Oxford University Press, 2008), 56–65. Man and woman need each other so that they can live in obedience to God.

80. In *De bono coniugali* 10, Augustine answers the question "What if no one gets married anymore?" He replies that such a turn of events, if inspired by true charity, would be acceptable and merely hasten the end of the world.

81. *De sancta virginitate*, 13, CSEL 41, 245–46.

82. *Contra Iulianum* 5.34; *Against Julian*, 278.

83. See also *Contra Iulianum* 5.41.

riage of believers turns the evil of concupiscence to the use of justice."[84] Procreation of spouses in marriage, therefore, is allowable and good (though not required) within the Church. Outside the Church, however, for those without faith, even procreative use of sex cannot put the evil of concupiscence to good use. Outside of the ecclesial context, sex—even for procreation—is sin.

For Augustine procreation is a divine activity, not properly a human one, in which spouses participate biologically and celibates spiritually. Of course, "God makes man from the parents," writes Augustine; "not even parents are able to make man."[85] Procreation is a good that the couple participate in by their posture of receptivity and openness to what God is doing. "You cannot deny that God gave life to the dead womb of Sara for the reception of seed, and to the dead body of Abraham for generation in the way in which young men generate."[86] Procreation is "the good which marriage possesses in the end to which its office tends, even if none [children] be actually born. The man sows the seed; the woman receives it; and *precisely this much the married are able to accomplish by their own activity.*"[87] "That offspring be conceived and born is the *divine work,* not the human, yet it is with this intention and wish that marriage achieves even that good which belongs to its own work."[88] Even the "biological" aspect of procreation in marriage is good on account of its Christian theological meaning—on account of what God does in and with it. Christian spouses are not "making a baby" but setting

---

84. *De nuptiis et concupiscentia* 1.5; *Answer to the Pelagians II,* 30: "When those without the faith have this obvious good [the good of marriage], they turn it into an evil and a sin, because they make use of it without faith. Similarly, then, the marriage of believers turns even that desire of the flesh, by which *the flesh has desires opposed to the spirit* (Gal 5:17), into the practice of righteousness."
85. *Contra Iulianum* 3.18; *Against Julian,* 137–38.
86. *Contra Iulianum* 3.18; *Against Julian,* 137–38.
87. *Contra Iulianum* 5.8; *Against Julian,* 278 (emphasis mine).
88. *Contra Iulianum* 5.8; *Against Julian,* 278 (emphasis mine).

up material conditions necessary for the generation of a new child of Adam who may become a child of God.

No less than the married woman, the virgin, focused exclusively on leading people to regeneration in baptismal grace of rebirth, participates in God's fecundity spiritually. Virgins do not sacrifice motherhood by their vow: "There is no reason, therefore, why God's virgins should regret that they too cannot be mothers physically while still preserving their virginity." With Mary as her model, the virgin mystically participates even in Mary's motherhood of Christ: "They too are Christ's mothers, along with Mary, if they do the will of his Father."[89] These virgins, mothers like Mary to Christ and the whole Church, are worthy of special honor because their fertility goes beyond that of the married. They are able to procreate without making use of concupiscence of the flesh and, in fact, their procreation may be even more fruitful.[90] The married procreate well by using an evil, but the virgins procreate without recourse to an evil. The married preserve the total commitment to God as spouse by faith, whereas the virgin maintains total commitment to God as spouse in faith *and* in body: they "preserve even in their bodies what the whole Church preserves by faith, in imitation of the mother of its spouse and Lord!"[91] In their virginal motherhood, all the baptized call them mother and they call all the baptized children.[92]

What draws the states of life together is that they both make up the one Church and share in the great procreative good of Mary and

---

89. *De sancta virginitate* 5; *Holy Virginity*, 70.

90. *De sancta virginitate* 9; *Holy Virginity*, 72: "What then if some rich woman spends a great deal of money on the good work of buying slaves of various nations in order to make them Christians? Will she not procure the birth of members for Christ more abundantly and fruitfully than would be possible from her womb, however fertile? She still will not dare to compare her money to the gift of holy virginity."

91. *De sancta virginitate* 2; *Holy Virginity*, 68.

92. *De sancta virginitate* 2; *Holy Virginity*, 68.

Something New from Someone Old—Augustine

the Church as mother of all Christians.[93] Both are spiritually mothers of Christ, and both spiritually participate in the Church's motherhood of all Christians. How? For both married and virgins it is by "holy practices and with love" living in obedience to the Father's will with a pure heart. All that is unique to the virgin's participation in this motherhood is her closer, physical approximation to Mary: the physical preservation of their virginal state and abstinence from the evil of *concupiscentia carnis*. Herein Augustine has provided a deep consonance between these states in life, a consonance linked in the ecclesio-nuptial good of procreation. In other words, the good of *proles* belongs first to the Church. It is properly ecclesial and secondarily called nuptial.

With respect to the second nuptial good, *fides castitatis*, we see Augustine shows married and celibate sharing in the same spiritual good only available ecclesially—that is, to those in the Church. He understands this *fides castitatis* as faithfully pursuing holiness in relation to one other exclusively, giving life a cruciform shape—spouses, "in ministering, so to say, to each other, to shoulder each other's weakness."[94] For the married this means living continently and seeking the gift of continence from God for and with one's strictly human spouse. For the virgin this means living continently for and with one's heavenly spouse. Both participate in the same virtue of continence, ultimately in the same way. The holier spouses are, "the earlier they begin by mutual consent to abstain from carnal union."[95]

---

93. *De sancta virginitate* 6; *Holy Virginity*, 70–71.
94. *De bono coniugali* 7; *Marriage and Virginity*, 38.
95. *De bono coniugali* 3; *Marriage and Virginity*, 35. The position that growth in holiness among spouses leads to their cessation of conjugal intercourse is not the Church's teaching and may deserve critique in light of the role the Church accords to sexuality in married love. As Paul VI writes in *Humanae vitae* 12, "if each of these essential qualities, the unitive and the procreative, is preserved, the use of marriage fully retains its sense of true mutual love and its ordination to the supreme responsibility of parenthood to which man is called." Further-

Something New from Someone Old—Augustine

The virgin may already practice the virtue of continence to the degree that holy spouses may have taken much struggle to reach. Perhaps only after years do both spouses refrain from seeking the marriage debt. At the same time, though, married spouses may be more continent than a virgin if the "continence" is understood in the wider sense of resisting any and all evil desires.[96] For Augustine, when it comes to the spiritual virtue of continence, "the first thing to say, and demonstrate, is that continence is a gift from God." He continues:

> In the book of Wisdom we find it written that *unless God grants it,* no one is able to be continent (Ws 8:21). Speaking about the superior and more splendid continence, whereby one abstains from marriage, the Lord said, "Everyone does not accept this, but only those to whom it is granted" (Mt 19:11). Since even conjugal chastity is unable to be preserved without abstaining from illicit sexual union when the apostle was speaking about both ways of life, he proclaimed that both are God's gift.[97]

Fides castitatis, or faithfulness of chastity, then, like the other goods of marriage, finds its source in God and is shared in different ways by both celibates and married Christians.

We now move on to the third, integrating good of marriage, the *sacramentum.* Again, as with the *proles* and *fides,* the *sacramentum* is an ecclesial good shared by both celibates and married Christians. Nuptial language is used to describe the way these states of life can participate in these goods. When using *sacramentum* here I am referring to Augustine's use of the term as the signifying character of the marriage at a given point in salvation history.[98] Consecrated re-

---

more, John Paul II writes in *Familiaris consortio* 11 that sexuality "is realized in a truly human way only if it is an integral part of the love by which a man and a woman commit themselves totally to one another until death."

96. This position develops throughout Augustine's life and is clearly given in *De continentia* 2, 3, 13, and 28, CSEL 41: 142, 155–56.

97. Augustine, *De continentia* 1.1, CSEL 41: 141; *Marriage and Virginity,* 192.

98. See *De bono coniugali* 21, CSEL 41:215; *Marriage and Virginity,* 49–50, where Augustine speaks of the signifying character *sacramentum* of the Patriarchs' marriages.

Something New from Someone Old—Augustine

ligious persons share in this *sacramentum* inasmuch as they are baptized into the Church, the bride of Christ, whose own nuptials (at an allegorical level) have a signifying but also participatory and literal character (though spiritually and not physically). With the good of *sacramentum* in sight, I am now in a position to walk through an Augustinian counternarrative for understanding the relationship between consecrated and religious life. It is the narrative offered for understanding the meaning of marriage, the symbolic quality of marriage—that is, the *sacramentum* of marriage.[99] Augustine fashions this narrative in terms of salvation history, isolating three sections of salvation history to narrate a trajectory of the relationship of marriage and virginity among the people of God: (1) marriage before the fall; (2) marriage after the fall but before the incarnation; and (3) marriage after Christ.

For Augustine the nuptial union of man and woman in the garden was intended for and required for the perfect obedience to God, joyful rest in God, and eternal beatitude.[100] To express their social nature and capacity for friendship, to tend and till the garden, to increase and multiply, Adam and Eve needed each other in perfect partnership. In Eden their conjugal union, based as it was on Eve's origin in Adam, their mutual friendship (*amicitia*), and their way of life together (*societas*), was an image of the unity of human society, as well as the integral unity of the human mind in one individual.[101] The first couple needed gendered complements not for

---

99. See also Bennett, *Water Is Thicker than Blood*, chaps. 3 and 4. Unlike Bennett's narrative of an Augustinian marital spirituality, mine focuses more on Augustine's polemical debates as an inroad, as a perspective, and as a way to understand its relevance to our modern theological context.

100. See Augustine, *De genesi ad litteram* 4.17, CSEL 28, 1:113–14; and Oliver O'Donovan, *The Problem of Self-Love in Augustine* (New Haven, Conn.: Yale University Press, 1980), 30.

101. *De genesi ad litteram* 3.22, CSEL 28, 1:89; see also *De genesi ad litteram* 9.5.9; and *De bono coniugali* 1.1; *Marriage and Virginity*, 33. The nature of the friendship between the first man and woman and between subsequent men and women in Augustine has been treated

romantic interests or to satiate an irascible concupiscence of the flesh, but for a complete union of persons, of flesh (physical reproduction in the garden of Eden) and of spirit (perfect, mutual obedience to God). As their nature is social, they require and have the capacity for friendship, but, in Augustine's thought, if friendship were the greatest reason for creating mankind, then God would have created two males: "How much more agreeably, after all, for conviviality and conversation would two male friends live together on equal terms than man and wife?" The greatest good of humanity is not conviviality and human companionship, but obedience to God in the context of human companionship. God's command was to tend and till the garden and to fill it. Only a sexually complementary humanity could live in the great good of friendship while also fulfilling God's command to be fruitful and multiply. Furthermore, their acts of procreation would have expressed their friendship peacefully. Their procreation would have been a peaceful act of the will out of loving obedience to the divine command, and would not have been subject to the potentially destructive powers of inordinate desire required to arouse men and women to the conjugal act after the fall.[102] In the fall, humans encounter the freedom of their potency for interpersonal union of friendship. It is a potency that, because of its power for good, can be equally turned for harm. Physical virginity would have had no place for Adam and Eve before the fall, since procreation was a matter of obedience for filling up the number God desired, yet the virtue of continence would have been theirs.[103]

---

in many places. The most convincing shows Augustine identifying a mutual relationship between man and woman that requires male headship only because the fall has deranged the *ordo caritatis* (order of love), leading to an ever-present need to avoid the risk of *contrariae voluntates* (opposing wills); Willemien Otten, "Augustine on Marriage, Monasticism, and the Community of the Church," *Theological Studies* 59 (1998): 385–405, at 399.

102. Augustine later reemphasizes this fact clearly in *De Civitate Dei* 21, 23, CCL 48, 2:786–87.

103. *De genesi ad litteram* 9, 14, 15; *On Genesis*, 384: "For the earth to be filled through just two human beings—how could they possibly fulfill this social duty except by having children?"

Because of the fall, we will see that the *sacramentum,* or sacred sign and mystery of marriage, takes on a new meaning, a new, prophetic character.

What does this scene of the narrative tell us about the relationship between the consecrated and conjugal life? Before the fall, there was no place for virginity, since God had given the command to be fruitful and multiply, and since he gave the command in the context of sexual beings. Virginity would have been disobedient. The kind of friendship obtained between members of religious communities, though, has found its source in the friendship of Eden. It would be a friendship focused on the obedience of God for the sake of eternal life lived in the subjection of one to the other. What Eden tells us about the relationship between religious and married life is that the vowed religious can learn from the married. The kind of relationships needed for monastic life can be found in the first married life. This Augustinian insight countermands contemporary fears of a one-way street from monastic life into married life. It is married life, after all, that serves as the paradigmatic friendship. The key difference between monastic and married friendship, of course, is that their project of obedience to God would not involve the command to be fruitful and multiply in a physical way. Let us see, then, how all this changes after the fall.

For Augustine the fall requires that marriage become a different kind of sign. When humans fell there was a substantial wound to their desiring and thus their relationships: humanity's relationship to God, the human person's relationship to her own body and will, and the human relation of friendship between man and woman. Human nature was wounded so that persons lost their ability to order their passions in accord with their will. The rebellion of the soul from its master and maker, expressed in the rebellion of will and action from God's will, results in the rebellion of human body from

Something New from Someone Old—Augustine

its own master. The result is mortality. Additionally, the human will is no longer in the human subject's complete control. The result is our inability to have properly ordered affection for properly ordered goods and our inability even to choose the goods we may even know to be better.[104] Having been turned in on itself by pride, the human will disobedient to God is no longer free to choose the good as it was in Eden. Not only does this inward turning of the will derange humanity's relationship with God its master and creator, but it deranges and makes more difficult a true friendship between man and woman who were once equals but now seek to rule one another out of a *libido dominandi* rather than as an expression of the *ordo caritatis*. The hierarchical relationship that would have obtained between the two arbitrarily now exists in the form of a punishment. As Augustine has it, "It was God's sentence, you see, that gave this position to the man, and it was by her own fault that the woman deserved to have her husband as her lord, *not by nature.*"[105] Nonetheless, we must not think that men and women cannot reclaim the kind of friendship and service to one another indicated by the gospel. After all, "the apostle indeed says, *Serving one another through love* (Gal 5:13); but he would never have dreamed of saying, 'Lord it over one another.' And so married couples can indeed serve each other through love."[106] Their relationship, then, despite the fall, can

---

104. Thus the three marital goods are deranged but not lost after the fall. First, whereas we would have procreated with a peaceful movement of the will, we must now procreate by agitation of lust, which is not always subject to the decision of the will. Furthermore, the offspring we beget suffer from the wound of nature inflicted by the prevarication to which the devil persuaded man. Second, whereas our fidelity of chastity would have been an expression of the order of charity, after the fall it becomes a remedy for concupiscence. Third, whereas before the fall the bond of marriage represented the unity of the human species and the integral unity of the human person, after the fall, the bond represents in two persons the difficulty of overcoming the rebellion and division of the will and body in each of us. Additionally, the marriage bond represents, until the coming of Christ, the disunity of the people that will eventually be gathered together under one husband.

105. *De genesi ad litteram* 11.38; *On Genesis*, 459 (emphasis mine).
106. *De genesi ad litteram* 11.38; *On Genesis*, 459.

take on the character of service in friendship that it once had, provided they do not attempt to reverse the conditions of the punishment.

As it is, the fall produced a mutation of practice (e.g., polygamy) and meaning (e.g., subjection of women) in marriage, but even this modified institution retained a prophetic, signifying character. In the mind of Augustine the marriage of one patriarch to multiple wives was a *sacramentum* or sign of the plurality of peoples that will be brought together in the one Church in a union of perfect harmony of love.[107] These marriages, Augustine argues, were entered out of obedience, as well, and for the sake of bringing about the eventual, physical birth of Christ Jesus. "What this means is that in the earliest ages of the human race, especially because of the need to propagate the people of God, through whom the Prince and Savior of all peoples would be proclaimed and be born, holy persons had a duty to make use of the benefit of marriage that is not desirable for its own sake but necessary on account of something else"—namely, redemption in Christ.[108] Augustine sees these marriages as preparing what will be revealed and made present in Christ's wedding to the Church by his life, death, resurrection, and eschatological return.

Just as in the garden, there is little place for virginity in the age between the fall and before the incarnation. Marriages were entered for the sake of Christ's advent, and virginity required a special vocation. As noted previously, Augustine's arguments against Jovinian and the Manicheans put him at pains to show that the patriarchs

---

107. *De bono coniugali* 21, CSEL 41:215; *Marriage and Virginity*, 49–50.
108. *De bono coniugali*, 9; *Marriage and Virginity*, 41. See David G. Hunter, "Reclaiming Biblical Morality: Sex and Salvation History in Augustine's Treatment of the Hebrew Saints," in *In Lordly Eloquence: Essays on Patristic Exegesis in Honor of Robert Louis Wilken*, edited by Paul M. Blowers, Angela R. Christman, David G. Hunter, and Robin D. Young (Grand Rapids, Mich.: Eerdmans, 2002), 317–36. Also in this same volume, see the work of Joseph T. Lienhard, "Augustine, *Sermon* 51: St. Joseph in Early Christianity," 336–48. Lienhard explores Augustine's thought on why Joseph might have taken Mary as wife.

were equally as continent as any celibate person. What is more, they were not only continent but obedient and humble, for they would have rather chosen celibacy had it been an option. These great men and women possessed the virtues of the celibate *in habitu* (in habit).[109] In this second stage of salvation history, from the first sin to the first noel, virginity remains hidden in the lives of those who marry in hope for Christ out of obedience to the need for a nation to be the bearers of God's prophecy and the physical progenitors of the Christ. Again the direction of influence is turned. The virgins ought to read the scripture and learn from the virtue of Susanna, Abraham, and all the rest of the married Old Testament saints who excelled in secret, in their hearts, at the virtues these same virgins struggle to imitate.

In the mind of Augustine, no couple since the fall of man has demonstrated the spirituality of marriage better than Mary and Joseph; they are the paradigm of marriage and the fulcrum between the *sacramentum* of marriage before Christ and the *sacramentum* of marriage after Christ. Mary and Joseph offer us the climax of this Augustinian narrative relating conjugal and consecrated life. Augustine treats this ideal couple most explicitly in his later work *Sermon 51* (ca. 418), but the pair also appears in *Contra Faustus*, *De bono coniugali*, *De genesi ad litteram*, *De sancta virginitate*, *Epistle 262*, *De nuptiis et concupiscentia*, and *Contra Iulianum*.[110]

The marriage of Mary and Joseph overflows with spiritual wealth; it exemplifies the mutuality and friendship of marriage in Eden, and, more than any other marriage, it contributes to the advent of God's kingdom.[111] Augustine makes this claim despite knowing that Mary

---

109. See *De bono coniugali* 21–22; *Marriage and Virginity*, 51–53.
110. Of great help for this section was Joseph T. Lienhard, "Augustine, Sermon 51," 336–47.
111. According to Augustine in *De nuptiis et concupiscentia* 1.13; *Answer to the Pelagians II*, 37, Mary and Joseph are the paragon of the gift of continence in marriage. Augustine is adamant, though, that the marriage of Mary and Joseph demonstrates all three goods of marriage

Something New from Someone Old—Augustine

and Joseph never consummated their marriage. As a *ratum*, non-*consummatum* marriage it would be considered in principle dissoluble by today's canon law. Nonetheless, it was at once more fecund and more continent than any other marriage ever has been or will be. Augustine presents the relationship of Mary and Joseph as a model of holiness based on mutuality, friendship, and love of God above all else.[112] Mary and Joseph testify that "intercourse of the mind is more intimate than that of the body."[113] "Joseph," Augustine writes, "was not the less his [Jesus'] father, because he knew not the mother of our Lord, as though concupiscence (*libido*) and not conjugal affection (*caritas coniugalis*) constitutes the marriage bond." In this sense Joseph is Jesus' father in a more pure way than if had begotten Jesus by intercourse with Mary.[114] Furthermore, "a chaste man and woman are husband and wife 'because there is no fleshly intercourse, but only the union of hearts between them.'"[115] In fact, for Augustine, the marriage itself was ordered toward procreation, but was made valid by consent, the shared will of the spouses in their

---

(*proles, fides, sacramentum*): "Every good of marriage, then, was realized in those parents of Christ: offspring, fidelity, and sacrament. We recognize the offspring in the Lord Jesus, fidelity because there was no adultery, and the sacrament because there was no divorce"; *Answer to the Pelagians II*, 37.

112. In *De sancta virginitate* 4, CSEL 41:238; *Holy Virginity*, 70.

113. *Contra Faustus* 23.8; see Elizabeth Clark, "Adam's Only Companion: Augustine and the Early Christian Debate on Marriage," *Recherches Augustiniennes* 21 (1986): 139–62.

114. Augustine's scale of fatherhood places adopting parents at the highest end and parents begetting in adultery at the lowest end. The former is a father only by *voluntas*, whereas the other is by *natura*. Interesting, especially for those who think Augustine is a slave to natural law, is the fact that Augustine ranks the will (*voluntas*) over nature (*natura*); see Lienhard "*Sermon* 51," 345.

115. "Quia non sibi carnaliter miscentur sed cordibus connectuntur," in *Sermon* 51.21, quoted in the helpful article by Pierre-Patrick Verbraken, "Le sermon LI de saint Augustin sur les genealogies du Christ selon Matthieu et selon Luc," *Revue Bénédictine* 91 (1981) : 20–45, at 36. A good translation of the sermon itself is in *Saint Augustine: Homilies on the Gospels*, translated by R. G. MacMullen, edited by Philip Schaff, Nicene and Post-Nicene Fathers 1, (Buffalo, N.Y.: Christian Literature Publishing, 1888; repr. Grand Rapids, Mich: Eerdmans, 1974), 6:245–59.

decision to be married.[116] All marriages after the fall are based on *caritas coniugalis*, but only Mary and Joseph manifested the material fruit of matrimony without recourse to *libido* or *concupiscentia carnis*. Not only does Mary's fleshly offspring fulfill the promise of the kingdom of God prepared for by the Patriarchs' children, but Jesus is the fulfillment in himself. Therefore, even in its very materiality, the fruit of Mary's womb and Joseph's son is the greatest spiritual good the world will ever know.[117] The fruit of their marriage is not only a physical good, a child, but it is the greatest spiritual good, the salvation of the world.

Just as Mary remained Joseph's wife even though she had vowed virginity, Joseph did not seek another wife, even though there was no hope of sexual union with his wife.[118] In that sense the matrimony of Mary and Joseph is a sort of foil to that of the Patriarchs. Mary and Joseph embraced virginity in order that God's kingdom might be fulfilled, while the Patriarchs, out of the same motive, embraced their wives in conjugal intercourse. After Jesus is born, procreation is no longer a duty for the married couple, although it remains a good of marriage. Mary and Joseph, then, exemplifying the obedience of the Patriarchs in their willingness to have offspring and the virtue of continence as they remained virgins in both spirit and body, signal the paradigm-shift in the expression of the way marriage contributes to the kingdom's advent. With Jesus' birth into the marriage of Joseph and Mary, the kingdom has become available to the whole world.

116. Lienhard, "Sermon 51," 342, where he characterizes Augustine's statement as congruent with Roman law's necessity of consent as the binding factor of a marriage and against Julian of Eclanum's position that the physical consummation constitutes the marriage.

117. *De sancta virginitate* 6, CSEL 41: 239–40. "So that woman, and she alone, was both mother and a virgin, not only spiritually but also physically. She is not spiritually the mother of our head, as that is the Savior himself. On the contrary, she was born spiritually from him, as everyone who believes in him"; *Holy Virginity*, 70.

118. *Contra Iulianum* 5.12; *Against Julian*, 289.

Something New from Someone Old—Augustine

So what do we learn about the relationship between married and consecrated religious states from this great fulcrum in history? Here we have a nexus of consecrated and married life once and only once in history—Mary and Joseph. Mary is both vowed virgin and mother, both truly married to a man and truly consecrated to Christ.[119] For one moment in history, the disposition and the practice of conjugal love and continence are expressed in one conjugal *societas*, one *amicitia*. Here we have a return to Eden for a recapitulation of humanity in Christ. This holy couple receive the gift of procreation without recourse to the broken tool of concupiscence, as Adam and Eve might have without the fall. This pivot point in salvation history has shown us that consecrated and conjugal life are not inimical to each other. They existed at once, for once, in one couple. They show us, furthermore, that the true *origin* of the practice of continence is in fact marriage, the true though unconsummated marriage of Mary and Joseph, a marriage that for its absence of intercourse was no less fecund. Rather than consecrated life influencing and bringing about married life, it is conjugal life in Mary and Joseph that will inaugurate the age of consecrated life as a novel Christian possibility and a necessary complement to marriage. In Mary and Joseph religious and matrimonial life do not compete; they coexist and constitute the center from which both states of life once again move forward in light of the incarnation. Both spouses and virgins participate in Mary's spiritual and physical fecundity. Virgins model Mary's spiritual fecundity by bearing Christ in their heart and the hearts of those whom they serve and evangelize. Married persons

---

119. John Paul II has reflected in depth on the marriage of Mary and Joseph. He too finds herein a fulcrum of history where the redemption of the body at the "historical" level (freely given spousal gift in marriage) and the "eschatological" level (freely given spousal gift in continence for the kingdom) are united in one couple. He sees their marriage as inaugurating a new kind of "fruitfulness from the Spirit"; see, for example, John Paul II, *Man and Woman He Created Them*, 419–22.

model Mary's physical fertility. They cannot bear Jesus as she did, but they bear a fallen Adam and bring that Adam to rebirth in Christ through baptism. Both married and consecrated thus participate in Mary's motherhood of the Christ (as theoretically distinct from "Jesus"), born in their hearts to the extent that they obey the will of the Father "with a pure heart and good conscience and a sincere faith" (1 Tm 1:5).

The incarnation thus turns the tables on the relationship between the married and religious states. Mary and Joseph's climactic marriage serves as the transition to the marriage between Christ and the Church, the one pure and holy bride composed of all Christians (including Mary). After the incarnation the focus shifts from Mary the individual person to the Church as corporate bride. While Mary is the model, the virgin shares in Mary's motherhood of Christ only because she is a member of the *Church*. As a result, Christ may be born in their hearts not of their flesh (as he was for Mary). The signifying character, the *sacramentum* of marriage, shifts therefore with the life, death, and resurrection of Jesus. Christian marriage can now sacramentally image and make present the nuptial reality of Christ and Church—that is, Christ's bond of love for the Church.[120] After Jesus marriage serves as a *sacramentum* or sign of Christ's own practice of abiding with his Church, which gathers up all peoples into *one* bride exclusively for him the *one* bridegroom.

During this time-between-times, after the incarnation but before the eschaton, Christian marriage is related to consecrated virginity not principally by comparison of merit, but chiefly through

---

120. The fall of man in some ways added to the list of the goods of marriage. Before the fall, man and woman had no need for redemption, merely development. After the fall, they require rebirth and renewal in themselves and their relationships. The coming of Jesus and his redemptive marriage to the Church mediate this rebirth to the world. It is possible, then, for married partners, by grace, to be conformed in themselves and their relationship to the image of Christ's marriage to the Church as it was evident in Adam and Eve.

participation in the same goods. Both participate in and symbolize in different ways the one nuptial union of Christ and Church. Spouses represent the indissolubility of the bond between Christ and Church, while consecrated virgins represent the complete purity and integrity of the sanctified Church.[121] And so it shall be until both marriage and religious life are no more and Christ is all in all at the end of the ages.

---

121. In this I am developing Augustine's thought beyond what he has explicitly stated himself, though I consider it Augustinian.

5

EVERYONE'S DOING IT— HOUSEHOLDING WITH GOD

While the arrival of a kingdom where Christ is all in all has been already inaugurated, it seems to be ever on the horizon, in sight but beyond reach. We require, therefore, constant training in the practices that make us the kind of people who would actually be capable of looking for this kingdom and abiding in it with God. While the previous chapter dealt with theoretical aspects of patristic thought concerning an adversarial, egalitarian, or mutually participative relationship between religious life and married life, this chapter must contend with more practical matters. First, I take up the false conception of a one-way relationship between religious and conjugal life—that is, the idea that consecrated religious life has influenced marriage but marriage has had little to say as a standard of excellence for consecrated religious life. The first step is to develop the Johannine concept of "dwelling with God" to suggest that all Christian life is a domestic project, a cohabitation in the household of God. The second step shows the way vowed religious life has understood its own identity and practices in domestic, familial language. Particularly, this language occurs in early cenobitic life and in post–

Everyone's Doing It—Householding with God

Vatican II reforms of religious institutes. Finally, step three forwards and critiques principles and practices of Christian householding as they appear in the work of twentieth- and twenty-first-century scholars. The result of the chapter will be to undermine the claim that the dialogue between monastic and married life throughout the tradition has been a one-sided invasion of monastic spirituality into married life and to replace it with the understanding of "Christian householding" as a set of ecclesial principles and practices that undergird both consecrated and conjugal Christian community. In other words, I intend to fulfill the eleventh commandment of marriage theology—thou shalt not monasticize marriage.

Christian Life as Domestic: The Witness of John's Gospel

In this section I argue for householding as a primary ecclesiological principle and as a term that can contain and embrace the practices of both vowed religious and married Christians with respect to their identity as members of the Church. To understand this term I begin with scripture, particularly the Gospel of John, though one could easily begin with Paul's letter to the Ephesians or Timothy, which explicitly proclaim that the Church is properly called "the household of God" (Tm 3:15; Eph 2:19) or the "household of faith" (Gal 6:10).[1]

As Mary L. Coloe has proposed in her 2007 monograph *Dwelling in the Household of God: Johannine Ecclesiology and Spirituality*, a key symbol for understanding Johannine ecclesiology and spirituality is "household."[2] Coloe applies narrative criticism to John's Gospel

---

1. The word root of *oikos* appears in 1 Cor 16:15; 1 Cor 9:17; 1 Cor 4:1–2; Col 1:25; and Ti 1:7–8; Ekkehard W. Stegemann and Wolfgang Stegemann, *The Jesus Movement: A Social History of Its First Century* (Minneapolis: Fortress, 1999), 277. Among other household terms used by Paul are *adelphos/adelphe*, as well as "children," "father," and "sons"; Rom 16:1; 1 Cor 4:15; 1 Thes 2:11; Phil 10; Rom 8:16–17; and Acts 2:17.

2. Mary Coloe, *Dwelling in the Household of God: Johannine Ecclesiology and Spirituality*

and finds in the text an extended depiction of life in the household of God. The terms *"meine"* and *"oikos"* take central roles in John's Gospel.[3] The author repeatedly refers to Christian life as a dwelling with God (*meine*).[4] Jesus meets people in homes (Jn 12, Lazarus's home), takes disciples to his home (Jn 2:12, after Cana), and tells his disciples that he will make a home for them (*oikos*) (Jn 14:1–5, last supper discourse). An *oikos* becomes a temple when Jesus enters (Jn 12, anointing of Jesus), and both the Christian and the Christian community become the temple of God when the Father and the Son dwell (*meine*) within them (Jn 14:1–15:17, last supper discourse). Furthermore, the Gospel's narrative structure characterizes life with Christ in terms of the experiences of a household: chapter 1 presents an invitation to join the household and ends with a type of betrothal; chapter 2 continues with a marriage to formally begin the householding. We see a birth in chapter 3, a death in chapter 11, and a welcome and description of life in the household in chapters

---

(Collegeville, Minn.: Liturgical Press, 2007), begins by noting the shift in God's presence from the temple to the Christian community mediated by the use of the term "household," which refers to the temple itself (Jn 2:16, Jesus cleanses the temple; Jn 14:2, last supper) as well as a personal community (e.g., Gn 24:38; 28:21; 46:31; Jo 2:13; Jgs 6:15; 9:18; 16:31; 1 Sm 22:15; 2 Sm 14:9; 1 Chr 28:4). The temple represented God's place of dwelling in creation, but "the incarnation makes personal the mode of God's being in the world, first in Jesus; then, in and through his departure and gift of the Spirit, God's dwelling has its locus in the community of believers, born into the Father's household"; Coloe, *Dwelling in the Household of God,* 2–3. The temple raised up by Jesus is not only his body but is the Christian community, "my father's household"; ibid., 3.

3. The New Testament makes multiple references to "oikos" and "oikonomia"; see Karin Lehmeier, *Oikos und Oikonomia: Antike Konzepte der Haushaltsführung und der Bau der Gemeinde be Paulus* (Marburg: N. G. Elwert, 2006); Leo G. Perdue et al., *Families in Ancient Israel* (Louisville, Ky.: Westminster John Knox Press, 1997), esp. 223–58; and Craig R. Koester, *The Dwelling of God: The Tabernacle in the Old Testament, Intertestamental Jewish Literature, and the New Testament,* Catholic Biblical Quarterly Monograph Series 22 (Washington, D.C.: Catholic Biblical Association, 1989).

4. The question of Jesus coming to "dwell" is central to the Gospel of John. Scholars have used "dwelling" language to link Jesus to the wisdom tradition; Prv 8:34; Ws 7:28; see Richard Dillon, "Wisdom Tradition and Sacramental Retrospect in the Cana Account (Jn 2, 1–11)," *Catholic Biblical Quarterly* 24 (1962): 268–96.

13–17; chapter 20 shows us the promise that our householding with God never ends but continues in the resurrection.

What does Coloe mean by "household?" First, Christian householding is not coterminous with the extended or nuclear family-life of the first-century Jews or that of Hellenistic society. The term "household" has a historical shape linked to the time John's Gospel was written, and this shape has been filled in by sociological study,[5] but "household" must be allowed to exceed its sociologically narrated and historically descriptive meaning if it is to function as a symbol for dwelling with God.[6] Coloe uses the term as a metaphor—that is, as a linguistic double meaning.[7] While householding with the Trinity takes place within an earthly domestic setting, the structures of earthly households pass away and are not the end or defining characteristic of Christian householding.[8] We cannot reduce the gospel of Christ to the claim that Jesus came to replace this or that culturally conditioned form of householding with some other culturally conditioned form of householding. In other words, Jesus did

---

5. The classic text is Raymond Brown, *The Community of the Beloved Disciple* (New York: Paulist Press, 1979). More recent and more social-scientific are the attempts of Bruce J. Malina and Richard L. Rohrbaugh, *Social-Science Commentary on the Gospel of John* (Minneapolis: Fortress Press, 1998); and Wolfgang Stegemann, Bruce J. Malina, and Gerd Theissen, eds., *The Social Setting of Jesus and the Gospels* (Minneapolis: Fortress Press, 2002). Modern studies of household and Church are numerous; see, for instance, Carolyn Osiek and David L. Balch, *Families in the New Testament World: Households and House Churches* (Louisville, Ky.: Westminster John Knox, 1997); Joseph H. Hellerman, *The Ancient Church as Family* (Minneapolis: Fortress Press, 2001); and Roger W. Gehring, *House Church and Mission: The Importance of Household Structures in Early Christianity* (Peabody, Mass.: Hendrickson, 2004).

6. I am dubious of the explanatory power of social science for making sense of scripture. Social scientists apply theoretical frameworks to historical social realities that can no longer be directly studied. The explanatory frameworks brought to bear on the texts and the communities determine the theological conclusions and significance up front; see John Milbank, *Theology and Social Theory: Beyond Secular Reason* (Cambridge, Mass.: Blackwell, 1990), 114; Hellerman, *Ancient Church as Family*, 2–25.

7. Coloe, *Dwelling in the Household of God*, 11.

8. John Howard Yoder, *The Politics of Jesus: Vicit Agnus Noster*, 2nd ed. (Grand Rapids, Mich.: Eerdmans, 1994), chap. 9, esp. 164–65.

Everyone's Doing It—Householding with God

not come to replace first-century Jewish and Greco-Roman forms of patriarchal householding with twenty-first-century quasi-egalitarian householding.

While a strictly sociological study of John's Gospel might suggest that the Christian community was built upon prevailing patriarchal structures or acted to resist them, our concern with "household" here is explicitly rather than implicitly theological. The term "household" represents a reality that is not limited to this world. As Coloe puts it, "the household model for the Johannine community is not to be found in the social sphere of the first century, but must be located in the world of divine relationships."[9] The household of God is an eschatological, mutual indwelling of God and the believer(s); it is present now inasmuch as the believer participates in common in the life of God as Trinity—that is, communion of Persons. In John's Gospel, discipleship is *menein,* a dwelling with Jesus (e.g., Jn 1:39, the disciples of John go and stay with Jesus). John's Gospel explores the contours of this life and invites the Christian to participate in all its joys and sorrows.

Two symbolic events take place to signify the beginning of life of the household of God. First, John takes his reader through a narrative of "gathering the household"—introduction, betrothal, and wedding. Coloe compares John the baptizer to the role of "friend of the bridegroom," who would announce the bridegroom's intention to wed and negotiates with the bride's family to set up the betrothal. John is the preeminent disciple, inviting all who can hear him to a wedding with the bridegroom. The betrothal begins with this encounter, when Jesus gives a promise to Nathanael that he will see "greater things still." Nathanael and others follow Jesus to a wedding, where Jesus is both guest and benefactor for the festivities. The wedding banquet and the wine imagery would recall for the Jewish reader images of the escha-

---

9. Coloe, *Dwelling in the Household of God,* 11.

Everyone's Doing It—Householding with God

tological wedding banquet pictured in apocalyptic literature, as well as the wine of judgment and the cup of God's wrath.[10] Furthermore, Jesus' calling Mary, his mother, "Gyne" or "woman" emphasizes her recapitulating role as "Eve," as "woman" who gives birth to the new Adam whose hour is to come. It is here that the first confession of faith is made (Jn 2:11, "and his disciples believed in him") and the disciples are incorporated into the household of Jesus. "After this he went down to Caper'naum, with his mother and his brothers and his disciples; and there they stayed for a few days" (Jn 2:12).

Following close upon this nuptial scene comes birth, the second symbol for entering life in the household of God (Jn 3, Nicodemus's clandestine, shadowy conversation with Jesus).[11] In the context of second-temple Judaism, birth is not only a physical continuation of Israel, but it is an eschatological event pointing toward the restoration of Israel. Jesus' conversation with Nicodemus revolves around the eschatological meaning of birth. As Jesus tells Nicodemus, the birth of the flesh ends in death, while the birth of the spirit leads to life.[12] Physical birth in the ages of the patriarchs and throughout Israelite history eventually led to Christ's incarnation, but Christ's dwelling in the world makes possible our own spiritual rebirth into the eternal household of God. After this discussion of birth the bridegroom's friend John the baptizer makes his last appearance, testifying to the completion of the nuptial union. "He who has the bride is the bridegroom," says John; "the friend of the bridegroom,

---

10. Dillon, "Wisdom Tradition and Sacramental Retrospect," 268–96. The link between the wine of this feast and the eschatological, messianic age appears in Jer 31:12 and Hos 14:7; see Edmund Little, *Echoes of the Old Testament in the Wine of Cana in Galilee (John 2:1–11) and the Multiplication of the Loaves and Fish (John 6:1–15): Towards an Interpretation*, Cahiers de la Revue biblique 41 (Paris: J. Gabalda).

11. Coloe, *Dwelling in the Household of God*, 59. In the Old Testament, Israel is referred to as the "firstborn of God" (Ex 4:2; Ex 19:5; Jer 31:8). In the New Testament the "firstfruits" applies to the Christian community (Jas 1:18; and Rv 14:4).

12. John 11 takes up the theme again with Lazarus's death and resurrection.

who stands and hears him, rejoices greatly at the bridegroom's voice; therefore this joy of mine is now *full*" (Jn 3:28–30).[13]

Having described incorporation into the household of God with the symbols of marriage and birth, John's Gospel continues to characterize that householding, speaking in liturgical terms. In chapter 12, as in chapter 2, the disciples and Jesus are present in an *oikos*, here referring to a building. But this building takes on a liturgical dimension and characterizes the household of God as a unity of action (worship) and place (a material temple of God).[14] When Mary anointed Jesus' feet with "a pound of costly ointment of pure nard" and "wiped his feet with her hair," we see that the response to Jesus' presence and the power of Jesus' word to bring new life is worship. The house in which Jesus and the disciples are eating becomes a temple as "the house was filled with the fragrance of the ointment." This scene recalls Exodus 40:9 and Exodus 30:22–29, which instruct the Israelites to anoint with oil the instruments of worship. The scene also brings to mind liturgical images of aroma and God's presence and glory filling the tabernacle and the temple (Ex 40:34–35; Lv 2:2; 1 Kgs 8:10–11). The household of God, where Christ's presence, power, and word are known, is a household of worship.[15]

The household of God not only welcomes new life and invites the response of worship, but makes demands of obedience. At the

---

13. For Coloe this completes a narrative chiasm of A (1:19–34, witness); B (1:35–51 disciples of John and Jesus); C (2:1–12, wedding); D (2:13–25, My Father's House); C' (3:1–21, birth); B' (3:22–24, disciples of John and Jesus); and A' (3:25–36, witness of the bridegroom's friend).

14. There is a constant tension in the narrative between the temple of God as referring to Jesus, the temple in Israel, the temple as Christian community, and the temple as individual Christian.

15. Thomas has the same response of faith and worship to Jesus' presence and the revealed power of his resurrection ("My Lord and my God!" Jn 20:26–29). Coloe argues that the resurrection appearances in Jn 20 have a liturgical, eucharistic setting and form; Coloe, *Dwelling in the Household of God*, 171–81. The first to note this connection was John Suggit, "The Eucharistic Significance of John 20:19–29," *Journal of Theology for Southern Africa* 16 (1976): 52–59.

Everyone's Doing It—Householding with God

last supper Jesus teaches his disciples the hospitality of God's household. He washes his disciples' feet (Jn 13:3–12). This process of welcome is also an inclusion of the disciples into the introduction of Jesus' own hour by means of a deep, mutual indwelling of the Father, the Son, and the Spirit in this new Christian community. The uniting principle of all this indwelling is love manifested in obedience. "Abide in my love. If you keep my commandments, you will abide in my love, just as I have kept my Father's commandments and abide in his love" (Jn 15:9–10). Furthermore, "If a man loves me, he will keep my word, and my Father will love him, and we will come to him and make our home with him" (Jn 14:23). In the last supper discourse the disciples learn that dwelling with Jesus in God's household is going to mean sharing in the cross and acting out of the same love Jesus has shown them. As the response to new life in God's household was worship, here in the last supper discourse the demand and fruit of dwelling in the household of God is radically self-giving love that joins disciples to the cross and the resurrection.

What can be concluded from this domestic framing of John's Gospel? What does it mean that John uses domestic images and activities (betrothals, weddings, births, absences, deaths, rites of welcome, meals, and communal worship) to make sense of who Jesus is and what it means to be his disciple? First and most important, we conclude that *all* Christian life is domestic, a participation in the household of God. The domesticity of Christian life takes on three forms. (1) The Christian and the Christian community (the Church) can understand their participation in the household of God as a familial householding started by rebirth into that household begun now and fulfilled eschatologically. At the same time, though, we participate in this familial householding communally as Christ's spouse. These two aspects are contained in the mysteries of baptism and the Eucharist. (2) The Christian and the Chris-

Everyone's Doing It—Householding with God

tian community (the Church) can take on the domestic moments of John's Gospel (e.g., the radical hospitality demonstrated by the footwashing or John the Baptizer's role as friend of the bridegroom, betrothing people to this marriage and its fruit). (3) The Christian and the Church are the temple, the dwelling place of God the Father inasmuch as they obey the words of the Son by the power of the Spirit—that is, when they love as Jesus loved—completely and sacrificially. Vowed religious or nonvowed, single or married, Christian life is cohabitation with the triune God.

*From Manor to Monastery:
Domestic Language in Early Rules of Life*

This section countermands any assumption of a unidirectional relationship between married life and vowed religious life through study of the domesticity of vowed religious life in patristic, medieval, and modern sources.[16] A look at monastic *regulas* shows that consecrated religious life has always known that it shares the same domestic character as married life, a domestic character that of itself demands obedience to something beyond oneself (e.g., a *regula*). The ecclesial principles "householding," abiding, and "domesticity" are shared by both states of life.[17] In the earliest sources, the use of familial language by the *Rule of the Master* (attributed to Pachomius)

---

16. Marriage as the permanent, exclusive union of a man and woman was a key idea informing the theory and practice of consecrated virginal life in the fourth century, when communities of consecrated religious women started developing with great speed. Consecrated virgins and the bishops accepting their vows considered the women brides of Christ. The liturgies reflected as much (veiling, reception of ring and crown), as did the ecclesiastical laws related to those who broke their vows to be married (these women were to receive the same ecclesial discipline accorded to a bigamist); see Anscar J. Chupungco, ed., *Handbook for Liturgical Studies: Sacraments and Sacramentals* (Collegeville, Minn.: Liturgical Press, 2000), 4:333-37; see Canon 19 of the Council of Ancyra (314 A.D.), trans. Henry Percival, in *Nicene and Post-Nicene Fathers 2*, vol. 14, ed. Philip Schaff and Henry Wace (Buffalo, N.Y.: Christian Literature Publishing, 1900), at http://www.newadvent.org, accessed May 13, 2013.

17. See Thomas Breidenthal, *Christian Households: The Sanctification of Nearness* (Eugene, Ore.: Wipf and Stock, 2004), 43.

Everyone's Doing It—Householding with God

is apparent. In the centuries that follow Benedict uses domestic but less familial language to refine and explain the vowed religious life to his own community. Modern evidence of the influence of family on religious life appears after Vatican II with greater use of familial language among religious orders.

The *Rule of the Master,* a sixth-century precedent to and a primary source for Benedict's own rule, explicitly employs familial language to characterize monastic life.[18] The *Rule of the Master* follows a late antique understanding of family structure, where the abbot is the *paterfamilias* who delegates his power to subordinates, who rule over the household. The *Rule of the Master* calls the monks "sons" of the abbot and defines their relationship to the abbot in terms of the fourth commandment, as a matter of honoring one's parents. The abbot, in disciplining, "must show now the harshness of a master, now the affection of a father." Furthermore, he "will combine in himself the characteristics of both parents for all his disciples and sons, by offering them equal love as their mother and showing them uniform kindness as their father."[19] According to the *Rule of the Master,* the abbot "must always remember what he is, remember what he is called"—namely, *abbot* or father.[20]

Byzantine monasticism demonstrates the use of familial language throughout its tradition, even beyond rules of life, in some *vi-*

---

18. See Pachomius, *The Rule of the Master,* trans. Luke Eberle (Kalamazoo, Mich.: Cistercian, 1977), 73–75; Marilyn Dunn, *The Emergence of Monasticism: From the Desert Fathers to the Early Middle Ages* (Malden, Mass.: Blackwell, 2000); Timothy Fry et al., eds., *RB 1980: The Rule of St. Benedict in Latin and English with Notes* (Collegeville, Minn.: Liturgical Press, 1981); Douglas J. McMillan and Kathryn Smith Fladenmuller, eds. and intro., *Regular Life: Monastic, Canonical, and Mendicant Rules* (Kalamazoo, Mich.: Medieval Institute Publications, 1997); and Benedict of Nursia, *The Rule of Benedict: A Guide to Christian Living; The Full Text of the Rule in Latin and English,* ed. Georg Holzherr (Dublin: Four Courts Press, 1994).

19. *Rule of the Master,* nos. 25, 30–31, page 113. Further, the *Rule* states that religious, having dared to call God Father and to find in the Church their mother, should leave their earthly family; ibid., no. 2–3, page 96.

20. Ibid., 32, page 113.

tae.[21] Specifically, in communities of women, mother superiors use familial, maternal language to describe community's relationships. As one monastic foundation has it, the mother superior is to care for the nuns "as a true mother looks after her own daughters, and cares for them like her own limbs and organs."[22] More interesting still is the appropriation of the female, familial imagery on the part of male monastic communities. The *vita* of Euthymios the Younger describes a spiritual father "who labored to give birth to his disciple through the Bible, who wrapped him in the swaddling clothes of prayers and admonitions, and nourished him with the milk of virtue and the life-giving bread of divine knowledge."[23] Not only did the monastery take on this familial language, but it also took on familial functions. Monasteries offered what some families could not, and monasteries provided a spiritual family where no biological one remained. "Monasteries could offer a secure home for orphans, battered wives, the mentally ill, widows and widowers, the elderly."[24] Despite the attempt and ideal of leaving behind the biological family for the spiritual kin, the reality of monastic life witnessed to the difficulty of actually dissecting the two completely. Often members of the same biological family resided in one monastery or in double monasteries (which were rare in the East), or biological parents would visit or influence a monastery wherein resided their child or children.[25] Connections to families went even as far as this: some

---

21. See Alice-Mary Talbot, "The Byzantine Family and the Monastery," *Dumbarton Oaks Papers* 44 (1990): 119–29, at 120–23. The essay studies the witness of Byzantine *typika* (rules of life) to the relationship between the Byzantine biological family and the monastery in the ninth- to fifteenth-century Byzantine tradition.

22. Typikon for the convent of Beaia Elpis, H. Delehaye, ed., *Deux typica byzantins de l'époque des Paléologues* (Brussels: M. Lamertin, 1921), 397–98; quoted in Talbot, "Byzantine Family and the Monastery," 121.

23. "Vita of Euthymios the Younger," ed. Louis Petit, *Revue de l'Orient Chrétien* 8 (1903): 169.10–13; quoted in Talbot, "Byzantine Family and the Monastery," 121.

24. Talbot, "Byzantine Family and the Monastery," 121.

25. Ibid., 123–24. The rule of Theodora, for example, allowed relatives to visit with nuns

Everyone's Doing It—Householding with God

monasteries included funerary chapels or Church narthexes serving as mausolea.[26]

The most influential rule of life, Benedict of Nursia's, takes a step away from the heavy use of earthly parental paradigm and language used in Pachomius's *Rule of the Master* in favor of a more spiritual understanding of fatherhood.[27] Benedict's rule nonetheless characterizes the monastic life as a domestic enterprise, a project of living together in the daily tasks of life sustainably and in holiness.[28] Benedict simply emphasizes brotherhood and lessens the focus on the abbot's fatherhood and status as "master." He saw his rule as organizing a domestic life that would lead to Christian perfection. Laymen of all ages, young to old, formed the household in ordinary events and rhythms of daily life.[29] Benedict's rule is "not so much a treatise on spirituality or a strict regimen, but rather more a way of *simply being in life,* of setting up a household—Benedict's household of God."[30] The Benedictine life is a dwelling with God: "And so, brothers, we have queried the Lord about what is required of a *dweller in his tent,* and we have received the teaching about *dwelling there.* The question is—will we fulfill the duties of an *inhabitant?*"[31] Benedict calls the community to daily response to God through

---

and allowed the nuns to visit their relatives at home, provided they were accompanied by two nuns. Earlier, stricter rules allowed such visits only if a relative was terminally ill (125).

26. Ibid., 124.

27. This is a commonly cited distinction between the *Rule of the Master* and Benedict's Rule; see Benedict of Nursia, *Benedict's Rule: A Translation and Commentary,* trans. Terrence Kardong (Collegeville, Minn.: Liturgical Press, 1996), 6 (hereafter *Benedict's Rule*); and Augustine, *The Monastic Rules,* trans. Sr. Agatha Mary and Gerald Bonner, Augustine Series (Hyde Park, N.Y.: New City Press, 2004), 4:64–65.

28. See Breidenthal, *Christian Households,* 43; and Dolores Leckey, *The Ordinary Way: A Family Spirituality* (New York: Crossroad, 1982), 6, 8. Her goal is to import helpful categories and practices from monastic life into marriage, whereas mine is to argue why those helpful categories and practices are not really imports at all.

29. Leckey, *Ordinary Way,* 7.

30. Ibid. (emphasis mine).

31. *RB,* Prologue.39; *Benedict's Rule,* 5 (emphasis mine).

Everyone's Doing It—Householding with God

their common life.[32] The way of salvation in the monastery is a quotidian answer to God's invitation: "Today, if you hear his voice, do not harden your hearts."[33] This psalm was recited daily in Benedictine monastic life (*RB* 9.3; 10.10). Thus, "the Lord waits for us to respond by action every day to his holy warnings."[34] In chapter 4 of the rule, among the "tools of good works" is the counsel to "put the commands of God into action every day." The "tools of the spiritual craft," "if we have wielded them ceaselessly day and night, and returned them on Judgment Day," will win the reward of eternal life.[35] In the prologue Benedict defines the task of the monk as an effort to grow in holiness together through the works of every life constantly responding to God's call.

The body of the rule contains practical details and descriptions of how this domestic project of training in holiness ought to happen; the details of the rule order the humdrum tasks of daily life explicitly to the service and love of God and neighbor. Some examples are notable. Benedict notes that sleeping arrangements should be separate beds in one room rather than separate cells, emphasizing the communal nature of this aspect of daily life. Highlighting their need to be always ready for the continual task of domestic holiness, Benedict's rule commands the brothers to "sleep clothed and girt with belts or cords … so the monks will always be on the ready to rise without delay at the signal. They should hasten to beat one another to the work of God."[36] Chapters 23 to 30 of the rule detail the important task of discipline in the community. Even included is a sec-

---

32. Benedict calls his monks "cenobites"; RB 1.2; *Benedict's Rule*, 34–35. This word derives from the Greek "koinos" and "bios," thus "common life."
33. *RB*, Prologue.9–Prologue.10; *Benedict's Rule*, 3. Interestingly, the *Rule of the Master* (prologue 36) has another "cotidie" (daily) that Benedict removed from his prologue 36; see *Benedict's Rule*, 19.
34. *RB*, Prologue.33; *Benedict's Rule*, 4.   35. RB 4.75–76; *Benedict's Rule*, 81, 95.
36. RB 22.5–6; *Benedict's Rule*, 224, 226.

tion on the discipline of children. Benedict then describes the qualities required for the practical office of cellarer. This brother would be responsible for maintaining, organizing, and distributing the community's goods. "He should consider the pots of the monastery and all its goods as if they were holy bowls of the altar. He must not hold anything as negligible. Let him not be controlled by avarice, nor should he waste or dissipate the goods of the monastery. But he should take a balanced approach to everything and follow the abbot's orders."[37] Chapter 32 treats the monastery's tools and goods. Chapter 35 describes the task of serving in the kitchen. As with the instructions to the cellarer, the treatment of the everyday items and duties in the monastery takes on the character of and are ordered explicitly to spiritual growth. "The brothers should serve one another. Therefore no one may be excused from kitchen duty except for illness or occupation with an essential task, for thus is merit increased and love built up." As part of the weekly cleaning task, "both the one completing service and the one beginning it should wash the feet of all." Furthermore, the serving monks would kneel before the others and ask for prayers, as well as invoke God for help, saying "God, come to my assistance; Lord, hasten to help me."[38]

The rule goes on, detailing care for the sick in chapter 36, care for the elderly and young in chapter 37, the duties of the weekly reader in chapter 38, and the amount of food and drink to serve, when to eat, and when and what kind of daily manual labor to do in chapters 39 to 41 and chapter 48. The monastic concerns are the concerns of every household, every domestic situation, conjugal or otherwise. The monastic tradition is taking on the domestic life and infusing it with a divinely ordered pattern, using the language and principles of the early Church and the gospel to understand what it is we do

---

37. RB 31.10–12; *Benedict's Rule*, 258–59.
38. RB 35.1–2, 9, 15; *Benedict's Rule*, 289.

when we live together and how we ought to solve the real, practical problems that arise in common life—that is, in everyone's life.

We see the same kind of domestic concerns throughout another popular rule of the Middle Ages: St. Augustine's rule.[39] Augustine emphasizes the realities of life in a common household even more than Benedict. While Benedict's rule begins with a tone and language invoking wisdom literature ("Listen, O my son, to the teachings of your master"),[40] Augustine's begins with a call to unity imaging that of the apostolic community and its concern for all things in common. "In the first place—and this is the very reason for your being gathered together in one—you should live in the *house in unity of spirit* (Ps 67:7[68:8]) and you should have *one soul and one heart* (Acts 4:32) centered on God. And then, you should not call *anything your own, but you should have everything in common* (Acts 4:32)."[41] Not even garments are to be retained for exclusive, personal use, but returned to the store daily at the proper time.[42]

While Augustine's rule does not cloister the monks, it provides for permanent companionship: "When you go out, walk together; and when you come to your destination, stay together."[43] Interestingly, the monks worshiped at Mass with the rest of the diocese at a local parish.[44] Like Benedict's rule, Augustine's has less concern for "vertical" master-student relationships than he does for "horizontal" friend-companion relationships. This fact has much to do,

---

39. See *Monastic Rules*, 26; and Luc Verheijen, *Nouvelle approche de la Regle de saint Augustin*, Collection spiritualite orientale et vie monastique (Godewaersvelde, France: Editions de Bellafontaine, 1980).

40. *RB*, Prologue.1; *Benedict's Rule*, 3.

41. Augustine, *Praeceptum* 1.2–3, in *Monastic Rules*, 110 (emphasis mine).

42. *Praeceptum* 5.1, in *Monastic Rules*, 117.

43. *Praeceptum* 4.2, in *Monastic Rules*, 114.

44. *Praeceptum* 4.6, in *Monastic Rules*, 114, 71–72. Bonner comments that the monks' attendance at the local parish serves as a reminder that the monastery is association of non-ordained people wherein the presence of a priest is the exception.

no doubt, with Augustine's own commitment to deep friendships.[45] The friendship so central to Augustine's monastic community links back to Augustine's reading of the friendship between Adam and Eve in Eden. For Augustine, friendship requires obedience—whether between men or between men and women. His commentary on Genesis claims that, in Eden, one ruled and one obeyed, but only because ordered society requires an office of leadership—permanent or temporary—to avoid a clash of wills.[46]

As we have seen, the early monastic *Rule of the Master*, the later Rule of Benedict, and the Rule of Augustine adopted in the Middle Ages relied on language and practices of the households built around married people to frame their own patterns of life. The rules integrated the concerns of domestic life with the explicit desire to order those domestic activities toward prayer together and training in virtues together, the kind of virtues that help persons live in God's kingdom, God's household. All this has demonstrated that religious life and married life have a deeper connection than has previously been explored.

"Family" Language in Modern Consecrated Life

While the notion of cenobitic life as domestic project is well attested to in ancient and medieval sources, we also find an increased use of domestic, even familial language to describe consecrated life among modern documents of religious orders. For example, as a result of reforms following the Second Vatican Council, the Dominican Order changed the language it uses to describe the place of lay persons in the mission and charism of the order. At the 1974 General

---

45. Augustine, *Confessions* 9.22–25; Peter Brown, *Augustine of Hippo: A Biography*, 2nd ed. (London: Faber and Faber, 2000), 110–11.

46. See Augustine, *De genesi ad litteram* 9.5; *On Genesis*, ed. John E. Rotelle, intro., trans., and notes Edmund Hill, part 1 of *The Works of St. Augustine: A Translation for the 21st Century* (Hyde Park, N.Y.: New City Press, 2002), 13:380.

Chapter Meeting, the Dominicans did away with the terms "first order," "second order," "third order secular" or "tertiaries," and "third order regulars." Instead, they adopted the term "Dominican Family" as a way to render to all these ways of being Dominican an equal dignity and share in the responsibility for the mission and charism of the order.[47] The term "family" is newly employed for the purpose of reducing the seemingly liminal character of the lay associate to the mission and charism of the order. By calling itself the Dominican Family, the order attempts to assert that lay persons forming lay fraternities approved by the order are true and full members of a Dominican family; they are not merely partial or tertiary members unable to make the full commitment. Lay persons associated in the Dominican Family are making the full commitment to the mission and charism of the order that is commensurate with their own state in life.[48]

The Franciscans, too, now use "family" as a term that suggests an affective bond of love and cooperation between members. We can read in the Rule of life for the Order of Secular Franciscans that the Secular Franciscan Order "holds a special place in this family circle." "The Franciscan family, as one among many spiritual families raised up by the Holy Spirit in the Church, unites all members of the people of God—laity, religious, and priests—who recognize that they

---

47. As early as 1968 a new rule was created. By 1969 it was approved on an experimental basis and officially legislated in the Acts of the General Chapter of 1974. This rule deleted the term "third order" in favor of "Lay Fraternities of Saint Dominic." In 1983 the General Chapter in Bologna issued the first official document on "The Dominican Family." From 1983 forward, official documents use "Dominican Family" to refer to all the persons associated formally with the order.

48. The rule of the Dominican Laity states that lay persons "are incorporated into the Order by a special promise according to the statutes proper to them." Further, "they constitute with other groups of the Order, one Dominican Family." "As members of the Order, they share its apostolic mission by study, prayer and preaching according to the state proper to lay persons"; Rule of the Lay Fraternities of St. Dominic, nos. 2, 3, and 4, at http://www.op.org/sites/www.op.org/files/public/documents/fichier/RULELatinEnglish_o.pdf, accessed May 10, 2013.

are called to follow Christ in the footsteps of Saint Francis of Assisi. In various ways and forms but in life-giving union with each other, they intend to make present the charism of their common Seraphic Father in the life and mission of the Church."[49]

This use of "family" as a big-tent term to include all persons associated with a religious order is, of course, a mixed bag. On the one hand, it affirms the equal dignity and the sharing of responsibility for the charism and mission by all those formally vowed into the order. In addition, the use of "family" is typically accompanied by descriptions of the common end of the order. Both of these uses of "family" align well with the understanding of family as a social unit, with shared responsibility and benefits, that is ordered cooperatively through common practices toward a common good and common end.[50] There is a certain nonvoluntary character to the family that resonates with religious life. Both religious and spouses choose to enter into their particular domestic forms of life that predate them, but there is much about even one's spouse and the religious community that they will not choose and would not have chosen. Just as children do not choose their siblings in a conjugal family, members of a religious order do not always choose the sisters and brothers with whom they live and work. Domestic life must go on, whether in the monastery or in the home, regardless of whether or not a particular member of the community finds it easy to love her fellow community members on any given day.

49. The newest version of the Rule of Life for Secular Franciscan Order includes this familial language. The rule is available at http://www.nafra-sfo.org/sforule.html, accessed May 10, 2013. Additionally, the General Constitutions from 2000 also make family language official; see Rule 1: "There are many spiritual families in the Church with different charisms. Among these families, the Franciscan Family, which in its various branches recognizes St. Francis of Assisi as its father, inspiration, and model, must be included"; National Fraternity of the Secular Franciscan Order, *General Constitutions* (Rome: National Fraternity of the Secular Franciscan Order, 2001), at http://www.nafra-sfo.org/index.html, accessed May 10, 2013.

50. See David Matzko McCarthy, *Sex and Love in the Home: A Theology of the Household* (London: SCM, 2001), chap. 4.

Everyone's Doing It—Householding with God

The life of the community, if it is a domestic project of householding with God, continues not for the sake of the community itself, nor for the sake of the affective bonds between the members, but for the sake of the common good and end, the union of each and all with God and each other. Likewise, both the family and the religious order have a shared common end and a common good—the sanctification of the persons in the community and a ministry to those outside the community. The work done for this common end together will often create the affective bonds.[51] One common good that both vowed religious and matrimonial families share is training in chastity.[52] Another task common to both the religious "family" and the conjugal family is, as expressions of the life of the Church, "to bear the story of God from generation to generation, and for this reason and in this expansive sense, family is the way of the Church. To love with the love of God, we are called to live as community, as an embodied interpretation, through time, of the world as the household of God."[53] The religious family reproduces and regenerates and traditions the love of God incarnationally through the quotidian, domestic tasks of its "family" life, just as the conjugal family's daily round must embody its cross-bearing, love-building, and disciplined training of each other in holiness. There is much, then, to recommend the language of "family."

At the same time, though, the language of "family" employed by religious orders in contemporary documents unfortunately remains open to the problems of the modern understanding of family as "ha-

---

51. Ibid., 155: "Family love attains depth through an outward orientation, through common endeavors, and 'productive' relationships, through an ordering of roles and reciprocal duties." This position is held over against a popular thought that romantic love is best produced by escaping from normal quotidian situations and productive relationships.

52. See Patrick G. D. Riley, *Civilizing Sex: On Chastity and the Common Good* (Edinburgh: T. and T. Clark, 2000).

53. McCarthy, *Sex and Love in the Home*, 151.

Everyone's Doing It—Householding with God

ven in a heartless world."[54] Family, in Robert J. McAllister's account, "occurs as a spontaneous outgrowth of loving relationships."[55] McAllister, a psychologist devoted to study and treatment of vowed religious, argues that emotional love is the one vital ingredient to the family community. Once a group becomes a goal-oriented community it is no longer a family.[56] Whether or not he is correct (I believe his characterization is overly romantic and inaccurate), McAllister's position represents a common narrative of family life in twentieth- and twenty-first-century America. Religious communities are different from families on McAllister's account because communities are formed by "definite decisions and practical objectives ... they are established because common goals, similar beliefs, geographic propinquity, temporal need, or official fiat unite."[57] McAllister warns that vowed religious persons living in community set themselves up for disappointment and frustration when they expect the same affective bonds and fulfillments from their religious community that they should expect from their family. McAllister provides ample example of the kinds of problems that manifest in the lives of those entering religious life with misguided expectations for a "family life" in their religious community.[58] Religious communities should not advertise that their community life will "extend to include a sense of intimacy, which it cannot produce, and to promise an atmosphere of affection, which it cannot provide." Finally, he counsels that "religious communities should not mistakenly assume that they can proffer to candidates or to professed members a life that compares with family life or creates relationships similar to family relationships."[59]

---

54. Christopher Lasch, *Haven in a Heartless World: The Family Besieged* (New York: Basic Books, 1977).
55. Robert J. McAllister, *Living the Vows: The Emotional Conflicts of Celibate Religious* (Cambridge, Mass.: Harper and Row, 1986), 28.
56. Ibid., 27–29. 57. Ibid., 28.
58. Ibid, 29–36. 59. Ibid., 37.

Everyone's Doing It—Householding with God

While I agree with McAllister that a religious community's alignment with a definition of family along affective, romantic lines is potentially dangerous, I reach the conclusion from a different road. If the use of "family" in the documents of religious orders leads to a privileging of affective bonds rather than bonds of a shared charism and mission—that is, their common good—then these religious orders will be destabilized in the same ways as the modern family has been. In adopting a preference for affective bonds, culture becomes increasingly indifferent to structure, since structure is less and less determinative for the definition of "family" in twenty-first-century culture. In other words, the use of "family" in these documents easily corresponds to overly voluntaristic, romantic definitions of family, where family is entered for one's own fulfillment and abandoned when no longer emotionally satisfying.[60] "Religious life is intrinsically communitarian," writes Schneiders, "but it does not exist to provide a surrogate family, social rehabilitation, psychological therapy."[61] Too many people are joining religious orders for "community": "an expressed desire for community today, however sincere, does not necessarily imply an outward orientation toward the love of others in love," which is necessary for religious vocation.[62] In their charitable desire to embrace the world, some religious orders, with this new use of "family" vocabulary, may in fact be left open to the same debilitating effects of the modern destabilization of family life in general.

---

60. Sandra Schneiders develops a similar insight in her *Selling All: Consecrated Celibacy, and Community in Catholic Religious Life,* Religious Life in a New Millenium 2 (New York: Paulist Press, 2002), 246.
61. Ibid., 61.
62. Ibid.

Contemporary Concepts of Christian Householding
Principles and Practices

John's Gospel has suggested the domesticity of all Christian life: that being Church is the practice of cohabiting with God and being incorporated into his family by marriage and birth. Additionally, the tradition of the rules of life has shown an ever-increasing use of domestic, even familial language to understand the identity, mission, and practices of householding with God and each other. Modern scholars, too, have pondered how both religious and married persons might participate in the one practice of householding with God. In this section I will synthesize and critique the various principles of "Christian householding" that modern scholars have found that demonstrate the consonance between religious and married life.[63] While there are marked differences among the authors (e.g., Bonhoeffer is Lutheran, Breidenthal Episcopal, and Bennett Catholic), their common ground is wide enough for me to draw together their thought around certain themes.

First, the term "Christian householding" needs definition. According to Thomas Breidenthal, "Broadly speaking, a household is two or more people sharing the daily round of life to a significant degree and over a period of time, whether the sharing is freely chosen or not."[64] The fact of householding is nearly universal at some point in every person's life. The question at hand is to identify explicitly "Christian" householding. One may name this project "Christian"

---

63. I weave together threads common to the work of Dietrich Bonhoeffer, *Life Together*, trans. John W. Doberstein (1954; repr. San Francisco: HarperSanFrancisco: 1993); Breidenthal, *Christian Households*; Breidenthal, *Sacred Unions: A New Guide to Lifelong Commitment* (Cambridge, Mass.: Cowley, 2006); and Jana M. Bennett, "Mark 8: Support for Celibate Singles Alongside Monogamous Married Couples and Their Children," in *School(s) for Conversion: 12 Marks of a New Monasticism*, edited by Rutba House, 112–23 (Eugene, Ore.: Cascade, 2005).

64. Breidenthal, *Christian Households*, 2.

based on its ends and standards of excellence. Householding becomes properly Christian when it is an inhabiting of God's household, when its end is the sanctification of the householders through the very actions essential to the domestic project, and when the standards of excellence for the practice actually conform the householders ever more to Christ the poor, chaste, and obedient bridegroom.

If baptismal belonging really runs deeper than biological belonging, then we should feel free to explore the variety of forms Christian householding can take. Further, if we take the position that married and nonmarried ways of life are complementary, then it follows that married need the celibate single and the celibate need the married in real and practical ways.[65] Integrating single celibates with married Christians in one living situation might allow for a fuller sharing of prayer and apostolate and a more direct witness and accountability between the two. A recent movement called the New Monasticism has attempted this sort of living, with rules of life for each community—with twelve general marks characterizing the new monastic project.[66] The New Monasticism attempts to bring diverse forms of Christian community to the abandoned places of Western society.

If Christian householding is a participation in the Church, then the gathering around the household table ought to reflect (without replacing) the gathering around the eucharistic table. Christians need each other to learn how to live in love together.[67] The source and summit of this life together is the eucharistic meal and sacri-

---

65. Jana M. Bennett, *Water Is Thicker than Blood: An Augustinian Theology of Marriage and Singleness* (Oxford: Oxford University Press, 2008), 185.

66. Some of these communities are Catholic worker houses, communities founded during the '60s (Reba House in Chicago), or newer ecumenical communities (Rutba House in Durham, North Carolina, and the Simple Way in Pennsylvania); see Rutba House, ed., *School(s) for Conversion: 12 Marks of the New Monasticism*.

67. Bennett, *Water Is Thicker than Blood*, 186.

fice, where Christians unite to receive and become the very body and blood of Christ.[68] Married and consecrated religious have come together at the eucharistic table for as long as both have been practiced. The altar where all sacrifices become united in the one Christ broken for all ought to be imaged in the common table where Christians receive and break in thanksgiving our daily bread. A common life among those Christians related through baptism rather than blood provides a living expression of our mutual dependence and our radical re-understanding of "family" once we have been reborn and adopted into brotherhood and sisterhood with Christ.

Having in mind the kinds of communities these scholars envision, we can now move on to the principles and practices of Christian life in community shared by these authors. Inevitably, these practices relate to each other by a dynamic tension, or polarity. But this tension does not, must not, mean choosing only one or the other. It is the tension and the polarity that make the practices and principles solid footing for Christian householding. The tension insures against destructive extremes in either direction.[69] In treating the various principles that follow, we will note the polar interactions between them. I will identify four sets of principles in polar tension. First, the intentionality of Christian householding goes hand in hand with the nonvoluntary, "given" nature of householding itself. Second, the nearness, availability, familiarity, and vulnerability of inhabiting a space and sharing daily activities with other people

---

68. *Sacrosanctum concilium* 10: "The liturgy is the summit toward which the activity of the Church is directed; at the same time it is the font from which all her power flows"; http://www.vatican.va, accessed May 10, 2013.

69. Consider a chemical example. A water molecule is polar—that is, it has an area of higher negative charge and an area of higher positive charge. It is in part this polarity that lends water the marvelous properties of cohesion (water molecules stick to each other) and adhesion (result is capillary action that takes water up plant stems). Thus by calling them polar I mean to say that the seemingly opposed aspects actually attract one another and draw each other together. In other words, where there is exclusivity there must also be openness.

stand in a proper tension with the formal, ritual, patterned, even liturgical elements of the Christian household. Third, the exclusivity of the Christian household, especially the sexual exclusivity of the conjugal household, requires a polar tension with openness and permeability. Finally, the *ora* of the Christian household must always be directed to and energize the *labora* of the community for those within and without its borders. Without tension, principles and practices risk losing vigor or becoming overbearing. Proper tension helps to ensure that each principle and the whole practice of Christian householding is employed as a strong push or pull.

First, Christian householding appears under the complementary principles of intentionality and given-ness or stability. Christian life together must be chosen, willed with a firm conviction about the specific project entered. At the same time, though, Christian householding always surpasses our own ability to choose and often countermands our own willing. Dietrich Bonhoeffer is especially clear on this point—Christian life together is *not* about finding a cadre of people who like each other and want to live together for community's sake. In fact, it is quite the opposite. "Jesus lived among his foes," writes Bonhoeffer. "The kingdom," he continues, "is to be in the midst of your enemies. And he who will not suffer this does not want to be of the kingdom of Christ; he wants to be among friends, to sit among roses and lilies, not with the bad people but the devout people. O you blasphemers and betrayers of Christ. If Christ had done what you are doing who would ever have been spared?"[70] To love the dream of community more than the reality of community, to hold out for the dream of pleasant life as the norm, is to betray what Christ has done in the incarnation and to destroy community itself.[71]

---

70. Bonhoeffer, *Life Together*, 17–18.
71. Ibid., 27. Bennett makes a similar point in her cautioning that dreams for what the fam-

Everyone's Doing It—Householding with God

Not only is Christian householding sometimes contrary to our own will, but even when aligning with our will it goes beyond our will. For example, when two people marry, they choose to make an unbreakable covenant, yet we know that when we receive our spouse in matrimony, we receive a book half-written and as yet unread. Furthermore, the couple welcoming and hoping for children are welcoming a mystery, welcoming a stranger, an alien, a naked, begging, and homeless infant: "Children are strangers by nature, because they come into the picture as if out of nowhere."[72] At the same time, those "we thought we knew well become unfamiliar when they are filled with the pain of mental or physical illness."[73] Furthermore, when Christians choose to open their home to the stranger, their expectations may be shattered, often for better consequence than they had originally hoped.[74] In addition, not every person in a Christian household chooses to be there. Children, for example, do not choose their parents, or their siblings, or any of the members in their home. Likewise, monks profess vows in a particular religious institute and a specific community within that institute, but they did not elect the members of that community.

Ultimately, the common element behind the tension involving choice in Christian householding is the claim that true Christian community must be received as gift. We cannot demand community, only receive it gratefully. "The very hour of our disillusionment with [our] brother becomes incomparably salutary because it so

---

ily can be (a savior of society and a bastion of emotional warmth) are misplaced; Bennett, *Water Is Thicker than Blood*, chap. 1.

72. Breidenthal, *Christian Households*, 114.

73. Ibid., 114. Breidenthal continues, saying, "It may even be easier to open one's home to the homeless than to welcome offspring into one's life and bring them up with patience and kindness."

74. Dolores Leckey gives the examples of her own family welcoming strangers into their home during the many marches and protests of the '60s as well as the time a priest called to ask her to house a parolee into their home for some time when he was released from prison. She could not have sought or willed these events or their results; Leckey, *Ordinary Way*, 134–35.

Everyone's Doing It—Householding with God

thoroughly teaches me that neither of us can ever live by our own words and deed, but only by that one Word and Deed which really binds us together, the forgiveness of sins in Jesus Christ."[75] Christian householding, then, must be intentional—that is, it must be hoped for and desired; Christian householding, though, may only be desired as gift, as a grace that is supra-voluntary, beyond our will, better than what we in fact wanted, both in principle and practice.

As an expression of the relationship between intentionality and given-ness, Christian households commit to "stability" as a standard of excellence amidst the unanticipated events and contingencies of life. In marriage, the kind of openness and vulnerability spouses have with one another (i.e., economic, emotional, sexual) necessitates permanence and stability to prevent major damage to either spouse.[76] In religious life the vow of stability is not principally given by one individual to another individual; instead, permanence and stability are owed by a person to the community and the rule.[77] Stability is a continuity of place and practices or rituals.[78] According to Dolores Leckey, stability in Christian householding, apart from vowed religious life, is required for a similar reason. Those enter-

---

75. Bonhoeffer, *Life Together*, 28.
76. Breidenthal, *Christian Households*, 105–7. The demand of permanence in marriage has a long history in the Catholic Church. Arguments have shifted from the nature of the marriage bond to the requirements of parenthood to the nature of married love to anthropological and Christological grounds. For Augustine, the permanence is demanded on account of scriptural command (*De bono coniugali* 7) and the *sacramentum*, or signifying character, of the marriage. For Aquinas the demands of educating and caring for the child and the sacramental character of the marriage bond as a sign that makes present the bond of Christ to Church both demand that the marriage commitment be permanent; see *ST*, supplementum, q. 67, art. 1, response, and reply to objection 2. In twentieth-century theology, especially in Vatican II's *GS* and Paul VI's *Humanae vitae*, the Church began to articulate the permanence of the marriage bond because of the spouses' complete and total gift of self to one another in love. The quality of marriage as a covenant and partnership of the whole of life rooted in conjugal love is what demands and inherently creates the permanent bond; see *GS* 50; *Codex Iuris Canonici* (*CIC*) 1055, 1056; and John Paul II, *Familiaris consortio* 11, 20.
77. See Breidenthal, *Christian Households*, 99.
78. Leckey, *Ordinary Way*, 130–31.

Everyone's Doing It—Householding with God

ing it must realize the fact that their every action forever has wide and permanent consequences for those with whom they share life. The practice and principle of stability, or permanence, are an important medicine for short attention spans and the ever-driving force of the market asking us to seek and consume more and more, newer products, and newer persons. Leckey argues that stability "unmasks our temptations to flee people, work, and love."[79] Seeking and finding God with *this* person or family is more often harder than easier. It is perhaps in these moments especially when we must rely on or discover the fact that "God's stability is found in ever expanding boundaries of community and that the bonds of baptism are as real as the bonds of marriage or blood."[80]

At the same time, stability as a standard of excellence is normative rather than simply descriptive. Fracture attacks Christian households through the many contingencies of life. The brokenness of life manifests itself either in moral failure (i.e., infidelity or lack of perseverance in a religious vow) or historical accident (i.e., death, reassignment, loss of a job, sickness). The response to these fractures and commitments to stability is, in Leckey's mind, the same virtue needed to develop permanence at all: perseverance or, in terms of cardinal virtues, fortitude.[81] Perseverance is the continuing commitment to live honestly and completely the way of life of the community, despite the inevitable failings we encounter therein.[82]

The question that confronts so many attempting to live in Christian households is this: where can stability be found amidst failures and misfortunes? Leckey suggests the cross of Christ and the wider

---

79. Ibid., 121.
80. Ibid., 127. McCarthy, *Sex and Love in the Home,* chap. 5, and Bennett, *Water Is Thicker than Blood,* 181–85, share Leckey's strong claim for the ecclesial bonds of persons in Christian community. We must find ways to depend on, even need, people in local parishes if stability is to be true.
81. Leckey, *Ordinary Way,* 122–24.
82. Ibid., 123.

ecclesial, social community as of primary importance.[83] She gives the example of St. Catherine of Genoa, whose husband repeatedly broke faith in their Christian householding, yet St. Catherine continually forgave her husband, even paying off debts he had incurred through vice. Eventually they served the poor and sick in their city together.[84] John Paul II has explored this topic, as well. Despite the fact that many modern scholars have criticized him for focusing on the "ideal" of marriage rather than its "reality,"[85] John Paul II actually approached the difficult realities of marriage from a popular direction. As Karol Wojtyla he wrote a drama entitled *The Jeweler's Shop*, which dealt with marriages both smooth and difficult, broken and reconciled, with jealousy and coldness, joy and resentment. His psychological and theological depth allows the audience to see the true stability in marriage as the love of Christ that is always present to reconcile, take up, and transform the love of the spouses.[86]

In the practice of stability Christian households necessarily encounter the next pair of polar householding principles in Christian community: familiarity and formality. At the bottom of the relationship between familiarity and formality is the notion of "radical availability," or our susceptibility to *nearness*, "a condition of accessibility to others which cannot be chosen because it can never be successfully refused."[87] Why do Christians live together? Salvation, the

83. Ibid., 127.
84. Ibid., 124; and Florence Caffrey Bourg, *Where Two or Three Are Gathered: Christian Families as Domestic Churches* (Notre Dame, Ind.: University of Notre Dame Press, 2004), 118.
85. See, e.g., Christina L. H. Traina, "Papal Ideals, Marital Realities: One View from the Ground," in *Sexual Diversity and Catholicism: Toward the Development of Moral Theology*, edited by Patricia Beattie Jung, with Joseph Andrew Coray (Collegeville, Minn.: Liturgical Press, 2001), 269–88.
86. John Paul II, *The Jeweler's Shop: A Meditation on the Sacrament of Matrimony Passing on Occasion into a Drama*, trans. Bolesław Taborski (1960; repr. San Francisco: Ignatius Press, 1992).
87. Breidenthal is aware of Gabriel Marcel's term *"disponibilité."* A difference between the two notions of availability is in the matter of the will. For Marcel, *"disponibilité"* is an attitude

Everyone's Doing It—Householding with God

Church, the Trinity, and the human person are all social realities. We live together because we cannot live otherwise.[88] Just as Christ did, we experience life as a sanctification (or rejection) of unavoidable nearness. From the woman at the well (Jn 4), to the Syrophoenician woman (Mt 15:21–28; Mk 7:24–30), to the woman who grabs his clothes (Mk 5:24–34), to the crowd of his townsfolk clamoring to throw him from the cliff (Lk 4:14–30), to the crowd forcing him into the boat (Lk 5:1–3), to the crowd filling the house so that people stood outside to listen (Mt 12:46–50), to the five thousand who sat, listened, and ate with him (Jn 6), people compel Jesus to act by being physically present. Their very proximity held a claim on him. In our own householding it is this nearness, often nonvoluntary and intrusive, that provides the rough reminder of our calling to love and forces us to either grow in that love or reject it.[89]

Nearness cannot be avoided and it cannot be made safe. Nearness is an occasion of grace, as when one spouse nurses another back to health. But nearness is also an occasion of the cross, as in the case of marital abuse or coldness. The dialectical tension of Christian householding comes in the fact that the nearness of grace always depends on the nearness of the cross. Attempting to insulate Christian householding from the cross inevitably insulates household from the nearness of grace. The less we allow ourselves to need each other, the less we experience the grace of receiving aid. At the same time, the less we allow ourselves to need each other, the less we can be let down or injured—the less we experience the cross and give mercy.[90] Both the career-driven go-getter spouses who can-

---

of availability to be chosen, whereas for Breidenthal we cannot avoid our availability; Breidenthal, *Christian Households*, 32.

88. Ibid., 20. Leckey's version of the "familiarity" and "nearness" is "intimacy"; *Ordinary Way*, 10–13; 21–31.

89. Breidenthal, *Christian Households*, 23, 24.

90. Bonhoeffer, *Life Together*, 114–15, 116, 121–22, emphasizes the need for regular, interper-

not make time for a family meal or a dinner with friends and the tired father who "needs" to be left alone in front of the TV after work equally make themselves unavailable. Our refusal to hide from availability to the neighbor, our willingness to embrace nearness to others comes from a nearness to Christ, the kind of nearness ironically rejected by those living near Jesus in his own home town (Lk 4:14–28; Mt 13:53–58; Mk 6:1–6). Ongoing Christian life together in the household is a compilation of events of nearness: waking, dressing, meals, washing, prayers, play, study, work, and more. Christian householding "takes these occasions of nearness and, as it were, stretches them out, so that we come to life in the constant knowledge of our extreme availability to one another, as persons who are in each other's power."[91]

The task of Christian householding maintains a dialectical tension between familiarity on the one hand and formality on the other. Every form of Christian householding fits somewhere on the continuum between the formality of the Church's public, universal gathering and the familiarity of the home as a place of nearness and vulnerability.[92] At the institutional level the representatives of this distinction are the married household (familiarity) and the Church (formality). According to Breidenthal, "The Church's claim to universality is a necessary check to our tendency to let familiarity be an excuse for insularity, exclusivity, and bigotry. Familiarity must be balanced by a genuine welcome to the stranger, even if the stranger does not wish to be made into a friend." "The Church in its essence

---

sonal confession, for in its absence we live with the lie that we are a pious fellowship and we will be shocked when we find a real sinner among the "righteous." Confessing solely to God is so easy because it is "living on self-forgiveness and not a real forgiveness." It is the reconciliation reached through confession that prepares us for true communion with our fellow householders, the wider Church, and ultimately with Christ in the Eucharist.

91. Breidenthal, *Christian Households*, 35.
92. Ibid., 43, 49.

is always city, it is never hearth."[93] Breidenthal's concern is to distinguish ultimate eschatological reality from earthly provisional society. In the kingdom of God, eschatologically speaking, we will love each person with the same familiarity and affective power that people often have for those in their own households. On earth such familiarity on a large scale would be untenable. Christian households are necessary as "spiritual workplaces," as training ground for the kind of familiarity we will have in heaven but that would be dangerous on earth. Each household has its unique "liturgies" of the eating, playing, and working together built upon familiarity and unwritten rules. The parochial nature of these domestic "liturgies" means they are more closed off to the outsider, who would not know how to navigate them. Therefore, in worship and communal activities of people who may or may not live together, practices of the Church require a certain amount of formality, enough so that the stranger is welcomed.

The formality of the Church's liturgies counterintuitively makes them hospitable to the stranger, who knows that no "inside, informal knowledge" is required but that participation is standardized and therefore open to all. The formal, standardized liturgies of the Church protect against insularity that can become a barrier to hospitality. For example, on Breidenthal's reading of 1 Cor 11, Paul sees the Eucharist as a public, formal rite, not a household dinner. "Church is not essentially a household marked by familiarities, but a mystery where there are not outsiders and no insiders."[94]

While the practice of householding should be a familiar embrace

---

93. Ibid., 14. Bonhoeffer finds familiarity and universality more antonymous than Breidenthal. "Life together under the Word will remain sound and healthy only where it does not form itself into a movement, an order, a society, a *colloquium pietatis*, but rather where it understands itself as being a part of the one, holy, catholic, Christian Church"; Bonhoeffer, *Life Together*, 37.

94. Breidenthal, *Christian Households*, 15.

Everyone's Doing It—Householding with God

and sanctification of our nearness, households (Christian and otherwise) must decide whose nearness they will embrace. Who is part of the household and who is not? Who shares responsibility for its charism and mission, and who is a temporary participant or guest? Thus the next two principles of *exclusivity* and *permeability* address this point.

On the one hand, the great vulnerability presented in daily life together demands a kind of exclusivity. "The gift of familiarity is a gift to be honored and protected, and the inclusion of strangers inside the circle of privacy presents understandable problems if it has not been agreed to by every other member of the group."[95] Furthermore, in order to live the Christian household according to the Benedictine principle that life together is a school of virtue, it will need to involve the same group of people over a long term. The virtues required for life in the kingdom of God as social habits (whether infused or acquired) can only be actualized in community and over time with repeated practice and correction. Additionally, a community committed to availability for each individual must not exceed a certain size lest members begin to be ignored or generalized. Finally, members must share the goals of the community and the willingness to work for their completion in fidelity to the household's practices. A group that welcomes every person to all aspects of its life together will reach no goal other than increased size.[96] Thus, Christian householding requires a kind of exclusivity. All Christian households have central members and many layers of persons participating in, aiding, and being helped by that household; among the crucial tasks of the household, then, is to identify those categories and negotiate the way they are entered and left.[97]

---

95. Ibid., 101.
96. Ibid., 99–101.
97. Authors suggesting creative forms of Christian householding have been vague on this

Everyone's Doing It—Householding with God

While the Christian household needs to be exclusive, it also requires permeability. Households require boundaries, but they must not be hermetically sealed. Permeability is as important to the life of the household as it is to the life of a living cell. A human blood cell's membrane physically distinguishes it from the surroundings, but the cell can only exist and achieve its telos because that boundary is selectively permeable. The cell exists *not* as an individual unit but as part of an interwoven system.

The relationship of the Christian household to the Church is similar. In the form of accountability, the wider society (principally the Church and the neighbor) demand a kind of access to the activities, resources, and persons within the household's boundaries. The household is permeable to the needs and standards of the wider ecclesial community. At the practical level the Church as public gathering cannot survive without the financial and bodily participation of households in liturgy and evangelism. Furthermore, the Church as public gathering cannot survive as "Christian" unless participating households are themselves "Christian." In other words, the households participating in the institution constitute its character. If the households comprising the Church do not feed the poor out of love for Christ, then the Church they constitute can hardly be called Christian and can hardly be called a sacrament of Christ's love in the world. The family's vocation, moreover, especially as described by John Paul II's four tasks of the family in *Familiaris consortio,* is intrinsically extroverted and missional—that is, ordered outward to

---

topic. Bennett suggests more robust marriage prep programs and that intentional Christian communities need to set up communal discernment practices for dating, novitiate, and engagement; Bennett, *Water Is Thicker than Blood,* 173–75; and "Mark 8," 119–20. Bennett mentions Michael Lawler's proposed betrothal process as a possible means for re-understanding marriage and better preparing people to live it as a means of Christian householding, though Bennett is critical of the idea (ibid., 173). I share her critiques. For more on Lawler's proposal, see, e.g., "A Marital Catechumenate: A Proposal," *INTAMS Review* 13 (2007): 161–77.

the service of life, society at large, and the Church in particular.[98] The Christian household, then, exists not as an isolated nucleus but as an organ within the Church, and it can only accomplish its end within the context of the whole. It must be permeable then to the demands and benefits of presence within the ecclesial body.

How does accountability to the primary context, which is the Church, work? First, there is accountability to the share each form of Christian householding has in the common destiny of the ecclesial body. As Bennett writes, "Neither state of life [married or consecrated religious] should be seen as having a different ultimate purpose than the other."[99] At times, she continues, the role of an abbot-figure or a member of the hierarchy outside the community may be necessary to hold members to account for these goals and practices.[100] As Breidenthal has it, "outsiders can call us to account for our tendencies to collusion and complicity against God and neighbor," especially in matters wherein we may have blinded ourselves.[101] Therefore, he continues, "most monastic communities have an official 'visitor,' often someone who is not a monastic, who can be counted on to speak the truth in love."[102] Left to themselves, the idolatrous tendencies of familiarity would take over Christian

---

98. *FC* 17. The domestic church is to be a communion of persons, to serve life, to serve the development of society, and to share in the mission of the Church. In addition, Paul VI, in *Evangelii nuntiandi* 71, writes, "One cannot fail to stress the evangelizing action of the family in the evangelizing apostolate of the laity.... In a family which is conscious of this mission, all the members evangelize and are evangelized."

99. Bennett, "Mark 8," 119.

100. Ibid.

101. Breidenthal, *Christian Households*, 104. In Lonergan's terms, these biases are *scotoma*, or blind spots; see Bernard Lonergan, *Insight: A Study of Human Understanding*, ed. Frederick E. Crowe and Robert M. Doran, 5th ed. (Toronto: University of Toronto Press, 1992), 244–57.

102. Breidenthal, *Christian Households*, 104. Furthermore, "the Church, especially the local Church, can act as a collective 'observer' of every household, helping each household stay on track" (104). This is related to what Stanley Hauerwas has said when he means that for Christians sex is public; Hauerwas, *A Community of Character: Toward a Constructive Christian Social Ethic* (Notre Dame, Ind.: University of Notre Dame Press, 1981), chap. 10.

households, and they could soon become sectarian and self-serving.

At the same time, though, households are permeable to the needs of the wider ecclesial community because the households need the wider ecclesial community. For example, a household may feed the hungry and clothe the naked, but with a small kitchen, two bedrooms, and one bathroom, the ability to provide hospitality is limited. A parishioner needs the Church's kitchen and meeting area, not to mention its parishioners, to put on meals and clothing giveaways. The answer to the family's problems will not be found within the encapsulated nuclear family, but in the neighbor who helps paint your house and those friends from the Church down the street who have you over for dinner.[103] Seeing other Christian practices of life together, participating in them, and even contributing to them is more helpful for the good life of one's own household than any managerial, specialist counseling session a person could buy. Seeing how a neighbor deals with his picky toddler at dinner, relying on a neighbor to shovel one's sidewalk in a pinch—these little interactions do more for the good life of a household and a community than hiring an expert in child-rearing or a professional service to shovel.

Christian households must be permeable to the wider community to accomplish their apostolic mission, but they must also allow wider community to pass through their boundaries in order to support them with resources and accountability along the way. For example, a few families living in a lower-middle-class neighborhood where kids go unwatched in front of drug houses and street corners might decide to invite all the neighborhood kids to a park once a week for a "neighborhood recess." Pretty soon, the neighborhood kids need no invitation. Instead, they are ready and waiting, or are even approaching their neighbors' doors to play on other days. The households of

---

103. McCarthy, *Sex and Love in the Home,* chap. 8.

all these children are permeable to the influence of the people putting on the "neighborhood recess," and likewise the household putting on the neighborhood recess opens itself up to the influence and even potential risk of being affected by the children and parents of the other families in the neighborhood (for better or worse).

The final pair of principles for Christian householding, which emerges from the household's permeability, is prayer (*ora*) and ministry (*labora*). The tension between these two is found in the attempt to be always at work on both. St. Paul exhorts the Christian to "pray constantly, give thanks in all circumstances; for this is the will of God in Christ Jesus for you" (1 Thes 5:17–18). Prayer is on the one hand introverted and on the other integrating.[104] Leckey emphasizes the importance of liturgical devotionals such as the rosary and the sacraments, especially the Eucharist,[105] but Bonhoeffer emphasizes the need of the community to make meditative prayer in solitude available for every member of the community individually: "we have a right to this time, even prior to the claims of other people, and we may insist upon having it as a completely undisturbed quiet time despite all external difficulties."[106] Not only prayer in solitude is necessary, but also regular liturgical action as a household. Typical suggestions include common morning prayer, meal prayers, and midday prayer, evening prayer, as well as daily meditative prayer and scripture reflection for each member in solitude.[107] Prayer together must serve as the organizing principle of the household's day, as it did for the early cenobitic communities. Prayer provides daily anchor-points. Far from overly determining daily life, the structure offered by daily prayer and the liturgical year function as a kind of skeleton for creative overlay.[108]

---

104. Leckey, *Ordinary Way*, 75. 105. Ibid., 70–72.
106. Bonhoeffer, *Life Together*, 87; Leckey, *Ordinary Way*, 73–74.
107. See Bonhoeffer, *Life Together*, 40–80; Leckey, *Ordinary Way*, chap. 5.
108. Leckey, *Ordinary Way*, 63.

Everyone's Doing It—Householding with God

If taken as primarily reflective and contemplative, the most complementary characteristic of the Christian household for prayer is ministry, which is active and focused both within and without the walls of the home.[109] For Bonhoeffer, Christian households of all kinds exemplify the following ministries: holding the tongue, meekness, listening, helpfulness, bearing, proclaiming, and authority.[110] Bonhoeffer focuses on how the members of the community practice these ministries first among each other as a requirement for authentic community in Christ. His vision does not have in focus the work of Christian householding for the wider community. Breidenthal, though, incorporates Bonhoeffer's intramural ministries as part of an outward direction for the Christian household. Christian householding is "a vocation to life together which is both familiar (family-like) and universal (Church-like)."[111] Prayer itself can be a ministry of Christian household, which daily offers up to God the needs of neighbors and the world. Leckey sees the ministry of the Christian household more in terms of the scriptural and monastic tradition of welcoming any stranger as Christ himself. She begins her chapter on hospitality with a reflection on Abraham's generous, unknowing hospitality to three angels (Gn 18) and continues reflecting on chapter 53 of Benedict's rule, where the monks are reminded to welcome any as they would welcome Christ, allowing them to enjoy a week of leisure before giving them a share in the community's work.[112] Becoming the kind of household that not only welcomes the stranger but seeks and finds the outcast takes practice and prayer, but in

---

109. Herein the dynamic in religious life between contemplative and active orders is relevant. The contemplative is no less extraverted in mission than religious with a specific active missionary end, however. As John Paul II writes in *Vita consecrata* 8, "They contribute, with hidden apostolic fruitfulness, to the growth of the People of God"; http://www.vatican.va, accessed May 10, 2013.

110. See Bonhoeffer, *Life Together*, 92–109, where he summarizes these connections.

111. Breidenthal, *Christian Households*, 113.

112. Leckey, *Ordinary Way*, 134–35.

light of how we have conceived of the Church as the household of God and Jesus' practice of inviting people to life in that household, we must conclude that active hospitality to strangers, as a fruit of prayer, is essential to the identity of any Christian household.[113]

Many of the principles used heretofore are helpful for drawing together married and religious life, and they will appear again the next chapter, which seeks to add principles to this discussion that have been left out: namely, the language of poverty, chastity, obedience, a rule of life, and a long-term preparation program along the lines of a novitiate.

---

113. This practice is especially important as a means to counteract the modern dichotomization of the public and private aspects of householding.

6

CONSECRATING CONJUGAL LIFE—
A CONSTRUCTION SITE

If previous chapters cleared a space in the forest of arguments in fundamental theology, scripture, and tradition, then construction can begin on a new-yet-old practice of Christian marriage. But what is the building material? It is precisely the language that until now had been typically reserved for consecrated religious life. The foundation for building an edifice with this linguistic material is the common baptismal consecration that married life and religious life possess: namely, their origin in the Trinity as communion of Persons and their end in being conformed to Christ the poor, chaste, and obedient bridegroom. The various rooms of this edifice are the evangelical virtues of poverty, chastity, and obedience. A *regula matrimonii,* or rule of marriage, constitutes this edifice's walls and roof, which synthesize, contextualize, and connect its rooms. No one, though, should build or buy a home without *at least* a down payment, a participation in the fullness of the project prepared for by diligent work and prudent saving. This down payment is the long-term marriage preparation couples undertake, possibly something along the lines of a novitiate or postulency. Finally, no home ownership is complete without a mortgage and home maintenance. A continual program of marriage formation constitutes just such steady journeying toward making the house of Christian marriage a home.

Recalling the Blueprint: Marriage Is an Ecclesial Practice of Living as Christ

In this section I will recall MacIntyre's definition of "practice" as it was applied to Christian marriage in chapter 1, but now in light of the principles of Christian householding from chapter 5. I take this step to remind us that, while the materials themselves are the language of the evangelical virtues, regular life, and long-term preparation and formation, the edifice itself is a domestic ecclesial practice. The blueprint is the notion of marriage as practice of being conformed to Christ by householding with God. MacIntyre defined "practice" thus:

> Any coherent and complex form of socially established cooperative human activity through which goods internal to that form of activity are realized in the course of trying to achieve those standards of excellence which are appropriate to, and partially definitive of, that form of activity, with the result that human powers to achieve excellence, and human conceptions of the ends and goods involved, are systematically extended.[1]

A key component of this definition is that, if marriage is a practice, it is socially established. If it is socially established, then its establishment and continued existence have a history. Furthermore, contemporary practitioners become sharers in this history. When they choose to begin the practice they elect to place themselves in relationship with all others currently living the practice, all who have lived it before them, and those who might follow them. In other words, to enter a practice is to enter an intergenerational relationship, whether or not one likes it. Here we see two Christian house-

---

1. Alasdair MacIntyre, *After Virtue: A Study in Moral Theology*, 3rd ed. (Notre Dame, Ind.: University of Notre Dame, 2007), 189.

holding principles rising into view: the nonvoluntary aspect of Christian householding and the permeability of Christian householding across the boundaries of the nuclear family.

These two principles carry implications for the practice of Christian marriage. Married Christians must understand they exist within a network of relationships beyond their choosing, particularly with in-laws. At the concrete level a respect for intergenerational relationships will mean greater permeability of the home to them. One example of this increased permeability is a greater openness to and even provision for intergenerational living. In light of the increasing privatization of eldercare, a privatization linked in no small part to the increasing cost of healthcare, the increasing life expectancy, and the already stressed position of most dual-income couples, ever more mothers and fathers, husbands and wives end up spending their last, weakest, and sometimes loneliest and most frightening years with rare or occasional contact with family. Because they have become radically dependent, they are no longer included in the practice of householding. The society of individualism has created a situation where our practices of householding cannot abide those who need help, those who cannot make it "on their own." Living with and caring for these people is becoming less a task of the Christian household than of private businesses or state-funded institutions. Take, for example, the company named Extended Family.[2] There is much to praise about this business's endeavor to "promote independence, good health, and engagement in life" for the elderly. Its services include all the kinds of things biological family or kin would do if they lived near their parents or could afford to take the time: opening mail, filling out and paying bills, taking the parents to doctor appointments, helping with domestic maintenance. It

2. See Home Free Extended Family, http://www.extended-family.net/, accessed February 3, 2011.

helps keep elderly people in their home, but as an exercise of independence rather than as a domestic practice of life together toward shared goods. That this kind of company exists is evidence that we live in a society that prefers contractual relationships to open-ended and asymmetrical ones.[3] Contractual relationships are easier, neater, and less risky, but they are also less human.

In light of the fact that Christian householding is per se intergenerational and that commitments to sacrificial care do not end when people become "independent," we need to find cooperative activities within the practice of Christian householding to account for these facts. For example, Christian spouses ought not only to be open to intergenerational living arrangements but to plan for them. There are many ways this kind of planning could work. The Becker family, for example, decided to buy a house with and begin living with one set of their parents, even though they did not yet need extra care. The idea behind the move was twofold. First, the grandparents could, while still able, contribute to the childcare of the children during the day. Second, anticipating a future need for eldercare, the children and grandchildren could accustom themselves to intergenerational living before it became a necessity. Learning to live together and love each other now would be much easier than when the stress would be much higher.

The move, of course, involved challenges for all parties. For one spouse it meant a decision to live with in-laws. For all it meant sacrificing independence. The decision was made, though, in the spirit of Christian householding, with Dietrich Bonhoeffer's notion in mind that Christian life together is not about finding "the community

---

3. See David Matzko McCarthy, *Sex and Love in the Home: A Theology of the Household* (London: SCM, 2001), 140, 141, 155, and chap. 9. McCarthy pointed out other examples of preferences for contractual relationships. For example, rather than hiring the neighbor kid to help paint a house, a person might hire a painter because it is easier and less risky. No need to teach a kid how to paint, worry if he will be late or slow, or if he will spill paint everywhere.

we've always wanted." Christian life together is *not* about finding a cadre of people who like each other and want to live together for community's sake. Rather, says Bonhoeffer, "The kingdom is to be in the midst of your enemies. And he who will not suffer this does not want to be of the kingdom of Christ."[4] As much as we love those who have traditioned the practices of Christian marriage to us, we can at times seem to be each other's enemies.

This insight about intergenerational Christian householding takes on a new character when we understand that, as ecclesial practices of householding, religious life and Christian marriage widen the scope of those to whom we have nonvoluntary relationships, those to whom we should consider offering hospitality and a share in our own householding. Intergenerational living within the biological household is not the only option. What if, in light of the rising need for eldercare, a new association of the lay faithful or new religious order arose whose apostolate was to hold house with the elderly in need? If our truest family are those who are incorporated into Christ, then this suggestion need not sound so strange. What if large, lonely Church rectories housing one priest became places of Christian householding for new kinds of Christian life together involving elderly from the parish? If true religion is to care for the widow, and if Christian householding is truly a task of the whole Church, then these options should not sound all that far-fetched.[5]

At this point another of MacIntyre's criteria for practice comes to the foreground. In the excellent pursuit of a practice, there are times

---

4. Dietrich Bonhoeffer, *Life Together*, trans. John W. Doberstein (San Francisco: HarperSanFrancisco, 1993), 17–18.

5. See M. Therese Lysaught, "Practicing the Order of Widows: A New Call for an Old Vocation," *Christian Bioethics* 11 (2005): 51–68. Lysaught argues for a revival of the Order of Widows, a version of the kind of Christian householding I hypothesize here, in light of the 1998 document from the Pontifical Council for the Laity entitled, "The Dignity of Older People and Their Mission in the Church and the World."

in which external goods associated with the practice may be harder to attain or may even be temporarily sacrificed for the sake of the internal goods and standards of excellence essential to the practice itself. As MacIntyre put it, faithfulness to the excellent performance of a practice and its standards leads "from time to time [to] the taking of self-endangering and even achievement-endangering risks."[6] Furthermore, "the possession of the virtues may perfectly well hinder us in achieving external goods."[7] This is frequently the case in the practice of Christian marriage and householding, particularly if we keep in mind the householding principles of familiarity and formality.

Familiarity, as explored in chapter 4, requires nearness, a quality of domestic life that cannot be made safe. It relies on the virtue and internal good of *fides*—fidelity in its fullest sense. For example, spouses must keep faithful to the common goods of their practice of Christian marriage. One of those goods might be time spent together in productive activity. Fidelity to a commitment to this kind of presence in the home may bar one or both working parents from greater job promotions that would result from or lead to extended absence from the life of the home. Faithfulness to standards of excellence in Christian householding as a spouse and parent include eating, praying, playing and working together for common goods (i.e., cleaning the house or repainting a wall) on a daily basis may involve achievement-endangering risks. The Bryant couple, before committing to marriage, considered the career path of the spouse who planned on being a primary income-earner. This spouse had already prepared for a career in medicine, but determined that the particular career of interest within medicine would require an infidelity of time and energy to the non–wage-earning aspects of their

---

6. MacIntyre, *After Virtue*, 193.
7. Ibid., 196.

future householding. The couple, through prayer and research, discovered a new, less auspicious and prestigious career path that enables one spouse to work from home on two days of the week and allows the couple to work for income together part-time.

A second example also touches financial matters and emphasizes the ecclesial character of marriage as a consecrated way in Christ. As MacIntyre reminds us, a practice's purposes and ends are in part defined by the social body in which the practice takes place. For Christians marriage takes place in the ecclesial body, so the purposes and ends of the Church are in part determinative of the purposes and ends of the marriage. The Roberts household, in an effort to make the Church's ends their own, give a tithe of 10 percent from the top of their gross income to their geographical parish. For them faithfulness to the mission of this parish means a steady, planned financial commitment rather than a chunk here or a piece there. This kind of commitment, though, at a middle-class wage, is a substantial portion of their income. It means the loss of some external goods for this family—in their case cable TV and cell phone. Members of religious orders often make an even more radical statement of fidelity to the mission of their ecclesial institutions. For example, employees of educational institutions who are also members of religious orders often give (with their order's permission) a substantial or even the entirety of their salary back to the institution. In both of these cases, the standard of *fides* (fidelity) to the internal goods of the practice leads to a sacrifice of goods external to the practice of their Christian householding.

A final aspect of MacIntyre's definition that brings Christian marriage, as consecrated way, into discussion with the principles of householding from chapter 5 is that the cooperative activities and virtues determinative of the practice contribute to the internal good of "living as X." In the case of a painter, the virtues and activities of her practice extend the internal good of "a painter's life, or living as a painter." In the case of the consecrated conjugal life, the virtues and activities of Christian householding integrate the internal goods of the practice into "living as Christ, or the life of Christ."

In particular, the householding principles of *ora et labora* are at work integrating the practice of Christian marriage into "living as Christ."[8] For example, the Jenkins household try to envision their household practices as part of Christ's own actions through the work of the Church. To that end the household members commit to daily prayer for the hungry and homeless as a support for the ecclesial ministries that aid them. In addition, they offer a weekly fast and hour of eucharistic adoration for one person or family in particular. This *ora*, though, as a shared work for a common good internal to the practice of being Church (feeding the hungry and sheltering the homeless) extends the capacity of the family to achieve that good in the concrete. In other words, it extends their ability to express the virtues of "living as Christ." One Saturday of the month, as a fruit of and natural companion to their prayer, the household, young and old alike, go to the parish and set up the tables, food, and clothes for the wider ecclesial household who live in need. The two- and three-year-old children push chairs into places, the four-year-olds set out napkins, five-year-olds fold and set out clothes, the older children help cook hot meals and pack bag lunches. Meanwhile, homeless and poor from the neighborhood make their way in and interact with the members of the Jenkins household (and other households). The ecclesial dining hall is transformed into a hearth where hospitality is offered in a familiar way to strangers who become friends. For the Jenkins household, this kind of activity is not a "service activity," an accidental aspect of their householding done

---

8. See Kenneth Russell, "Marriage and the Contemplative Life," *Spiritual Life* 24, no. 7 (1978): 48–57. Russell argues that *ora* can be considered the vocation of the family.

because of their participation in a voluntary association. It is part of the practice of Christian householding done out of the standards of excellence built into the practice of living in the household of God. If "living as Christ" is the internal good achieved by integrating the virtues and activities of their practice of Christian householding, then doing the things the Church (as sacrament of Christ) does is a standard for the achieving this internal good. "Living as Christ" is the integration of their activities of *ora* and their *labora* toward their share in the common purposes, ends, and goods of God's household.

Constructing Consecrated Rooms: Conjugal Poverty, Chastity, and Obedience

Conjugal Poverty

The chief difficulty in suggesting concrete practices for marriage and family life is, well, reality. Families inhabit a wide variety of socio-economic and cultural situations. How can any practice of poverty be universally applicable, especially when a majority of the world's people already live in conditions Americans would consider impoverished? Furthermore, when the poverty of vowed religious is materially richer than the life of those whom they serve, how prophetic or exemplary can that poverty be? This section will look to Christ as the exemplar and the source making the virtue of poverty possible in the spouses. Traumatic material poverty may or may not be a reality for the married couple, but regardless, the state and virtue of poverty are necessary for the couple to live marriage as a consecrated way in Christ. In other words, poverty has a deep theological meaning about dependence and reliance on God, but this section will avoid reducing poverty to a pious metaphor by attempting to maintain a connection to the material and economic aspects of poverty, as well.

This notion of common possession goes beyond shared bank accounts and cars to common possession of goals, practices, values, and narrative. Practicing poverty in marriage means working toward what theologian Bernard Lonergan calls a "common consciousness."[9] The household of Christian spouses and their children (along with anyone else who might live with them), as place of formation, become a community where spouses achieve ever greater sharing in the capacity to write and tell the narrative of their union in love with one another. Spouses must hold in common the ends, purposes, and goods of marriage if they are to come to the same understanding, judgments, and decisions about their common marital activities such as parenting and domestic management. Achieving a common consciousness takes time but begins, almost accidentally, early in the couple's relationship. By the time of formal engagement, though, the couple must explicitly address the issue and begin sharing in ever more common activities for common ends. Once the couple enter marriage they begin to share in the whole of life together through activities that constitute the path toward a common consciousness or toward decline and division. Arriving at and living in the common consciousness necessary for sharing in such a narrative is only possible within a state of poverty, a realization that nothing in the marriage is one's own, least of all the authority to determine the goals, values, and practices of the married household. This, as all other things, belongs to God.

What is the state of spouse, *coram conjuge*, in the face of the other spouse? If the spouses enter into an institution that images the incar-

---

9. Lonergan treats the relationship of "common consciousness" and "common conscience" to marriage explicitly in "Finality, Love, Marriage," *Theological Studies* 4 (1943): 477–510, at 494–96, 503, and 507. Lonergan expands on the terms and ideas involved with "common consciousness" and "common conscience" as they relate to meaning and communication, progress and decline in all human community in *Method in Theology*, 2nd ed. (Toronto: University of Toronto Press, 1979), 50–51, 79, and 356–58.

nation, then we should find an answer if we ask the same question of Christ: what is Christ's state, *coram conjuge*? As argued in chapter 2, Christ's state is one of poverty. Christ made himself poor so that we (his spouse) might be rich. He puts himself in relationship with us so that we might share his inheritance. All his merit can become ours. His reign can become our reign as we rule with him eternally. His kingdom becomes our kingdom if we are joined to him as his spouse. The clearest practice suggested by this theological description is that the marital consent is implicitly a vow of poverty *coram conjuge*. There is no more "mine," there is only "our." Whereas consecrated religious become canonically incapable of owning property personally, spouses become morally incapable of owning property personally.[10] There must be no financial, material aspect of conjugal life that belongs solely to one spouse. All property should be held in common, as in a religious order.

Once this commitment is made, the couple and the religious order, then, must determine the poverty they will embrace at the institutional level. For married Christians in the middle class and for the wealthy, embracing poverty (both spiritual and material) presents a challenge that must be met. Embracing poverty means rejecting the myth of economic, social, and moral independence by creating conditions that require economic and spiritual reliance on others and fidelity to being reliable in answering the economic and spiritual needs of neighbors. One possibility that has worked is for households or members of a parish to share a car, a grill, washer and dryer, lawnmower, construction skills, childcare.

Married persons ought to practice the virtue and state of poverty by putting themselves in positions of dependence, as well as mak-

---

10. In terms of civil law, assets gained after the marriage are considered marital property held equally by both spouses, even if the property is not held in the name of both spouses; see, for example, Wisconsin's Marital Property Act of 1986, at http://nxt.legis.state.wi.us/nxt/gateway.dll?f=templates&fndefault.htm&d =stats&jd=ch.%20766, accessed January 7, 2011.

ing themselves more available to those who necessarily depend on them. Householders can only develop the virtue of poverty from within real conditions of need. Take, for example, a common family practice: the babysitting co-op. The babysitting co-op, in many ways, is an example in the practice of poverty. Couples understand their poverty; they need babysitting and they cannot afford to pay for the service. Networks of families who are friends turn to each other for help. The currency for the co-op system is hours. Families begin with a certain number and spend or accrue hours as they have their children watched or as they watch other children. A system like this one has much to recommend it: availability to others, dependence on others, accountability, justice, and a disconnection from monetary economy. The co-op is a practice born of the state of poverty and fulfilled with the virtue of poverty.

At the same time, though, the practice decidedly maintains a market inspiration and economic structure. In other words, it does not go far enough to address the problems of the contractual individualism that has invaded practices of householding (even among Christians). Yes, it is relational and expresses availability and dependence, but it does so on a client-customer level. This co-op system operates on the market logic of saving and spending currency. Unfortunately, it attempts to concretize, contractualize, and monetize friendships in terms of interpersonal capital. Once the forty hours are spent, the currency has vanished. I cannot ask for babysitting help until I have accrued more hours watching other people's children. There is only one kind of currency to spend—namely, hours. So, while there is a certain justice in having symmetrical reciprocation and a standard currency, the project does not allow for the way friendships typically work: asymmetrically.[11] A meal and

---

11. McCarthy defines "asymmetrical reciprocity" and its practical and theological implications well in *Sex and Love in the Home*, 133–51.

hospitality, or help in some other way, can serve as an expression of gratitude for babysitting and asymmetrically reciprocates the time and energy spent by the other family or single person. For example, occasionally my brother's family watches our children. Occasionally, my wife and I help my brother paint his house or work on landscaping. There is no logging of hours and no attempt to reciprocate in exactly the same way. There is only the understanding that we need each other and a willingness to be available for each other. Our needs arise from poverty and are fulfilled in poverty. As a second example, not all persons have the same skills or the same needs. A babysitting co-op might make sense for some groups of married persons, but some married couples with children are not in a position to look after their friends' kids. They may need to rely on non-married friends for help. With the co-op model, the married folk cannot repay the favor symmetrically. They will have to informally, asymmetrically show gratitude to that friend by being available to answer the call of their friend's poverty. Spouses, then, ought not to seek to insulate themselves from poverty, but to experience true need and make themselves available to fulfill the poverty of people who need them.

Among the activities that create conditions requiring reliance and fidelity in poverty, though, is inviting God's gift of fertility in a marriage. Such an activity is an openness to the Augustinian, ecclesio-nuptial good of *proles*. The activities of conceiving, preparing for, and parenting a child demand mutual reliance and fidelity more than any other activity in the Christian household.

Just as for Christ, poverty meant complete dependence on God the Father for all he was to receive (his flock) and all he was to do (the will of God), so for the married couple, the state of poverty and the virtue of poverty will be to exist in a similar, radical dependence on God the Father for the children they may *or may not* receive in

Consecrating Conjugal Life—A Construction Site

marriage. A great number of couples find themselves faced with the specter of infertility. This heavy cross highlights the fact that spouses are dependent on the will of God for children. They are received as gift; they are not ordered and patiently awaited like items on a restaurant menu. They are given to the couple as Christ's flock is given to him—by the Father's will.[12] As Christ cares for and shepherds his sheep, so parents shepherd theirs, with the same trust Christ has—that not a single sheep given him will be lost. This was the trust St. Monica showed in her persevering prayer for Augustine. This is the trust parents show when they fulfill their wedding vow to boldly raise their children "according to the Law of Christ and the Church."

Especially early in marriage, before couples are accustomed to dual-income and upper-middle-class life, the gift of pregnancy develops the virtue and state of poverty. Parenting is an activity for which only a rare soul finds herself "ready." At least in Middle America, "not being ready" economically is all too often an excuse for Christian households to remain closed to God's gift of fertility. This state of affairs relates to a misconception of the economic resources parenting actually demands. Too often parenting is construed according to the logic of the market rather than the logic of the cross. A household can never be prepared for children if parenting is construed as a consumer activity. Often the gap between what a child needs and what parents want for that child and what things the parents will train their children to want is large, indeed. The current plague of obesity in America testifies that the middle-class problem (and especially the problem among the poor) is not that parents can't give their children *enough* but that parents can't give children enough of *the right stuff.* Our most scandalous poverty is our over-

---

12. See Jn 11:11–18, 29, where Jesus refers to his flock as those given to him by the Father, and for whom he will lay down his life, and Jn 17:9–10, where Jesus prays during the last-supper discourse for those whom God has given him and whom he has guarded.

abundance of junk that is bought, eaten, and played with by and for children. Parenting is an opportunity for voluntary and nonvoluntary poverty at the economical level that Christian households must embrace. They must embrace poverty not merely because it is an accurate reflection of their relationship to God in Christ, but also because the alternative is a scandalous affront to the solidarity called for in Catholic social teaching.

Parents often feel a complete poverty of knowledge and "things" when it comes to their first child. A positive pregnancy test is often accompanied by a rush to the store for all the newest parenting books and the mountain of things the latest parenting magazine says all mothers and fathers who love their children really need. Before a baby is even born, parenting is cast as a consumer activity. Loving the child has become buying the right material goods. For Christians the story is no different. They are just told to buy different, "Christian" material goods (i.e., the Noah's ark pajamas instead of the Batman pajamas). This moment is a touch-point for nourishing the virtue of poverty in the Christian household. This is a moment of renunciation for the parents, who can declare that raising their children for Christ is not principally a consumer activity. It is economic activity, but most concerned with salvation economy and home economy, the creation of practices that will form the kind of person who can inhabit God's household. Relying on secondhand children's clothes, furniture, and toys can be a way to resist the economy of consumption and embrace reliance on God and neighbor. A couple might find they can receive all their most useful children's furniture secondhand, for example (cribs, beds, changing table), either purchased or received as gift from neighbors.[13] A family in the neighborhood, upon expanding to four children, needed a larger ve-

---

13. Catholic pregnancy help centers often share and give material goods, along with preparation and training programs, to expecting mothers.

hicle. They bought a minivan from a family in the parish who had just welcomed their sixth child (they too needed a bigger vehicle). The same family that bought the minivan sold their smaller car to a first-generation college student who needed a deal. Personally receiving and giving used goods contributes to the development of the virtue of poverty by building relationships of reciprocity. Furthermore, teaching children to participate in shared resources like libraries and parks develops the virtue of poverty through learning care for common goods.

Practically speaking, each couple should choose at least one "thing" they will do without as a practice of poverty. Absence of this item should be obvious for the couple. Examples might be a cellphone, a television, cable TV, a second car, five degrees on the thermostat. In deciding on this voluntary poverty, couples should be thinking about things that would be normal inclusions on a budget rather than luxury items or discretionary spending. This activity could be increased periodically to coincide with liturgical seasons or days. For example, Lent could be a time to increase a household's voluntary poverty for the sake of households who have no choice about their material lack of necessities. (Drop five degrees on the thermostat for Lent and send the savings to that neighbor whose car just broke down.) Furthermore, developing the virtue of poverty requires friendship with the poor. Friendship is different from institutional or even patron-client charitable relationships with the poor. Friendship means a reciprocal relationship wherein people seek and work for the same ends together. This embrace of poverty challenges middle- and upper-class families to take steps to not only help the poor, but enter solidarity with them—to be with the poor. Families—yes, families—might consider moving to less than desirable locations to live among those with less, might consider serving *and* eating at soup kitchens, might consider taking in a person (e.g., a foster child, a single pregnant woman) in need and working with them toward stability.

These practices help remind spouses and parents of their radical poverty in the face of their own children. Parents can buy the newest and best material goods for their children, but they cannot ensure their children will become Christian disciples, or even that they will be happy in this life. Christian parents who realize their poverty also understand that the greatest gifts they can give their children are those that initiate the child into the consecrated way in Christ (the first of which is baptism) and those that form them in the practices of Christian householding. Baptism expresses the virtue of poverty inasmuch as it declares before the Church that the life the biological parents give to the child is secondary to the life the parents cannot give the child but that God offers the Child—namely, God's own life. The Church and the parents as members of the Church claim the child for Christ, and the child is reborn into a life given by God and cared for by the parents. The child's life is not the parents' but Christ's to be formed and guided by the parents.

Again, the reason to live in a state of poverty with the virtue of poverty is not because it makes life easier. In fact, needs make life difficult, and being available for the needs of others makes life messy. The reason marriage requires poverty is, again, because it accurately represents our own position *coram Deo* and Christ's own position *coram conjuge*. In other words, we find poverty in Christ. Christ, the creator of the universe, becomes a naked, cold, crying, and hungry infant. Christ has radical need. He will die if Mary and Joseph do not make themselves available for his needs. Christian parents are continually reminded of this fact whenever they tend to their children's daily needs. Christ the king of kings becomes a babbling one-year-old, a teary-eyed two-year-old, a curious five-year-old, who needs training and formation in the virtues of a holy life. Christ cannot symmetrically repay his mother, nor can she repay her child. We too find ourselves in a situation of radical need with the impossibility of repayment. Dead and lost in the darkness of sin and ignorance, of disordered desires and misdirected intellect, only baptism into Christ and formation in the virtues of faith, hope, and love can fill us with the riches we require. Ours is the need, God's the gift. Ours is a need we cannot fulfill; his is a gift that cannot be repaid, symmetrically or otherwise. Our state is poverty, but a poverty fulfilled. Our posture is gratitude and joy at giving back to the one who fulfills our need all that we have to give, which is both nothing and everything at once. Arriving at an understanding of one's radical dependence and responding with gratitude leading to availability is the reality of conjugal living. The realization that it was "not good for the man to be alone" is a moment of poverty. Adam did not need Eve to complete him, but the two needed each other to fulfill their human vocation. All persons find themselves in the state of poverty, in need of human and supernatural fellowship. Some will fulfill their human vocation in community without vows; some will fulfill their human vocation vowing poverty in a particular religious community; and others with a vocation to marriage will fulfill their human vocation vowing a life of poverty in complementary, sacramental union with one other person.

Conjugal Chastity

Perhaps no aspect of marriage has received as much attention as sexuality—with good reason. Sexuality is an essential part of the human person; the partnership of the sexes has a primal connection to our sexuality, and our desire for holistic sexual, personal, complementary partnership can express in part our deepest desires for perfect union with God.[14] Just as the consent to marriage, a consent to

---

14. In married sexuality we know and are known, we see and are seen, we give and receive, we transcend ourselves yet are at home. Yet all of these relationships are conditioned, tempo-

give all that one is and receive all that another is, includes the vow of poverty, so too does it include the vow of chastity. Spouses promise to "be faithful to you" (*promitto me tibi fidem servaturum*). The *fidem* promised has been developed throughout Christian history to be understood in a totalizing sense of complete personal fidelity, but from the earliest sources it has always included sexual fidelity. Even in the days of Christ, conjugal fidelity included more than merely genital exclusivity: "Every one who looks at a woman lustfully has already committed adultery with her in his heart" (Mt 5:28). Christ assumes that spouses will maintain chastity in a full sense—that is, a self-possession of not only their bodies but also their thoughts and desires. For his part Augustine continues this thought. The virtue associated with marital fidelity was chastity. He calls this fidelity *fides castitatis* (faithfulness of chastity).[15]

The virtue associated with the sexual fidelity of the marriage vows is the same virtue associated with the sexual fidelity required by the vows of religion: chastity. For Aquinas chastity exists as a species of temperance, which is the power of properly ordering pleasures.[16] Among twentieth-century theologians (and even in the *Catechism of the Catholic Church*), expressions of chastity given shape by the phenomenology of personalism and advances in psychology

---

rary, and imperfect. Only in the beatific vision will we be fully known while knowing all that can be known; will we be fully seen while seeing all that we can see; will we be fully given and fully receive the love of God; will we entirely transcend while entirely being at home.

15. In Augustine's mind *fides* cannot be reduced to sexual exclusivity. He scolds a woman for a breaking of faith regarding the greatest end of the marriage, the sanctification of the spouses. While her husband was away she entered a life of poverty and celibacy, giving their wealth to two traveling monks. The husband eventually ended up committing adultery; Epistle 262, in Augustine, *Letters 211–70*, ed. Boniface Ramsey, trans. Roland Teske, in part 2 of *The Works of Augustine*, edited by John E. Rotelle and Boniface Ramsey (Hyde Park, N.Y.: New City Press, 2004), 4:204–7.

16. See Aquinas, *ST* II-II, q. 151. In the mind of Aquinas, the conjugal act was not only allowable but virtuous; see *ST* suppl., q. 41, a. 4 and q. 49, a. 4 (though as an expression of the virtue of religion).

prevail.[17] The human person is a unity of spiritual and bodily existence. Both of these aspects of the human person become especially expressive and vulnerable in sexuality and especially open to dislocation from one another. In summary, "chastity is the successful integration of sexuality within the person and thus the inner unity of man in his bodily and spiritual being. Sexuality, in which man's belonging to the bodily and biological world is expressed, becomes personal and truly human when it is integrated into the relationship of one person to another, in the complete and lifelong mutual gift of man and woman."[18] This lifelong mutual gift is clearly expressed in the conjugal vows, but may also be expressed in the vows of religious profession.

All couples will need formation in chastity as they enter the sacrament with varied levels of the virtue or its opposing vice. If chastity is a virtue, then it not only expresses a person's character, but also forms that character. Just as sound practice of religious life must offer a set of conditions and formative activities that aid in the development of chaste celibacy, no less does married life require apt conditions and formation for developing chaste married sexuality. Specifically, the Church recommends the program or skill of natural family planning. Among the benefits of natural family planning is that it offers a set of conditions that disposes couples to growth in the virtue of chastity toward the practice of chaste married sexuality integrated into the rest of married life.

Because there is much confusion over the use of natural family planning in marriage, I would like to contextualize it within the wider practice of chaste married sexuality. I will offer below some clarity on these two terms: (1) natural family planning (hereafter NFP)

17. John Grabowski, *Sex and Virtue: An Introduction to Sexual Ethics*, Catholic Moral Thought (Washington, D.C.: The Catholic University of America Press, 2003), 85–95.
18. *Catechism of the Catholic Church*, 2337:561.

and (2) a new term that I am offering as a practice (in the MacIntyrian sense) of chastity in marriage—chaste marital sexuality (hereafter CMS).[19] It is easy to equate NFP with CMS, as if the use of the method is itself a virtuous expression of married sexual love. I think NFP must remain distinct from CMS as a potentially necessary but not sufficient condition for excellent practice. By way of analogy we can say that the Kieninger trap is to chess as NFP is to CMS. The skill of NFP is nested within the practice of CMS, which sits within the overall practice of Christian marriage, a consortium of the whole of life and love.

Here I will offer definitions of NFP and CMS. *NFP is a method of timing conjugal intercourse to either avoid or invite pregnancy based on data gathered from female physiology.* Two parts constitute natural family planning: (1) gathering and analyzing data from physiological signs to determine the probability that conception will result from conjugal intercourse on any specific day; (2) employing the conclusion of the first part as a datum for deciding whether or not to engage in the marital intercourse on any specific day. CMS, on the other hand, is *an integration of a couple's sexuality into the* consortium vitae et amoris *that is Christian marriage. CMS is a complex set of activities, virtues, and skills necessary to love the spouse as "man" or "woman" in all the quotidian interactions and activities of Christian marriage.* Only occasionally do spouses embody conjugal love in sexual intercourse. For the most part spouses enact CMS in the small, seemingly insignificant touches, glances, smiles, words, and

---

19. Michael Therrien has offered a definition of "responsible parenthood" as a practice along MacIntyre's lines; see Therrien's "The Practice of Responsible Parenthood, NFP, and the Covenantal Unity of Spouses," in *Leaving and Coming Home: New Wineskins for Catholic Sexual Ethics*, ed. David Cloutier, 173–205 (Eugene, Ore.: Cascade, 2010); see also the USCCB's document "Responsible Parenthood," http://www.usccb.org/issues-and-action/marriage-and-family/natural-family-planning/catholic-teaching/upload/Responsible-Parenthood.pdf, accessed May 10, 2013.

gestures throughout the day, in the way they dress, in the way they communicate with each other about sexuality, the way they pray about and for each other and their children, the way they talk about each other to their children and coworkers, the kinds of media they consume, and the way they interact with persons of the opposite sex in general. CMS is a practice that orders sexuality within marriage for the goods internal to that practice (procreation and the mutual aid of the spouses in sanctification).

This orientation sees the invitation to life as the status quo and avoidance of pregnancy as an exceptional situation. Responsible or (as Janet Smith translates it) "conscious" parenthood is the mission of the married couple.[20] The virtue of generosity disposes spouses to an expansive procreation and education of children, whereas prudence helps them judge whether their invitation to life is within reason.[21] Chastity is the fulcrum between these two virtues. It allows a couple to honor each other and the dignity of their children, who deserve to be the fruit not of lust but of a sincere gift of self and reception of the other. Abstinence with NFP, in this understanding, would only be necessary in cases of "serious reasons" to avoid conception.[22] These would be cases where the possibility of

20. Paul VI, *Humanae vitae* 1, 7; see Janet Smith, "Conscious Parenthood," *Nova et Vetera* 6, no. 4 (2008): 927–50.
21. Generosity and prudence are the two virtues and standards of excellence central to the Church's description of responsible parenthood; see *GS* 48 and *Humanae vitae* 10, 16.
22. *Humanae vitae* 10, 16; *Catechism of the Catholic Church* (Boston: Pauline Books, 1994), no. 2368. The catechism uses the word "just reason." The question "what is a just reason?" can be answered by looking at other definitions of when avoidance of pregnancy constitutes responsible parenthood. *Humanae vitae* 10 uses the language "grave reasons/motives" regarding the "tendencies of instinct or passion," as well as "physical, economic, psychological and social conitions." *Humanae vitae* 16 uses the language "serious reasons/motives." *GS* 50 uses the language of "common counsel and effort," "thoughtful account," "trusting in divine Providence and refining the spirit of sacrifice" to make decisions in light of the personal good of the spouses, the children already born, and the society they inhabit. Both *Humanae vitae* 10 and *GS* 48, 50 use the language of "generous decision" and "generous human and Christian sense of responsibility" respectively. In *Evangelium vitae* 97, John Paul II writes that a

another pregnancy seriously endangers the goods internal to the practice of marriage. The endangerment of external goods is sometimes required for the excellent performance of any practice, including CMS, so it is difficult to make the case that endangering these goods alone would constitute a serious (and therefore just) reason to avoid pregnancy. NFP is a skill helpful for determining the *when* of conjugal intercourse, but CMS is the practice concerned with the *how* and the *why* of loving the spouse and children as *man* and *father* or *woman* and *mother* as a whole.

CMS, as a richly ecclesial practice, ties in especially well with one pair of principles from chapter 5 on Christian householding: familiarity (nearness) and formality (universality). Here the familiarity of the home and the universality and formality of the Church meet. This section treats the more obvious of the two: familiarity. The link between chastity and familiarity is intuitive. No other part of the marital practice involves as much physical and emotional nearness. As a primary practice wherein couples experience the powerful affective love of familiarity, CMS can contribute to making the entire household into what Breidenthal calls a "spiritual workplace."[23] The Christian household and especially chastity within it are a training ground for the kind of familiarity we will have in heaven but that would be dangerous on earth. Training in sexual self-possession teaches us that genital expression is not the only or even greatest way to love those to whom we are nearest. Frequently, it is washing out the diapers, shoveling the sidewalk, giving the kids a bath,

---

responsible procreation "obedient to the Lord's call . . . happens when the family is generously open to new lives, and when couples maintain an attitude of openness and service to life, even if, for serious reasons and in respect for the moral law, they choose to avoid a new birth for the time being or indefinitely." This discernment remains the solemn duty of each unique married couple.

23. Thomas Breidenthal, *Christian Households: The Sanctification of Nearness* (Eugene, Ore.: Wipf and Stock, 2004), 15.

watching a daughter's soccer game, and offering a shoulder massage to a tired spouse that more deeply manifest and embody conjugal love than does expressing one's interest in sexual intercourse. The key of chastity is that it allows a person to put in action the statement, "I love you with my whole body."

This viewpoint is helpful especially for the formation of teens in Christian households. Many teens and young college students engage in sexual intercourse "when they are ready for that next step" or "to give the deepest expression of our love for each other." Genital contact is not in most cases a "next step" or the "deepest expression of love."[24] Genital contact is a consequence and physical expression of a personal, public (ecclesial), and sacramental vow to love one person unconditionally and without fail. Apart from this context, it is unintelligible to say that sexual intercourse is the greatest expression of love for each other or that it is a "next step" in romantic love. Genital contact in the context of Christian householding requires chastity because chastity is the capacity to order one's sexuality to this kind of exclusivity. Before marriage chastity enables a person to love without genital contact.[25] Within marriage chastity does the same thing: it gives the person the capacity to love with the whole body, except now there is occasional genital expression of love. Without an actualized capacity to love with the rest of the body—that is, without chastity—conjugal intercourse (even in marriage) expresses not married love, but lust. The familiarity of the

---

24. See David Matzko McCarthy, "Cohabitation and Marriage," in *Leaving and Coming Home*, 119–46. McCarthy explores the individualist-expressivist vision of marriage, cohabitation, and sexual intimacy as a "personal capstone" while suggesting an alternative that is more institutionally grounded; see in the same volume David Cloutier and William C. Mattison III, "Bodies Poured out in Christ: Marriage beyond the Theology of the Body," 206–25.

25. In fact, a recent study by Donna Freitas shows that when nonmarried people are asked about the most romantic experience of their life, they do not mention genital contact; see Freitas, *Sex and the Soul: Juggling Sexuality, Spirituality, Romance, and Religion on America's College Campuses* (Oxford: Oxford University Press, 2008), 109.

bed is then more a concession to weakness than an embodiment of self-donation.

What often goes unnoticed in marriages, and even in discussions of familiarity and chastity, is the dynamic tension between this familiarity and nearness against the pole of universality and formality. Christ comes to redeem and sanctify our nearness, part of which is sexual. To redeem our nearness to each other, Christ becomes near to us, formally, in a universal way. Christ incorporates any person into his body through the sacramental grace of baptism, an incorporation continued and enlivened in the participation in the grace of the Eucharist. If each of us is in Christ, all of our nearness to each other is nearness to Christ, a nearness manifested and actualized liturgically and formally. Sexuality, as part of the nearness of spouses in a Christian household, benefits from this formality. At the concrete level the formal, liturgical practices initiate the activities of sexual familiarity in Christian marriage through a universal, liturgical rite of matrimony. The formal is bound to the familiar, commencing the ratified marriage created in the public words of consent. Soon after this formal rite the familiarity of Christian marriage formally consummates the marriage. The very nearness, the intimate familiarity of the conjugal act between spouses in Christ, completes the marriage's formal, universal, ecclesial foundation and inception. Consider, too, the liturgical, formal context for the consummation of marriage in the book of Tobit. After making consent but before consummating their marriage, Tobias and Sara fervently pray. Tobias even declares to God, "Now, not with lust, but with fidelity I take this kinswoman as my wife. Send down your mercy on me and on her, and grant that we may grow old together" (Tb 8:7). Would that all married intimacy could be so contextualized.

The link between the familiarity and the formal, liturgical aspects of marriage in the Church is also a source of concrete actions for developing goods internal to CMS and destroying its contrary vice of lust. For example, a couple who makes the formal pattern of the liturgical year their own could decide to incorporate it into their pattern of sexual intimacy. If a couple truly experiences their conjugal union as an expression of joy, a celebration of their love, then they might consider the relationship between this expression of joyous, superabundant love and the days and seasons of fasting and penance in the liturgical year. The Church recommended abstinence from conjugal sexuality on a great many days in years past, and it is easy to think that any effort to renew or make a similar suggestion would betray a negativity about sexuality. If anything, asking couples to reconsider the relationship between sexuality and the liturgical year must be cast as an exceptionally positive understanding of conjugal intercourse. Because it is an authentic good and contributes to the joy of couples and their superabundant love for each other, it can be sacrificed not "as something bad" but as something whose absence will be felt as a loss of a good that reminds us of the loss of Christ in death, as a good we hold away from ourselves in penance, and as a good that eventually reminds us in a small way of the return of Christ and his gift of eternal life to the world.

Couples who want to grow in CMS, then, ought to attempt a greater integration of their conjugal familiarity into the formal seasons of the liturgical year. Specifically, couples could consider abstaining during Lent, or on Fridays in addition to abstaining from meat, on Wednesdays, during ember days, for the period of a novena. Such commitments would necessarily take seriously St. Paul's letter to the Corinthians. "Stop depriving one another," he writes, "except by agreement for a time, so that you may devote yourselves to prayer" (1 Cor 7:6). Their time of abstinence must, however, be intentionally discerned and must follow the words of St. Paul, lest it lead to even greater lust, coldness, or legalism. In other words, the time of abstinence must be *for prayer together*. This is not because sexual intercourse detracts spouses from prayer per se, but because practically speaking it in fact does detract from prayer. By the time spouses (especially those working long hours or those with kids) have enough time and energy to relax together, they may be faced with the option to either pray or be physically intimate. If they choose conjugal intimacy first, they may fall asleep together without prayer. If they spend time in prayer first, they may have little energy or time left for physical intimacy. These are concrete realities of married life. Sexual intercourse is splendid, but it takes time and energy that could be put into prayer, wiping the floors, discussion of what to do about Johnny's behavior problem, or just sleeping. This is in part why a temporary, intentional abstinence from conjugal intercourse entirely can be such a boon. It can relieve some of this pressure to find time for it all and the unspoken tension that can accompany that pressure.

To bear fruit this time should include daily prayer and scripture together (perhaps the Divine Office), spiritual reading, and communication about the goods, ends, and purposes of sexuality in marriage. Prayer together during a time of abstinence should remind spouses that their conjugal intercourse is a physical expression of their marital love, a love that is a participation in Christ's own love for the Church. This is a time for spouses to evaluate their practice and reconsider the standards of excellence and virtues necessary to help them live the life of chaste persons in the household of God. This is a time to remember and relearn how to live Christ's love in nongenital ways. Without these little ways of love, after all, there is no chaste married sexuality, and there will be little desire to express love sexually—even when not in a time of abstinence.

Chaste married sexuality, in a MacIntyrian sense, extends the couple's capacity for and understanding of the goods internal to its practice. The more chaste spouses become the more they will see their sexuality as integrated into their service to each other's sanctification and the sanctification of the world. Furthermore, the more chaste spouses become the more they will see their sexuality integrated into the larger mystery of Christ's love for the Church. At the practical level chastity will increase the ease with which couples love each other in the quotidian activities of life and with which they determine the demands of responsible parenthood through obedient attention to God's will in the education of their children and their openness to or avoidance of a new pregnancy. With CMS, the more spouses possess their whole bodies and can love them in nongenital ways, the more fully they understand what it means to give freely, fully, faithfully, and fruitfully to each other and God when they love in the greatest physical intimacy. NFP, on the other hand, does not of itself extend these goods. This skill can serve as a path toward lust, frustration, infidelity, and ruin or as a road toward sanctity, chastity, responsibility, and true conjugal love. The skill of NFP must be contextualized within the practice of CMS if it is to be intelligible.

As with attempts at any practice, though, practitioners will encounter difficulty.[26] Couples having difficulty with CMS, especially those growing in lust as opposed to chastity, might be suffering because they have unintentionally reduced CMS to NFP. If CMS is reduced to the question of *when,* it is clear that there exists some lack not in the practice of CMS itself, but in the couple's own formation in that practice. They may not have the formation required to achieve the standards of excellence appropriate to and definitive of the activity. In this case the fault lies as much with the Church as with the couple. CMS requires formation especially in prayer; the

---

26. Mary Shivanandan, *Crossing the Threshold of Love: A New Vision of Marriage in the Light of John Paul II's Anthropology* (Washington, D.C.: The Catholic University of America Press, 1999), chap. 8.

internal goods of poverty, chastity, obedience, communication, attentiveness, patience, and well-ordered conjugal sexuality are ineptly achieved without it. Prayer, especially celebration of liturgy together as spouses, garners the gifts of the Holy Spirit and the infused virtues (especially infused temperance, fortitude, and prudence) required for the practice.

Another standard of excellence is communication. One partner's impatience may result from a lack of communication—about stress in the spouse's life, about an unstated conflict, about the woman's place in her cycle, about the decision to avoid or achieve pregnancy. In other words, inasmuch as a couple actually practices CMS, they grow in virtue.

When it is a part of the practice of CMS, there is no way to use the skill of NFP with a "contraceptive mentality," as some fear.[27] The formation of a life-giving mentality is an internal good of CMS itself. There is a clear distinction between NFP and CMS. NFP is the skill of assessing probabilities of conception and abstaining from or engaging in sexual intercourse accordingly. The practice of CMS is a practice that may or may not require the skill of NFP to achieve and extend the internal goods of chastity or responsible parenthood. In chaste marital sexuality, as a Christian practice involving responsible parenthood, couples should be able to identify their fertility and prayerfully, thoughtfully, and virtuously discern God's will for their openness to inviting growth of the Christian family during any given cycle of fertility. Then, ordered by chastity, they can positively act to express conjugal sexuality appropriately based on that discernment.

27. John Paul II has warned couples not to use NFP as the result of a "decision to be closed to life which would be substantially the same as that which inspires the decision to use contraceptives"; see John Paul II, "Pope Calls Spouses to a Sense of Responsibility for Love and for Life," in *L'Osservatore Romano* (Dec 17, 1990): 3, no. 5. John F. Kippley argues that couples using NFP for selfish reasons are in fact selfish but not guilty of a contraceptive mentality, since a contraceptive mentality is a disposition to engage in contraceptive actions; see Kippley, *Sex and the Marriage Covenant: A Basis for Morality*, 2nd ed. (San Francisco: Ignatius Press, 2005), 69–70.

Conjugal Obedience

Less studied, but perhaps equally as incendiary as chastity, is the virtue of conjugal obedience. The question of marital obedience in the last sixty years has been largely controlled by the feminist debates on patriarchy in the Christian tradition, which inevitably take up the endless exegetical arguments over biblical *Haustafeln*—moral exhortations appearing in Colossians 3:18:4–1, 1 Peter 2:18–3:6,[28] and Ephesians 5:21, 22–6:9.[29] Of course, both spouses must submit to each other out of conjugal love, out of reverence for Christ residing in each, and as a general precept of Christian life (see 1 Cor 13; Eph 5:21). This kind of giving way is important and requisite for Christian marriage, but it is not the subject of the marital obedience I am speaking of here.

Within marriage there are two kinds of obedience to consider: obedience of one spouse to the other and the couple's united obedi-

---

28. The most common modern reading of the household codes is to say that they were accommodationist—that is, they were attempts by Christians to baptize current social structures or deal with the inadequacy of the evangelical message for designing long-term societies. They can, therefore, be either continually accepted (evangelical protestant writing) or summarily rejected (feminist scholarship). With Yoder, I challenge the accommodationist position, stating that the Church's use of these moral lists was a radical witness to the contingent and nonpermanent nature of social structure in light of the gospel message. Yoder agrees that the household codes may have been a less revolutionary modification of an original vision of equality in Christ, but he adds the argument that the use of the household codes carried a Christological component, a witness to Christ's revolutionary subordination to structural evils, subordination that destroys the power of the evil and witnesses to its impermanence. John Howard Yoder and David Schroeder have challenged this position; see Yoder, *The Politics of Jesus: "Vicit Agnus Noster,"* 2nd ed. (Grand Rapids, Mich.: Eerdmans, 1994), 162–92; and David Schroeder, *Die Haustafeln des Neuen Testaments: Ihre Herkunft und ihr theologischer Sinn.* 2 *Anmerkungen* (Hamburg: Universitaet Hamburg, 1959).

29. As to Ephesians 5:21–6:9, the same kind of reading strategies applies as to the household codes. I read the text with John Paul II, who has read the passage with an emphasis on 5:21, 25–26. He reads 5:21 as the beginning of the new section (5:21–33). He argues that the author of the letter asks spouses to be "reciprocally subject in the fear of Christ." He supports a use of the head/body analogy for the relationship of husband/wife and Christ/Church; see John Paul II, *Man and Woman He Created Them: A Theology of the Body*, ed., trans., with an introduction by Michael Waldstein (Boston: Pauline Books, 2006), nos. 89–93, pages 472–87.

ence to God the Father in Christ. The first kind of obedience emerges from two scriptural loci: the *Haustafeln,* or household codes, found in St. Paul's letters; and Genesis 1–3. The feminist interests that have dominated the debate on marital obedience for the last fifty years have a certain sense to them. A command to be subject to a man sets up a condition of vulnerability, even dependence, and might suggest reduced dignity. Considering the evidence men have given women since the beginning of the human race, submitting to a man sounds like one of the most dangerous and least intelligent things she might do. One needs not look far for the truth; Adam sets the tone of history in Genesis 3. First, Adam does nothing to prevent the serpent's tempting Eve. There is no statement in the text requiring the assumption that he is far away during the event. Second, upon accusation from God, Adam immediately shifts the blame from himself onto Eve. Even more ridiculous, he has the gall to blame God! Adam says, "The woman whom thou gavest to be with me, she gave me the fruit of the tree, and I ate it." By saying "whom thou gavest to me," Adam accomplishes two rhetorical ends: first to dissociate Eve and her guilt from himself, and second to suggest that God is at fault, since he is the one who put Eve with him in the first place. For her part, Eve does little better, simply blaming the serpent. The important insight is that the relationship between Adam and Eve, husband and wife, is marked by accusation, competition, and suspicion after the fall. It is no wonder women are skeptical of any command to submit themselves to a man. What evidence does woman have to believe that her husband will resist the Adamic urge to implicate her in an attempt to save himself?

    The only evidence a woman can have comes from the incarnation, the recapitulation of history where Christ becomes the new Adam who, rather than blaming Eve and God for sin, takes the guilt and punishment of sin upon himself. In Christ a man reverses the garden narrative; rather than implicating his bride to save himself, he implicates himself to save and purify his bride. How different things might have been had Adam been equal to his duty and shouldered the guilt that was his, if not his wife's as well. Christ, though, has accomplished where Adam failed. In marriage, a wife submits to her husband as to Christ—not Adam.

When submitting to Christ, what does the Christian submit to? A look at John's account of the last supper is helpful. Submitting to Christ there means joining Peter's confusion yet allowing Christ to reign through an act of humiliating service (Jn 13, the washing of the feet). In Mark's Gospel submitting to Christ means joining Peter's confusion again at learning that the disciple must allow Jesus to hand himself over and suffer for one's own sake (Mk 8:33, Jesus rebukes Peter, who says he will prevent Jesus' death). Submitting to Christ means throwing away our false notions of independence and, even more, self-salvation. Submitting to Christ means accepting that one will be saved not through one's own works or piety but in and through another person being handed over and poured out for oneself. Submitting to Christ means allowing ourselves to be a burden to others, even asking others to carry the load we cannot. The application to marriage becomes plain. The Holy Spirit, when inspiring St. Paul to write, "submit to your husband as to Christ," might be interpreted as calling wives to allow and expect their Christian husbands to participate in Christ's handing over of himself, to submit to the husband's pouring out of his life to purify his bride by large and small acts of self-giving and perhaps humiliating service. By submitting to her husband, a wife is expecting him to fulfill St. Paul's call to husbands: "love your wives, as Christ loved the church and gave himself up for her, that he might sanctify her, having cleansed her ... that she might be holy and without blemish" (Eph 5:25–27). Sometimes this "giving up" might involve the unhappy task of calling a

Consecrating Conjugal Life—A Construction Site

spouse lovingly to account for ways they have not lived up to the standards of Christian married holiness. Sometimes this "giving up" might involve allowing and expecting a man to give up sexual desire during a time of prayer or when intending the conception of a child would be irresponsible. On this account, contraception is among the ways women have been tempted again by the serpent, fooled into thinking that they need not expect and ask their husbands to chasten their bodies for their wife's sake. When sexual availability is a given, sexual self-possession is unnecessary and eventually considered impossible. When sexual self-possession is impossible, so too is sexual self-gift. Man's relation to woman becomes mutual use rather than gift and receipt.[30]

Obedience or submission of one spouse to the other is indeed part of the Christian marriage as a consecrated way in Christ, but only inasmuch as the submitting spouse obediently submits to being loved and served, to being called into accountability and loved into holiness. This kind of submission or obedience requires a heroic trust and high expectations from the wife and heroic holiness in the husband, yet a Christian should expect no less. It seems rather far-fetched to hope that husbands will succeed in serving their wives where Adam failed. It seems equally far-fetched to hope that wives obediently expect and demand this love from their husbands rather than offering them the alternative "fruit" of mutually attempted domination. Yet this is the hope of the Christian spouses consecrated in the evangelical virtue of obedience in the sacrament of marriage.

---

30. Another real life example is this: A woman suffering from a serious auto-immune disease has reached the point of needing to attempt treatment with medicine that would certainly cause serious birth defects or death to any child conceived. The couple, therefore, will need to abstain entirely for at least nine months (but potentially for the remainder of their marriage). The wife is reasonably tempted not to undergo the treatment, as it would not only impart a burden on herself but also her husband. Assuming she can bear the burden of her own sexual desire, she should submit to her husband's assurance that he supports this course of medical treatment.

The second kind of obedience within marriage is the couple's unified obedience (as a two-in-one-flesh union) to the will of God the Father. It is this virtue of obedience that takes primary place in any Christian marriage. Spouses ought together to seek obedience to the Father inasmuch as together they are in Christ, who perfectly loved, knew, and obeyed the Father's will—so much so that he possesses that selfsame will. The difficulty of this obedience is that it involves spouses discerning and holding each other accountable to a will that is at once neither the husband's nor the wife's, but God's. Nonetheless the couple prays each day that their own wills conform ever more closely to God's.

As previous chapters have argued, the primary social location for Christian marriage as a consecrated way in Christ is ecclesial, and it is this focus on the ecclesial location of marriage that offers a distinct vantage point for finding a common obedience in Christian marriage. Instead of reifying one individual spouse as "Christ" and the other as "Church," I ground marital obedience in the same foundation that grounds religious obedience—namely, Jesus, the Son of God, whose perfect obedience to the will of the Father was so encompassing that Jesus possessed the divine will itself. Perhaps we can understand conjugal obedience better if we focus on the couple's common share in Christ's obedience to the Father. After all, as baptized Christians the couple is joined in Christ. They are two parts of Christ's body linked forever for a mission in the service of the Church. Their conjugal love together is to be Christ's love for the Church. Their love is a share in God's own love; therefore, it is fruitful, free, and faithful. Furthermore, if the couple are seen corporately as Christ, rather than individually as Christ and Church, their mutual participation in the Son's obedience to the Father comes into sharper focus. What the couple are aiming at in their conjugal love is not only a mutual submission to one another in reverence to

Christ. The couple are aiming even more at a united, corporate submission to the will of God *together*—that is, *as, in, and with Christ*. They are to be a sacrament of Christ's own obedience.

Because each is Christian, each must share in Jesus' obedience to the father, but because together they are one flesh in Christ, they now have a unique specification of that obedience. They are enjoined to a common obedience to the Father's will together. God's will is for both to hear and for both to obey as one flesh and in one flesh, because the separate parts they were in Christ are now irrevocably joined in mission and identity. The spouses marry in Christ and serve the Church as Christ served her—unto death and resurrection. The sacrament of the spouses' marriage is a sacrament of Christ's love for the Church, so the spouses' conjugal love binds the couple in Christ for the Church. When they marry their spousal unity in Christ makes present Christ's love for the Church, a love that is indissoluble and generative, chaste and obedient. As Christ did what he saw the Father doing and said what he heard the Father saying, so must married Christians. Their practice of Christian marriage must incarnate Christ's obedience to the Father, an obedience that was at once painful and dreadful (from Gethsemane to the cross) and life-giving and glorious (at Cana, at Tabor, at Lazarus's tomb, and at the resurrection).

Because the religious and conjugal obedience are linked in Christ, I can look to the religious life for language and example of how conjugal obedience might be practiced. For vowed religious, obedience to a superior is a mediation of obedience to the Father and an attempted participation in Christ's own obedience to the Father as a complete gift of one's own will to the service of God. While a larger social institution such as a religious congregation has the numbers and structure to make a superior necessary and possible, the consortium of man, wife, and whoever else holds house with them does not initially seem to lend itself to the notion of a superior, even on a temporary, rotational basis.

In considering obedience and the relationship between spouses, we can recall chapter 4's earlier mention of Augustine's thought that any association of friends (even among two men) would necessarily include one who commands and another who obeys.[31] Marriage, though, is a unique kind of friendship wherein the two are not simply a leader and a follower, but, as Augustine points out, the spouses are joined as two side-by-side walking the same direction together.[32] Given this image, the question for spouses remains—whose will to follow?

The couple must give united obedience to what they have discerned to be their shared understanding of God's will for the marriage. This will is at once their own and always other-than-their-own. It is within them yet ever over and apart from them. It is at once their will and (they hope) a mediation of the Father's will. When they consent to Christian marriage in the Church, they express their will to enter a consecrated way of life in Christ, a practice of Christian householding with ecclesially established standards of excellence, internal goods, and virtues necessary for the achievement of those goods. The couple does not create these standards, goods, and virtues, but rather consents to them. Recalling MacIntyre, we are reminded:

the goods [of a practice] can only be achieved by subordinating ourselves within the practice in our relationship to other practitioners. We have to

---

31. Augustine, *De genesi ad litteram* 9.5; *On Genesis*, ed. John E. Rotelle, intro., trans., and notes Edmund Hill, part 1 of *The Works of St. Augustine* (Hyde Park, N.Y.: New City Press, 2002), 13:381; see also *De bono coniugali* 1.1, CSEL 41, 187–88; *Marriage and Virginity: Holy Virginity; The Excellence of Marriage; The Excellence of Widowhood; Continence*, trans. Ray Kearney, intro. and notes David G. Hunter, part 1 of *The Works of St. Augustine* (Hyde Park, N.Y.: New City Press, 1999), 9:34.

32. Augustine, *De bono coniugali* 1.1; *Marriage and Virginity*, 34.

learn to recognize what is due to whom; we have to be prepared to take whatever self-endangering risks are demanded along the way; and we have to listen carefully to what we are told about our own inadequacies and to reply with the same carefulness for the facts.[33]

The sacred task of the couple then, is to mediate God's will for the marriage to each other by holding each other accountable to what they mutually discern that will to be.

Concretely, working with this kind of obedience means that, at various times on various matters, spouses must mediate this common will, God's will, to each other—serving as a kind of "superior" for the other. Let us presume that a couple have a common will and intention for their marriage—namely, that it sanctify them both through their actions of daily life together. This shared will and intention, which they have discerned to be compatible with God's will, create a nonvoluntary given-ness in their marital practice. The shared will should supersede their own personal wills whenever the two come into conflict. For example, say a husband, Charlie, skips breakfast and lunch to save money and accomplish more at work. He remains late at work in order to increase productivity. He knows that these goods (productivity and riches) are external to the practice of marriage and are beginning to conflict with the will for marriage that he and his wife share. This husband would be well served by the virtue of obedience. In a conversation with his wife about the situation, he can ask her to mediate for him their shared will for these activities in marriage for the time being. The topic will be revisited in a determined amount of time. Their shared will to "sanctify each other in daily activities" supersedes his own will to business achievement and college savings. This husband, then, will submit himself in obedience to his wife's reasonable regulation of

---

33. MacIntyre, *After Virtue*, 191.

these activities: that he eat at least a small breakfast and lunch; that he not stay late more than once a week. The wife is mediating their shared, spousal will to him, which is also hopefully the will of God the Father. In time his own personal will shall be reshaped into their shared will.

Four Walls and a Roof: A Regula Matrimonii

If poverty, chastity, and obedience are essential virtues for Christian marriage as a consecrated way in Christ, there must be something to integrate them within that practice. Unsurprisingly, an answer comes from a method that has enlightened the life of the Church for sixteen hundred years: the *regula* or rule of life.[34] The rule of life encompasses the virtues and states of poverty, chastity, and obedience and integrates them within the wide varieties of Christian householding. In this section I will treat a general format of a married rule, how it should be formed, and how it integrates the evangelical virtues.

A rule of life should begin with a couple's own statement of what they discern to be their unique mission, or charism, as a married couple. This statement summarizes their common will or consciousness for the marriage. They can feel free to include a narrative account of how God worked in their lives to bring them together, as this is often helpful in discerning a mission or discovering a charism.

---

34. Alphonsus Liguori wrote a rule for lay persons; see Liguori, *The Christian Virtues and the Means for Obtaining Them*, trans. and ed. Robert A. Coffin (New York: Dunigan and Brother, 1855), 413–18; and "Rule of Life," in *The Way of Salvation and of Perfection*, edited by Eugene Grimm, rev. ed. (Brooklyn: Redemptorist Fathers, 1926), 2:502–10. A popular author has promoted the idea of a family rule of life with a book and a popular blog; see Holly Pierlot, *A Mother's Rule of Life: How to Bring Order to Your Home and Peace to Your Soul* (Manchester, N.H.: Sophia Institute Press, 2004); see also Margaret Guenther, *At Home in the World: A Rule of Life for the Rest of Us* (New York: Seabury, 2006); Anthony Marrett-Crosby et al., eds., *The Benedictine Handbook* (Collegeville, Minn.: Liturgical Press, 2003); Wil Derkse, *The Rule of Benedict for Beginners: Spirituality for Daily Life* (Collegeville, Minn.: Liturgical Press, 2003); and the ecumenical Dennis Okholm, *Monk Habits for Everyday People: Benedictine Spirituality for Protestants* (Grand Rapids, Minn.: Brazos, 2007).

Consecrating Conjugal Life—A Construction Site

A couple would likely be aided by a spiritual director in making their rule, especially one with experience in religious orders. An example of such a statement of mission or charism could include a section like this one:

> Imitate Jesus in our everyday interactions with each other, friends, neighbors, and strangers. Specifically, being present, generous, and hospitable to people in our neighborhood; joyfully and thankfully accepting the difficulties and delights God gives us; and praying constantly for needs of others that we see, hear about, and remember.

This statement identifies a Christological foundation and a two-part charism for the household's practices of a consecrated way in Christ. This household sees God calling them first to imitate Jesus through an incarnational presence and an intentional outreach to their neighbors (both inside and outside the walls of their house). Second, they see prayer as part of their unique charism; they commit to praying together as an act of solidarity with those in need and beyond their material reach.

Beyond this general statement of charism or mission, a *regula Matrimonii* should include a description of roles within the household and explanations of virtues and goods internal to the common life of the household. For example, the distinction between child and parent, the general roles taken by each parent, the expectations of each and the role of each in the working of the household should be spelled out. If possible, the general methods of discipline should be included, as well. Following this description of roles should come the daily activities, from rising to bedding down. As with all rules, the point is not to constrain but to free. The question is not whether to live by an order, for we all do. We all live according to a rule of life, even if that rule is "to never live the same way two days in a row." The question is whether to live by a good one that we rationally and prayerfully choose to fit the purposes and goals of our common life in Christ or a haphazard one that we simply fall into in an unthinking manner.

In this regard a rule can be specific with times or it can be general, merely stating the kinds of things that happen at certain times throughout the day and the week. The couple's married *regula* ought to include times and direction for prayer (both common and individual), work (domestic, for pay, and directly ecclesial—i.e., works of mercy, missionary activity, Church council), and relaxing time for the household together. The rule ought to be ordered toward the household's stated mission and charism. For example, a household who see their mission as one principally of intercessory prayer for the world will build in more time in for this activity. A household who see their mission as related to educating their children in the home will have a rule designed uniquely for this purpose. A household who see their mission as oriented toward their neighborhood will include regular time for outreach and being present for the people living around them. One example might be that shown in table 6-1. This daily order is general enough to allow for flexibility regarding what time and how long certain activities take, but the shape of the day is, on the whole, set. This is an order for a typical weekday, and so no provision is made for errands and outings, which ordinarily take place with a modified daily order included in a rule. An order for Saturdays and Sundays should also be included. The rule is concerned principally to ensure that those standards of excellence and virtues necessary to achieve the goods of the consecrated way in Christ are maintained. Here, the rule attempts to frame the entire day with prayer, ensure time for both parents to contribute to the children's education (understood in a wide sense), create time for parents to spend together, share work among all for common goods of the household, and promote the charism of the household.

The consecrated way in Christ for married Christians is a living

Consecrating Conjugal Life—A Construction Site

Table 6-1. Order for a Typical Weekday

6:00 a.m.	Wake up—dress—pray morning offering in "chapel area."
6:30 a.m.	Children and father prepare breakfast—mother prepares self—scripture reading.
7:00 a.m.	Meal—thanksgiving prayer, gospel, psalm, daily petitions, meal cleanup.
8:00 a.m.	Father to work—children and mother begin school day.
11:30 a.m.	Mother prepares meal—children clean up school and toys.
12:00 p.m.	Meal—midday prayer/family Mass.
1:00 p.m.	Nap/reading with mother/devotional reading.
3:00 p.m.	Children play outside—household maintenance by mother.
4:00 p.m.	Father returns—meeting with mother—outside play or home maintenance with children.
5:00 p.m.	Clean house—set table.
5:15 p.m.	Meal—thanksgiving prayer/scripture devotion after meal.
6:15 p.m.	Cleanup with children—prepare for bed.
7:00 p.m.	Read with children/one-on-one school time/piano lesson.
7:30 p.m.	Evening prayer—children to sleep.
8:00 p.m.	Mother and father prepare for tomorrow—household maintenance.
9:00 p.m.	Mother and father pray and relax together.
10:00 p.m.	Mother and father to sleep.

practice, and thus its charism, mission, and the activities required to achieve these purposes will change throughout the course of its existence. Therefore, a Christian household must revisit its rule occasionally and in prayer and discussion decide whether and how to amend it—for example, with the entrance of children, the change of a job, children leaving the home.

The power of the *regula matrimonii* is that it integrates the virtues and states necessary to excel in the practice of Christian householding. First, the rule is a matter for obedience. Married couples mutually submit in obedience to the *regula*. Spouses understand the rule to be an expression of their shared will, which they have discerned to be compatible with God's will, for their consecrated way in Christ. Even if, at times, their own will is contrary to the rule's (and it certainly will be), the rule is a supravoluntary aspect of their Christian householding to which they owe obedience. The spouses should prefer the will represented by the rule rather than their own, momentary will if a conflict arises. Spouses, after all, in constructing this rule, are prayerfully intending that this rule mediate God the Father's will for their practice of a marriage as a consecrated way in Christ. Through obedience together to the rule, the household hope they are obedient together in Christ to the will of God the Father.

Second, the *regula matrimonii* encompasses chastity. The spouses' sexuality is subject to the ordering of the rule. The rule may build in times of abstinence that coordinate with liturgical days or seasons, annual novenas. Additionally, if a couple finds need to delay pregnancy, the rule can be helpful in ordering the skill of NFP to the service of CMS. If a couple is discerning their stance toward further pregnancy, this process can be intentionally built into the rule. Couples following this kind of a rule will be encouraged to see their sexual expression as another regular part of their consecrated way in Christ, but it will allow them also to be spontaneous. By building in extra time in the evening a couple may or may not decide to be physically intimate, but the option exists if the couple has interest. By incorporating times of abstinence, the couple will likely experience less unexpected coldness toward physical intimacy. The periods of abstinence can act to kindle the spouses toward one another.

Finally, the rule incorporates a commitment to poverty. The rule might state, for one, that no person in the household exclusively owns any goods therein. The mother and father should be given the role of determining just appropriation of goods to each person, though this task can be shared with other, older members of the household. Second, the rule should specify the level of economic

Consecrating Conjugal Life—A Construction Site

simplicity a household hopes to achieve and what steps the household will take to achieve them. Traumatic material poverty may strike any household, and this is to be avoided, but intentional poverty of some kind ought to be sought. Households should put themselves in positions of reliance on others and positions where others rely on them, even if it something as simple as buying a snowblower together with a neighbor or as complex as owning a home together with another household, vowed religious, or single, nonvowed persons.

The couple will also have daily orders that will account for home economics—that is, they will include shopping and errands. These daily orders encourage the virtue of poverty inasmuch as they resist the reigning economic milieu that seeks to make consumption the ordering principle of life. Greater intentionality and planning in shopping leads to greater frugality and attention to Christian economic principles a household may find difficult to do when shopping more spontaneously. For example, a group of neighboring families decided to buy a farm share from a local family farm: an organic CSA (community-supported agriculture enterprise that provides food to thirty families). Each week a share of the farm's harvest is picked up or delivered. Because their money has been invested upfront in the farm, the family is not in a financial position to buy any vegetables from grocery during the spring, summer, or fall, even if the farm share gave them vegetables they did not prefer. (There is such a thing as too many beets.) Beyond the upfront cost, though, is the true risk involved; if the farm has a low yield, the family will not have many vegetables to eat. In previous years the family has bought a less expensive "work-share" in the farm with two other families. The mandatory hundred hours of work was too much for one family, so three families in the neighborhood split the share and the work. This meant adjusting and creating a rule to cooperate with the other families. One day a week they cooperated to put in their hours, some car-pooling to the farm, some staying at their paid jobs, and another staying with the children for the day.

Families can also build poverty, or a dependence on God, into their rule of life by using it to determine tithing practices. Regardless of how little comes in, or how much expenses may grow, a household can commit to giving the same percentage of income.

Finally, the rule of life builds the virtue of poverty by telling the truth about a person's identity before God and before her spouse. Before God spouses have nothing; the husband is entirely dependent upon the divine economy as God has revealed it, and the spouses rely upon God to be faithful to it. Before one's spouse a husband has only himself to give, and even that does not belong to him. He depends entirely upon his spouse faithfully to give herself in obedience to the rule just as he does. The spouses' happiness, their salvation, depends upon the fact that the spouses are mutually obedient to the rule. The success of the marriage is not rooted in the resources the spouses bring to the table, but their willingness to be faithful as God brings great works to fruition in each.

As we have seen, a *regula matrimonii* has the potential to integrate poverty, chastity, and obedience of married spouses into a consecrated way in Christ. The promises of this kind of rule, though, extend beyond married households alone. One of the promises of a wider application of *regulas* in Christian life is the ability for a rule to unite conjugal and celibate life in one Christian household. Among the authors who spoke of principles of Christian householding, the rule did not take a central place, though Bennett and the "new monastic" movements have taken a big step in that direction with their charter of the twelve characteristics of the "new monasticism."[35]

---

35. See Rutba House, ed., *School(s) for Conversion: 12 Marks of a New Monasticism* (Eugene, Ore.: Cascade, 2005).

Consecrating Conjugal Life—A Construction Site

Living in community, in obedience to a rule, celibates and married persons can serve each other and share in common and distinct ministries. Shared domestic endeavors in the household of God can provide unique ecclesial solutions to problems faced both by celibates and married families as well as new possibilities for missions and ministries. Of course, such efforts must not be rushed into, as they require clear vision, expectations, goals, and roles, but neither should they be avoided. After all, it has been the claim that both married and religious people are sharing in one domestic project, cohabiting in the household of God.

Preparing the Down Payment: Preliminary Suggestions for a Marriage Novitiate

Pulling off this consecrated conjugal way in Christ requires hard work and grace. How many couples are prepared to do this, let alone *want to*? In this final section I will make some suggestions regarding a marriage novitiate. This topic deserves its own monograph. In fact, there are already two strains of thought at work within the Catholic scholarship on this topic. Michael Lawler and Paul A. Holmes have both proposed versions of a married catechumenate.[36] Their approaches are at once similar and radically different. Both want to recover from the tradition rites and practices that prepare people for sacramental married life in a stepwise, liturgical, and pedagogical fashion. The radical difference, though, is that Lawler believes he has found strong support in the tradition for arguing that marriage begins at betrothal. Lawler's catechumenate, therefore, involves co-

---

36. See Paul A. Holmes, "A Catechumenate for Marriage: Presacramental Preparation as Pilgrimage," *Journal of Ritual Studies* 6, no. 2 (Summer 1992): 93–113; Holmes, *Betrothal: A Liturgical Rite of Passage: The Anthropological Perspective of Victor W. Turner as the Basis for the Development of a Catechumenate for the Betrothed*, S.T.D. diss. (Rome: Pontifical University of St. Thomas Aquinas, 1991); and Michael Lawler, "A Marital Catechumenate: A Proposal," *INTAMS Review* 13 (2007): 161–77.

habitation and sexual intimacy. For his part, Holmes finds the historical and current teaching to say that marriage begins with the rite of matrimony. His catechumenate, therefore, involves many recovered and translated rites from the tradition, but no cohabitation or sexual intimacy.

Holmes's position is closer to my own in that I suggest no change to the current magisterial teaching and canon law, but my research takes marriage preparation more into the direction of the novitiate. A novitiate is, perhaps, more along the lines of *how* engaged couples ought to prepare and *for what* they are preparing. The couples, like seminarians, are preparing for a sacrament of service, not a sacrament of initiation. Similarly, like those preparing for full entrance into religious life, they are preparing to make a complete gift of themselves in service to the other. In that sense "novitiate" may be a more apt analogy for describing the time of engagement. Furthermore, if catechumens were to die during preparation, they can be said to possess their end by intent. Such is the concept of baptism by desire. Conversely, if a fiancé were to die before marriage, he or she would not be considered married by intent, nor would a survivor be considered a widow or widower. Again, in this sense the novitiate seems more apt. Also, marriage is entered by spoken consent and requires at least a minimum of faith in the candidate, as in religious life, whereas baptism is an action done *to* the new Christian requiring the faith of the parents and community but not the recipient of the sacrament. Finally, the novitiate preparing for religious orders or for the priesthood is not fully initiated into the order until the liturgical rite of profession. Until that time, he is not permitted the fullness of that life's practice. Just as the seminarian does not celebrate Eucharist until after celebrating ordination, the fiancés do not enact conjugal intercourse until after celebrating the rite of matrimony. Thus, their participation in the whole of married life, including cohabitation and sexual intimacy, is unintelligible as a way to prepare for the marriage.

Challenges to the analogy could be leveled, though. Three come to mind. First, while fiancés are preparing for a sacrament, novices in a religious order are not preparing for any of the seven sacraments. Second, while novices in a religious order do cohabit, fiancés ought not. To the first argument, whether either is a sacrament, each is a form of Christian householding directed toward the sanctification of all sharing the household. They are, therefore, similar kinds of activities. Furthermore, marriage is a sacrament because it is a natural institution made by God, denatured by humanity's fall, and now raised beyond its original stature. Marriage requires the grace of redemption more than does religious life, since marriage attempts to integrate concupiscence at the sexual level into the authentic, free, irrevocable gift of self to another. To the second argument, whereas cohabitation among novices generally helps develop the virtue of chastity with accountability, cohabitation among fiancés gravely threatens the virtue of chastity. In fact, it is seen as helpful toward the development of chastity through accountability. Chastity is a standard of excellence and internal good of both religious and married life, which cannot be sacrificed. Any activities that mitigate the virtue should be eliminated from the practice.

This section will lay out some ground for new studies by making suggestions for how engaged persons might prepare for their consecrated way in Christ by beginning to practice poverty, chastity, and obedience as a process of formation and partial participation.

First, a moment on poverty. Engaged couples, no less than spouses, should begin to work toward poverty as a state of common possession and a virtue of radical dependence on God. Engaged couples need to begin discussing their current spending habits, expenses, goals, career aspirations, budgets, and moral criteria for consumption. For some couples this will be a discussion about how they see themselves getting out of poverty. For others this will be a discussion of how to embrace intentional forms of poverty, dependence on God, and solidarity with the poor. Couples should also be introduced to the evangelical counsel of poverty explicitly through discussions with a priest and spiritual readings.[37] On those grounds couples could consider renting or buying in a poorer section of their city than they otherwise might have, or even living in community with other Christians. The couple must decide if their marriage will be subject to the prevailing economic winds of ever-increasing consumption. Mentors and priests should encourage couples to tithe together to their parish and a charitable cause. They ought to work out lists of "things" that are necessities and wants. Together they should anticipate expenses and hold each other accountable to their spending while still unmarried. They should talk about how they will put into action the notion of common possession. They should also talk about how money will affect their willingness to be open to God's gift of fertility—that is, whether their poverty or lack thereof constitutes a serious reason to avoid pregnancy temporarily. They should ask how they see themselves entering relationships of interdependence with neighbors and Church. Co-ownership, especially a future place of residence, before marriage is risky, but under the right circumstances could be an opportunity for developing habits of fidelity to common goals and practice in working together. Rather than a practice in sharing and work for a common good, co-ownership could easily amount to a serious occasion for sin. Couples should be prepared for a distinct change upon beginning their

---

[37.] I would suggest excerpts from the gospels, especially the Sermon on the Mount and the Sermon on the Plain, as well as Masie Ward, ed., *Be Not Solicitous: Sidelights on the Providence of God and the Catholic Family* (New York: Sheed and Ward, 1953); Robert Farrar Capon, *Bed and Board: Plain Talk about Marriage* (New York: Simon and Schuster, 1965).

marriage, and holding off on economic co-ownership helps reinforce the difference in state from single to married. The life they prepare to enter is a paradox requiring all they have, while reminding them that they have nothing to give but themselves.

Second, if chastity is as important and as difficult in entering the conjugal state and reaching its goals as it is in the religious state, then the Church must identify and effect bold practices to form marrying couples in this virtue. Remote preparation for marriage in childhood and adolescence should provide a formation in the virtue of chastity, but the fact is that many couples will approach their parish priest with little or no training in the capacity to regulate and integrate their sexuality into the Christian conjugal life. Formation in chastity must begin from the very moment they approach a pastor for marriage. I suggest the following practice: require couples to make a verbal commitment to a chaste period of engagement as a condition for their celebrating matrimony in the Catholic Church. This requirement would hold for any couple, whether cohabiting or not. The couple would not have to succeed to perfection, but their most earnest attempt should be expected. There would be no documentary record of the couple's success or failure to keep the commitment, but the couple would be encouraged to avail themselves of the sacrament of penance if necessary. Regular conversations with mentor couples and/or a pastor should not hesitate to broach the topic. With respect to the wide variety of moral development and the uniqueness of each couple's situation, the definition of "chaste" should be discussed and defined along a spectrum with at least the pastor, but hopefully also with a mentor couple. The definitions will include clarity on chaste ways for the couple to express affection. For example, some couples may choose to refrain from any kind of touch or kiss that can typically cause sexual arousal. The definition will include clarity on the kinds of situations, media, language, and clothing to avoid or encourage (again, determined uniquely for each couple). The definition will also institute positive practices to advance in chastity—for example, conversations on sexual expectations and experience, on struggles relating to body image, and on struggles relating to current sexual sin.

Chastity training should also include a course in human sexuality, including sessions on natural family planning. The priest and mentor couple should be sure to talk about prayerfully discerning what is meant by "responsible parenthood" and what might constitute "serious reasons" for the couple to avoid a pregnancy. Explanation of the virtues of generosity and prudence are also essential. These explanations should be paired with commitments to reflect on and practice both virtues over the course of the engagement. These pastoral actions of formation may lead to a decline in the number of marriages in the Church, at least initially. Some way must be found, though, to avoid any decline on account of the hurdles of material poverty and a lack of education. Extra resources must find their way to aid parishes that marry Catholics for whom the leisure time necessary for this kind of preparation is greatly difficult to come by. Baptized Christians have a right to not just any marriage in the Church, but to a *valid* marriage. Without adequate preparation they are not free to exercise that right, and a pastor may be compelled by canon law to delay the wedding. Couples seriously lacking in or unwilling to commit to chastity demonstrate their incapacity to make the marriage vows. As the body of Christ we must insist on the public nature of married sexuality with the understanding that joining Christians ill-prepared does the spouses as well as Christ's body a disservice and a great irreverence.

Finally, couples should prepare for obedience by common prayer, spiritual reading, and common works of mercy (soup kitchens, Habitat for Humanity). These kinds of activities will help engaged couples understand that they are becoming one in Christ, and their obedience is primarily to God the Father. They are to embody Christ's own perfect obedience to the Father, doing what he saw the Father doing and saying what he heard from the Father. Knowing what the Father says and does requires being in his presence through prayer, readings, and liturgy together. Common prayer, spiritual reading, and works of mercy will additionally help the couple discern God's initial calling for them in their marriage. Through this discussion, reading, prayer, and action, the couple should develop a *regula* for each fiancé until marriage and at least an initial *regula matrimonii* with the help of a mentor couple, a priest, or religious person. They should consider the virtues and goods they want to privilege, the roles they want to inhabit, and the form of life they hope to live. The engagement would be an opportunity for couples to make an extended visit to mentor couples' homes to see how others living according to a rule order their lives as a consecrated way in Christ. They might even consider different or creative forms of Christian householding at this point with vowed religious or with single nonvowed persons in community. By the time the couple reach their wedding day, they should be ready to hit the ground running with a well-ordered rough draft of their *regula matrimonii*, one that will certainly change, but that will guide them in the early days as they discover God's will for their Christian householding together.

Conclusion

This chapter has sought to integrate creatively the insights of those before it into a constructive proposal for Christian marriage understood as a consecrated practice of being conformed to Christ the poor, chaste, and obedient bridegroom. Marriage is a form of Christian householding participating in the ecclesial states and virtues of poverty, chastity, and obedience.

Consecrating Conjugal Life—A Construction Site

The first section recalled the way that MacIntyre's definition of "practice" and the principles of Christian householding contribute to understanding marriage as a consecrated way in Christ. The second section explored the place of poverty, chastity, and obedience as virtues and states in marriage as a consecrated way in Christ. In poverty households resist the economy of consumption as the ordering principle for their practice of householding. Instead, they choose solidarity with the poor and conditions of real interdependence, reliance, and reliability. The notion of poverty as a virtue and state in marriage must avoid remaining at a merely metaphorical level. If it does, then the Christian household will remain under the power of the same economy of desire and consumption that has in part led to its current crisis. In conjugal chastity, couples integrate their entire being as sexed and gendered into their spousal love by realizing that love in the daily, bodily actions of their Christian householding. Far from being reducible to natural family planning, the practice of chaste married sexuality might incorporate this skill in service to marriage's internal good of the child (or responsible parenthood). In obedience, members of a conjugal household submit themselves to each other as mediators of their common will for the marriage, a will they hope corresponds to God the Father's will. In doing so the couple act together to live in Christ obeying his Father.

The third section considered how a *regula matrimonii* integrates poverty, chastity, and obedience into one consecrated way. The rule contains a statement of charism, a description of principles and roles, and a daily order for each kind of day. Among the benefits of a rule is its ability to order forms of Christian householding that might include spouses with children along with vowed religious, single-nonvowed, or multi-generational domestic arrangements. Finally, I suggested some hypotheses and sources for further research on how Christians might prepare for their consecrated way of pov-

Consecrating Conjugal Life—A Construction Site

erty, chastity, and obedience in Christ along the lines of a novitiate.

Admittedly, the lion's share of this volume has been to make way for the constructive effort, which is little more than a framework, certainly not a definitive account. A more detailed, complete account of marriage as consecrated way in Christ will have to be enfleshed in a subsequent work. Among aspects requiring further development is the possibility for mixed Christian householding among spouses, children, parents, vowed religious, or single non-vowed persons. In addition, the notion of parenthood as a practice shared by the whole Church, especially under the lost rubric of "spiritual parenthood," deserves renewed focus. More exploration is required before a construction of marriage preparation with the language of novitiate would be feasible or wise. This volume focused on the conjugal side of the conjugal-consecrated consonance. A complementary volume on the consecrated life and its participation in the ecclesial-nuptial goods of *proles, fides,* and *sacramentum* could prove a worthwhile project.

I can only end by recalling the central claim with which I began: the language of the evangelical virtues (poverty, chastity, and obedience), a rule of life, and a robust preparation period (i.e., a novitiate) belongs as properly to conjugal life as it does to consecrated religious life. I have hopefully shown that consecrated religious life has called upon the language of evangelical virtues for the same kinds of reasons married people might. As *Lumen gentium* and the marriage liturgy show, people in these ways of life are both called and consecrated to be conformed to Christ who possesses these virtues. As Augustine argued, they both share in these goods principally as members of Christ's bridegroom rather than individually. As John's Gospel and the practices of religious life through history have demonstrated, all Christian living is a domestic practice—householding with God in anticipation of the time when Christ is all in all. Finally, having shown that consecrated conjugal life and consecrated religious life share a deep consonance, I set forth an experimental structure for practicing poverty, chastity, and obedience in marriage, a *regula matrimonii*, and a preparation along the lines of a novitiate. I hope this structure for a practice of consecrated marriage, if it proves sound, and if it be built on the rock, might facilitate growth in holiness for all those inhabiting the household of God—a household conceived and built by a far better carpenter than I.

BIBLIOGRAPHY

Abbot, Elizabeth. *A History of Celibacy*. Toronto: HarperCollins, 1999.

Abercrombie, Nigel. *The Origins of Jansenism*. Oxford: Clarendon Press, 1936.

Ablondi, Alberto. "Dalla Trinità alla comunità," *Consacrazione e Servizio* 28, no.10 (1979): 7–17.

Ahearne-Kroll, Steven. "'Who Are My Mother and My Brothers?' Family Relations and Family Language in the Gospel of Mark." *Journal of Religion* 81 (2001): 1–25.

Aquinas, St. Thomas. *The Religious State, The Episcopate, and The Priestly Office: A Translation of the Minor Work of the Saint on The Perfection for the Spiritual Life*. Edited by F. J. Procter. Westminster, Md.: Newman Press, 1950.

———. *Summa Theologiae*. http://www.corpusthomisticum.org/. Accessed February 7, 2011.

Atkinson, Joseph C. *Structures of Christian Priesthood: A Study of Home, Marriage, and Celibacy in the Pastoral Service of the Church*. Translated by Rosemary Sheed. New York: Macmillan, 1968.

———. "Family as Domestic Church: Developmental Trajectory, Legitimacy, and Problems of Appropriation." In *The Church, Marriage, and the Family*, edited by Kenneth D. Whitehead, 378–91. South Bend, Ind.: St. Augustine's Press, 2004.

Augustine. *Homilies on the Gospel According to St. John, and his First Epistle by Saint Augustine, Bishop of Hippo*. Translated, with notes and indices. 2 vols. Oxford: J. H. Parker, 1848.

———. *Corpus Scriptorum Ecclesiasticorum Latinorum (CSEL)*. Vienna: 1866–.

———. *Corpus Christianorum*. Series Latina *(CCL)*. Paris: 1953–.

———. *Saint Augustine: Against Julian*. Translated by Matthew A. Schumacher. Fathers of the Church 16. New York: Fathers of the Church, 1957.

———. *Saint Augustine: Homilies on the Gospels*. Translated by R. G. MacMullen. Edited by Philip Schaff. Nicene and Post-Nicene Fathers 1. Vol. 6. Buffalo, N.Y.: Christian Literature Publishing, 1888. Reprinted Grand Rapids, Mich.: Eerdmans, 1974.

———. *Tractates on John 10.4*. Translated by John W. Rettig. Washington, D.C.: The Catholic University of America Press, 1988.

Bibliography

———. *Letters 211–70*. Edited by Boniface Ramsey. Translated by Roland Teske. Part 2, vol. 4 of *The Works of Saint Augustine: A Translation for the 21st Century*. Edited by John E. Rotelle and Boniface Ramsey. Hyde Park, N.Y.: New City Press, 2004.

———. *On the Trinity*. Edited by John Rotelle. Introduction, translation, and notes by Edmund Hill. Brooklyn, N.Y.: New City Press, 1991.

———. *Sermons III: 51–94 on the New Testament*. Edited by John E. Rotelle. Translated by Edmund Hill. Part 3, vol. 4 of *The Works of St. Augustine: A Translation for the 21st Century*. Hyde Park, N.Y.: New City Press, 1992.

———. *The Rule of Saint Augustine*. Translated by Raymond Canning. Cistercian Studies 138. Kalamazoo, Mich.: Cistercian Publications, 1996.

———. *Answer to the Pelagians II*. Edited by John E. Rotelle. Translated by Roland J. Teske. Part 1, vol. 24 of *The Works of St. Augustine: A Translation for the 21st Century*. Hyde Park, N.Y.: New City Press, 1998.

———. *Marriage and Virginity: Holy Virginity; The Excellence of Marriage; The Excellence of Widowhood; Continence*. Translated by Ray Kearney with introduction and notes by David G. Hunter. Part 1, vol. 9 of *The Works of St. Augustine: A Translation for the 21st Century*. Hyde Park, N.Y.: New City Press, 1999.

———. *De bono coniugali; De sancta virginitate* [*The Good of Marriage; On Holy Virginity*]. Translated and edited by P. G. Walsh. Oxford: Clarendon Press, 2001.

———. *On Genesis*. Edited by John E. Rotelle. Introduction, translation, and notes by Edmund Hill. Part 1, vol. 13 of *The Works of St. Augustine: A Translation for the 21st Century*. Hyde Park, N.Y.: New City Press, 2002.

———. *Corpus Augustinianum Gissense 2*. Edited by Cornelius Mayer. Basel: Schwabe, 2004.

———. *The Monastic Rules*. Translated by Sr. Agatha Mary and Gerald Bonner. Augustine Series. Vol. 4. Hyde Park, N.Y.: New City Press, 2004.

———. *The Manichean Debate*. Edited by Boniface Ramsey. Translation and notes by Roland Teske. Part 1, vol. 19 of *The Works of St. Augustine: A Translation for the 21st Century*. Hyde Park, N.Y.: New City Press, 2006.

Azevedo, Marcello de Carvalho. *Let Wives Be Submissive: The Domestic Code in 1 Peter*. Society of Biblical Literature Monograph Series. Chico, Calif.: Scholars Press, 1981.

———. *The Consecrated Life: Crossroads and Directions*. Translated by Guillermo Cook. Maryknoll, N.Y.: Orbis, 1995.

Banner, Michael. "Who Are My Mother and My Brothers? Marx, Bonhoeffer and Benedict and the Redemption of the Family." *Studies in Christian Ethics* 9 (1996): 1–22.

Barth, Karl. *Church Dogmatics*. Vol. 3, *Doctrine of Creation*. Part 4. Edinburgh: T. and T. Clark, 1961.

Barton, Stephen C., ed. *The Family in Theological Perspective*. Edinburgh: T. and T. Clark, 1996.

Bibliography

Beal, John P., James A. Coriden, and Thomas J. Green, eds. *New Commentary on the Code of Canon Law*. New York: Paulist Press, 2000.

Bellah, Robert, et al. *The Good Society*. New York: Knopf, 1991.

Benedict of Nursia. *The Rule of Benedict: A Guide to Christian Living; The Full Text of the Rule in Latin and English*. Edited by Georg Holzherr. Dublin: Four Courts Press, 1994.

———. *Benedict's Rule: A Translation and Commentary*. Translated by Terrence Kardong. Collegeville, Minn.: Liturgical Press, 1996.

Bennett, Jana M. "Mark 8: Support for Celibate Singles Alongside Monogamous Married Couples and Their Children." In *School(s) for Conversion: 12 Marks of a New Monasticism*, edited by Rutba House, 112–23. Eugene, Ore.: Cascade, 2005.

———. *Water Is Thicker Than Blood: An Augustinian Theology of Marriage and Singleness*. Oxford: Oxford University Press, 2008.

Bishops' Committee for Pastoral Research and Practices. *Faithful to Each Other Forever: Catholic Handbook of Pastoral Help for Marriage Preparation*. Washington, D.C.: National Conference of Catholic Bishops, 1989.

Bonhoeffer, Dietrich. *Life Together*. Translated by John W. Doberstein. San Francisco: HarperSanFrancisco; New York: Harper and Row, 1993. Originally published in 1954.

Bonner, Gerald. "Pelagianism and Augustine." In *Doctrinal Diversity: Varieties of Early Christianity*, edited and with an introduction by Everett Ferguson. New York: Garland, 1999.

Bourg, Florence Caffrey. *Where Two or Three Are Gathered: Christian Families as Domestic Churches*. Notre Dame, Ind.: University of Notre Dame Press, 2004.

Breidenthal, Thomas. *Christian Households: The Sanctification of Nearness*. Eugene, Ore: Wipf and Stock, 2004.

———. *Sacred Unions: A New Guide to Lifelong Commitment*. Cambridge, Mass.: Cowley, 2006.

Brown, Peter. "Pelagius and His Supporters: Environment and Aims." *Journal of Theological Studies* 19 (1968): 93–123.

———. *Augustine and Sexuality: A Protocol of the Forty Sixth Colloquy, 22 May 1983*. Edited by Mary Ann Donovan. Berkeley: Center for Hermeneutical Studies in Hellenistic and Modern Culture, 1983.

———. *The Body and Society: Men, Women, and Sexual Renunciation in Early Christianity*. New York: Columbia University Press, 1988.

———. *Augustine of Hippo: A Biography*. 2nd ed. London: Faber and Faber, 2000. Originally published at Berkeley: University of California Press, 1967.

Brown, Raymond. *The Community of the Beloved Disciple*. New York: Paulist Press, 1979.

Browning, Don. *Equality and the Family: A Fundamental, Practical Theology of Children,*

Bibliography

Mothers, and Fathers in Modern Society. Grand Rapids, Mich.: Eerdmans, 2007.

Browning, Don, and David Clairmont, eds. *Marriage and Modernization: How Globalization Threatens Marriage and What to Do about It.* Grand Rapids, Mich.: Eerdmans, 2003.

Buckley, Timothy. *What Binds Marriage? Roman Catholic Theology in Practice.* London: Continuum, 2002.

Burke, Cormac. "St. Augustine and Conjugal Sexuality." *Communio* 17 (1990): 545–65.

Cabra, Giordano. *Breve meditazione sui voti.* Introduzioni e trattati 22. Brescia: Queriniana, 1983. Originally published in 1978.

Cahill, Lisa Sowle. *Family: A Christian Social Perspective.* Minneapolis: Fortress Press, 2000.

Caldecott, Stratford. "The Drama of the Home: Marriage, the Common Good, and Public Policy." In *Marriage and the Common Good: Proceedings from the Twenty-Second Annual Convention of the Fellowship of Catholic Scholars,* edited by Kenneth D. Whitehead, 1–26. South Bend, Ind.: St. Augustine's Press, 2001.

Capon, Robert Farrar. *Bed and Board: Plain Talk about Marriage.* New York: Simon and Schuster, 1965.

Carlson, Allan. "The State's Assault on the Family." In *The Family, Civil Society, and the State,* edited by Christopher Wolfe, 39–51. Lanham, Md.: Rowman and Littlefield, 1998.

Catechism of the Catholic Church. Boston: Pauline Books, 1994.

Congregation for Institutes of Consecrated Life and Societies of Apostolic Life. *Starting Afresh from Christ: A Renewed Commitment to Consecrated Life in the Third Millennium.* Strathfield, N.S.W.: St. Pauls, 2002.

Cavadini, John. "Feeling Right: Augustine on the Passions and Sexual Desire." *Augustinian Studies* 36 (2005): 195–217.

———. "The Sacramentality of Marriage in the Fathers." Paper given for the USCCB Committee on Marriage and Family's 2006 Theological Colloquium on the Sacramentality of Marriage at Notre Dame. http://www.usccb.org/laity/marriage/Cavadini.pdf. Accessed July 8, 2009, February 7, 2011.

Christensen, Michael J., and Jeffrey A. Witung, eds. *Partakers of the Divine Nature: The History and Development of Deification in the Christian Traditions.* Grand Rapids, Mich.: Baker Academic, 2007.

Chrysostom, John. *Homilies on the Acts of the Apostles.* Edited by Philip Schaff. Translated by J. Walker, J. Sheppard, and H. Brown. Nicene and Post-Nicene Fathers 11. Buffalo, N.Y.: Christian Literature Publishing, 1889.

———. *On Marriage and Family Life.* Translated by Catharine P. Roth and DavidAnderson. Crestwood, N.Y.: St. Vladimir's Seminary Press, 2003. Originally published in 1986.

Bibliography

Chupungco, Anscar J., ed. *Handbook for Liturgical Studies: Sacraments and Sacramentals.* Vol. 4. Collegeville, Minn.: Liturgical Press, 2000.

Ciardi, Fabio. *Koinonia: Spiritual and Theological Growth of the Religious Community.* Hyde Park, N.Y.: New City Press, 2001.

Claiborne, Shane. *The Irresistible Revolution: Living as an Ordinary Radical.* Grand Rapids, Mich.: Zondervan, 2006.

Clark, Elizabeth. "'Adam's Only Companion': Augustine and the Early Christian Debate on Marriage." *Recherches augustiniennes* 21(1986) : 139–62.

———. *Ascetic Piety and Women's Faith: Essays on Late Ancient Christianity.* Studies in Women and Religion 20. Lewiston N.Y.: Edwin Mellen, 1986, 291–349.

Clapp, Rodney. *From Family Values to Family Virtues.* Harrisburg, Penn.: Trinity Press International, 1997.

Cloutier, David and William C. Mattison III. "Bodies Poured Out in Christ: Marriage Beyond the Theology of the Body." In Cloutier, ed., *Leaving and Coming Home*, 206–25.

Cloutier, David, ed. *Leaving and Coming Home: New Wineskins for Catholic Sexual Ethics.* Eugene, Ore.: Cascade, 2010.

Codex Iuris Canonici. http://www.vatican.va/archive/cod-iuris-canonici/cic_index_lt.html. Accessed on October 15, 2009.

Cole, Basil, and Paul M. Conner. *Christian Totality: Theology of the Consecrated Life.* New York: Alba House, 1997.

Coloe, Mary. *Dwelling in the Household of God: Johannine Ecclesiology and Spirituality.* Collegeville, Minn.: Liturgical Press, 2007.

Columba, Marmion. *Christ the Ideal of the Monk: Spiritual Conferences on the Monastic and Religious Life.* Translated by a nun of Tyburn Convent. London: Sands, 1926.

Cooke, Bernard. "What God Has Joined Together ..." In *Perspectives on Marriage: A Reader,* edited by Kieran Scott and Michael Warren, 353–60. New York: Oxford University Press, 1993.

Congar, Yves. *Lay People in the Church.* Westminster, Md.: Newman Press, 1965.

Connery, John R. "The Role of Love in Christian Marriage: a Historical Overview." *Communio* 11 (1984): 244–57.

Coontz, Stephanie. *The Way We Never Were: American Families and the Nostalgia Trap.* New York: Basic Books, 1992.

———. *Marriage, A History: From Obedience to Intimacy, or How Love Conquered Marriage.* New York: Basic Books, 2005.

Crawford, David S. "Christian Community and the States of Life: A Reflection on the Anthropological Significance of Virginity and Marriage." *Communio* 29, no. 2 (2002): 337–65.

Curran, Charles, and Julie Hanlon Rubio, eds. *Marriage.* Readings in Moral Theology 15. New York: Paulist Press, 2009.

Bibliography

Dacanáy, Adolfo N. *Canon Law on Marriage: Introductory Notes and Comments.* Loyola Heights, Manila: Loyola School of Theology, 2003. Originally published in 2000.

Davies, John G. "Tertullian, *De Resurrectione Carnis* 63: A Note on the Origins of Montanism." *Journal of Theological Studies*, new series 6, no. 1 (April 1955): 90–94.

Delchard, Antoine. "Religious Poverty in Canon Law." In *Poverty*, translated by Lancelot C. Sheppard, 126–39. Religious Life 4. Westminster, Md.: Newman Press, 1954.

De Haro, Ramón García. *Marriage and the Family in the Documents of the Magisterium: A Course in the Theology of Marriage.* Translated by William E. May. 2nd ed. San Francisco: Ignatius Press, 1993.

De Lubac, Henri. *Catholicism: Christ and the Common Destiny of Man.* Translated by Lancelot C. Sheppard and Elizabeth Englund. San Francisco: Ignatius Press, 1988.

De Margerie, Bertrand. "L'analogie familiale de la Trinité." *Science et Esprit* 24 (1972): 77–92.

Demming, Will. *Paul on Marriage and Celibacy: The Hellenistic Background of 1 Corinthians 7.* 2nd ed. Grand Rapids, Mich.: Eerdmans, 2004.

Denzinger, Henrico. *Enchiridion Symbolorum Definitiorum et Declarationum de Rebus Fidei et Morum.* No. 432. Freiburg: Herder, 1911.

Derkse, Wil. *The Rule of Benedict for Beginners: Spirituality for Daily Life.* Collegeville, Minn.: Liturgical Press, 2003.

De Vogüé, Adalbert, ed. *The Rule of Saint Benedict: A Doctrinal and Spiritual Commentary*, by St. Benedict. Kalamazoo, Mich.: Cistercian Publications, 1983.

Dillon, Richard. "Wisdom Tradition and Sacramental Retrospect in the Cana Account (Jn 2, 1–11)." *Catholic Biblical Quarterly* 24 (1962): 268–96.

Doms, Herbert. *The Meaning of Marriage.* London: Sheed and Ward, 1939.

Doran, Robert. "The Nonviolent Cross: Lonergan and Girard on Redemption." *Theological Studies* 71 (2010): 46–61.

Doyle, Dennis. *Communion Ecclesiology: Vision and Versions.* Maryknoll, N.Y.: Orbis, 2000.

Dunn, Marilyn. *The Emergence of Monasticism: From the Desert Fathers to the Early Middle Ages.* Malden, Mass.: Blackwell, 2000.

Elliott, Dyan. *The Family in Political Thought.* Amherst: University of Massachusetts Press, 1982.

———. *Spiritual Marriage: Abstinence in Medieval Wedlock.* Princeton, N.J.: Princeton University Press, 1993.

Evdokimov, Paul. *The Sacrament of Love: The Nuptial Mystery in the Light of the Orthodox Tradition.* Translated by Anthony P. Gythiel and Victoria Steadman. Crestwood, N.Y.: St. Vladimir's Seminary Press, 1985.

Fahey, Michael. "The Christian Family as Domestic Church at Vatican II." In *The Family*, edited by Lisa Sowle Cahill and Dietmar Mieth, 85–92. Maryknoll, N.Y.: Orbis, 1995.

Bibliography

Faul, Denis. "Ecclesia, Sponsa Christi: Origenes y Augustín ante la exegesis de Eph. 5, 27." *Augustinus* 15 (1970): 263–80.

Finley, Mitch, and Kathy Finley. *Christian Families in the Real World: Reflections on a Spirituality for the Domestic Church*. Chicago: Thomas More Press, 1984.

Flannery, Austin. *Vatican Council II: The Basic Sixteen Documents: Constitutions, Decrees, Declarations*. Rev. ed. Northport, N.Y.: Costello, 1996.

Freitas, Donna. *Sex and the Soul: Juggling Sexuality, Spirituality, Romance, and Religion on America's College Campuses*. Oxford: Oxford University Press, 2008.

Fry, Timothy, ed. *RB 1980: The Rule of St. Benedict in Latin and English with Notes*. Collegeville, Minn.: Liturgical Press, 1981.

Gardella, Peter. *Innocent Ecstasy: How Christianity Gave America an Ethic of Sexual Pleasure*. Oxford: Oxford University Press, 1985.

Gehring, Roger W. *House Church and Mission: The Importance of Household Structures in Early Christianity*. Peabody, Mass.: Hendrickson, 2004.

Gendron, Lionel. *Mystère de la Trinité et Symbolique familiale: Approche historique*. Rome: Gregorian University Press, 1975.

———. "La famille: Reflet de la communion trinitaire." In *La famille chrétienne dans le monde d'aujourd'hui*, 127–48. Montreal: Bellarmin, 1995.

Genovesi, Vincent J. *In Pursuit of Love: Catholic Morality and Human Sexuality*. 2nd ed. Collegeville, Minn.: Liturgical Press, 1996.

Grabowski, John. *Sex and Virtue: An Introduction to Sexual Ethics*. Catholic Moral Thought. Washington, D.C.: The Catholic University of America Press, 2003.

Grabowski, Stanislaus J. *The Church: An Introduction to the Theology of St. Augustine*. St. Louis: Herder, 1957.

Gudorf, Christine. *Body, Sex, and Pleasure: Reconstructing Christian Sexual Ethics*. Cleveland: Pilgrim Press, 1994.

Guenther, Margaret. *At Home in the World: A Rule of Life for the Rest of Us*. New York: Seabury, 2006.

Harrison, Carol. "Silent Majority: The Family in Patristic Thought." In *Family in Theological Perspective*, edited by Stephen C. Barton, 87–105. Edinburgh: T. and T. Clark, 1996.

———. "Marriage and Monasticism in St. Augustine: The Bond of Friendship." Studia Patristica 33. Louvain: Peeters, 1997, 94–99.

Hauerwas, Stanley. *A Community of Character: Toward a Constructive Christian Social Ethic*. Notre Dame, Ind.: University of Notre Dame Press, 1981.

———. "The Radical Hope in the Annunciation: Why Both Single and Married Christians Welcome Children [1998]." In *The Hauerwas Reader*, edited by John Berkman and Michael Cartwright. Durham: Duke University Press, 2001.

———. "Sex in Public: How Adventurous Christians Are Doing It [1978]." In *The*

Bibliography

Hauerwas Reader, edited by John Berkman and Michael Cartwright. Durham: Duke University Press, 2001.

Hays, Richard B. *The Moral Vision of the New Testament: A Contemporary Introduction to New Testament Ethics*. San Francisco: HarperSanFrancisco, 1996.

Heller, Karin. "The Interpersonal Communion of Trinity, Origin and Aim of Communion between Man and Woman." In *Dialoghi sul mistero nuziale: Studi offerti al Cardinale Angelo Scola*, edited by Gilfredo Marengo and Bruno Ognibeni, 115–29. Rome: Lateran University Press, 2003.

Hellerman, Joseph H. *The Ancient Church as Family*. Minneapolis: Fortress Press, 2001.

Hemmerle, Klaus. "Matrimonio e Famiglia in una antropologia trinitaria." *Nuova Umanità* 6 (1984): 3–31.

Hogan, Margaret Monahan. *Marriage as a Relationship: Real and Rational*. Marquette Studies in Philosophy 34. Milwaukee: Marquette University Press, 2002.

Holmes, Paul A. *Betrothal: A Liturgical Rite of Passage; The Anthropological Perspective of Victor W. Turner as the Basis for the Development of a Catechumenate for the Betrothed*. Ph.D. diss. Rome: Pontifica University of St. Thomas Aquinas, 1991.

———. "A Catechumenate for Marriage: Presacramental Preparation as Pilgrimage." *Journal of Ritual Studies* 6, no. 2 (1992): 93–113.

Hugo, John. *St. Augustine on Nature, Sex and Marriage*. Chicago: Scepter, 1969.

Hunter, David G. "Augustinian Pessimism? A New Look at Augustine's Teaching on Sex, Marriage, and Celibacy." *Augustinian Studies* 25 (1994): 153–77.

———. "The Virgin, the Bride, and the Church: Reading Psalm 45 in Ambrose, Jerome, and Augustine." *Church History* 69, no. 2 (2000): 281–303.

———. "Reclaiming Biblical Morality: Sex and Salvation History in Augustine's Treatment of the Hebrew Saints." In *Dominico Eloquio—"In Lordly Eloquence"—Essays on Patristic Exegesis in Honor of Robert Louis Wilken*, edited by Paul M. Blowers, Angela Russell Christman, David G. Hunter, and Robin Darling Young. Grand Rapids, Mich.: Eerdmans, 2002.

———. *Marriage, Celibacy, and Heresy in Ancient Christianity: The Jovinianist Controversy*. Oxford Early Christian Studies. Oxford: Oxford University Press, 2007.

Hurley, Dan. "Divorce Rate: It's Not as High as You Think." *New York Times*, April 19, 2005. http://www.divorcereform.org/nyt05.html. Accessed November 17, 2009.

Isaac of Nineveh. *Mystic Treatises by Isaac of Nineveh*. Translated by A. J. Wensinck. Amsterdam: Koninklijke Akademie van Wetenschappen, 1923.

Jenks, Richard J. *Divorce, Annulments, and the Catholic Church: Healing or Hurtful?* New York: Haworth Press, 2002.

Jerome. *Nicene and Post-Nicene Fathers* 2. Vol. 6. Translated by W. H. Fermantle, G. Lewis, and W. G. Martley. Buffalo, N.Y.: Christian Literature, 1893. http://www.newadvent.org/fathers/30091.htm.

Bibliography

John Paul II. "Pope Calls Spouses to a Sense of Responsibility for Love and for Life." In *L'Osservatore Romano* (December 17, 1990): 3, no. 5.

———. *The Jeweler's Shop: A Meditation on the Sacrament of Matrimony Passing on Occasion into a Drama*. Translated by Bolesław Taborski. San Francisco: Ignatius Press, 1992. Originally published in 1960.

———. Letter to Families (Gratissimam Sane). Rome: Libreria Editrice Vaticana, 1994.

———. *Familiaris consortio*. In *The Post-synodal Apostolic Exhortations of John Paul II*, edited and with an introduction by J. Michael Miller, 119–259. Huntington, Ind.: Our Sunday Visitor, 1998.

———. *Vita consecrata*. In *The Post-synodal Apostolic Exhortations of John Paul II*, edited and with an introduction by J. Michael Miller, 617–755. Huntington, Ind.: Our Sunday Visitor, 1998.

———. *Man and Woman He Created Them: A Theology of the Body*. Edited and translated, with an introduction by Michael Waldstein. Boston: Pauline Books, 2006.

Jones, Kenneth. *Index of Leading Catholic Indicators: The Church Since Vatican II*. St. Louis, Mo.: Oriens, 2003.

Kam-Lun Lee. *Augustine, Manichaeism, and the Good*. Patristic Studies 2. New York: Peter Lang, 1999.

Kardong, Terrence. *Benedict's Rule: A Translation and Commentary*. Collegeville, Minn.: Liturgical Press, 1996.

Kasper, Walter. *Theology of Christian Marriage*. New York: Seabury, 1980.

Kaufman, Peter Iver. "Augustine, Evil, and Donatism: Sin and Sanctity before the Pelagian Controversy." *Theological Studies* 51 (1990): 115–26.

Kazhdan, Alexander. "Hermitic, Cenobitic, and Secular Ideals in Byzantine Hagiography of the Ninth [to Twelfth] Centuries." *Greek Orthodox Theological Review* 30 (1985): 484–87.

———. "Byzantine Hagiography and Sex in the Fifth to Twelfth Centuries." *Dumbarton Oaks Papers* 44 (1990): 131–43.

Kippley, John F. *Sex and the Marriage Covenant: A Basis for Morality*. 2nd ed. San Francisco: Ignatius Press, 2005.

Knox, Ronald Arbuthnott. *Enthusiasm: A Chapter in the History of Religion, with Special Reference to the XVII and XVIII Centuries*. New York: Oxford University Press, 1950.

Koester, Craig. R. *The Dwelling of God: The Tabernacle in the Old Testament, Intertestamental Jewish Literature, and the New Testament*. Catholic Biblical Quarterly Monograph Series 22. Washington, D.C.: Catholic Biblical Association, 1989.

La Corte, Daniel Marcel, and Douglas J. McMillan. *Regular Life: Monastic, Canonical, and Mendicant Rules*. 2nd ed. Kalamazoo, Mich.: Medieval Institute Publications, 2004.

Bibliography

Lamberigts, Mathijs. "Was Augustine a Manichean? The Assessment of Julian of Aeclanum." In *Augustine in the Latin West*. Ithaca, N.Y: Snow Lion, 2002, 113–36.

Lancel, Serge. *Saint Augustine*. Translated by Antonia Nevill. London: SCM Press, 2002.

Lasch, Christopher. *Haven in a Heartless World: The Family Besieged*. New York: Basic Books, 1977.

Lawler, Michael G. *Marriage and Sacrament: A Theology of Christian Marriage*. Collegeville, Minn.: Liturgical Press, 1993.

———. *Family: American and Christian*. Chicago: Loyola University Press, 1998.

———. *Marriage and the Catholic Church: Disputed Questions*. Collegeville, Minn.: Liturgical Press, 2002.

———. "A Marital Catechumenate: A Proposal." *INTAMS Review* 13 (2007): 161–77.

Leckey, Dolores. *The Ordinary Way: A Family Spirituality*. New York: Crossroad, 1982.

Lee, Patrick, and Robert P. George. "What Male-Female Complementarity Makes Possible: Marriage as a Two-in-One-Flesh Union." *Theological Studies* 69 (2008): 641–62.

Lehmeier, Karin. *Oikos und Oikonomia: Antike Konzepte der Haushaltsführung und der Bau der Gemeinde be Paulus*. Marburg: N. G. Elwert, 2006.

Lienhard, Joseph T. "Augustine, *Sermon* 51: St. Joseph in Early Christianity." In *Dominico Eloquio—In Lordly Eloquence—Essays on Patristic Exegesis in Honor of Robert Louis Wilken*, edited by Paul M. Blowers, Angela Russell Christman, David G. Hunter, and Robin Darling Young. Grand Rapids, Mich.: Eerdmans, 2002.

Liguori, Alphonsus. *The Christian Virtues and the Means of Obtaining Them*. Translated and edited by Robert A. Coffin. New York: Edward Dunigan and Brother, 1855.

———. "Rule of Life." In *The Way of Salvation and of Perfection*, edited by Eugene Grimm. Vol. 2. Rev. ed. Brooklyn: Redemptorist Fathers, 1926.

Little, Edmund. *Echoes of the Old Testament in the Wine of Cana in Galilee (John 2:1–11) and the Multiplication of the Loaves and Fish (John 6:1–15): Towards an Interpretation*. Cahiers de la Revue biblique 41. Paris: J. Gabalda, 1998.

Lonergan, Bernard. "Finality, Love, Marriage." *Theological Studies* 4 (1943): 477–510.

———. *De Verbo Incarnato*. Translated by Charles Hefling. Rome: Gregorian University Press, 1964.

———. *Method in Theology*. 2nd ed. Toronto: University of Toronto Press, 1979.

———. *Insight: A Study of Human Understanding*. Edited by Frederick E. Crowe and Robert M. Doran. 5th ed. Toronto: University of Toronto Press, 1992.

Lössl, Josef. "Augustine, Pelagianism, Julian of Aeclanum, and Modern Scholarship." *Zeitschrift für antikes Christentum* 11, no. 1 (2007): 129–50.

Lysaught, M. Therese. "Practicing the Order of Widows: A New Call for an Old Vocation." *Christian Bioethics* 11 (2005): 51–68.

MacIntyre, Alasdair. *After Virtue: A Study in Moral Theology*. 3rd ed. Notre Dame, Ind.: University of Notre Dame Press, 2007.

Bibliography

Mackin, Theodore. *What Is Marriage?* New York: Paulist Press, 1982.
———. *Divorce and Remarriage.* New York: Paulist Press, 1984.
———. *The Marital Sacrament.* New York: Paulist Press, 1989.
Mahoney, John. *The Making of Moral Theology.* Oxford: Clarendon Press, 1987.
Malina, Bruce J., and Richard L. Rohrbaugh. *Social-Science Commentary on the Gospel of John.* Minneapolis: Fortress Press, 1998.
Marrett-Crosby, Anthony, et al., eds. *The Benedictine Handbook.* Collegeville, Minn.: Liturgical Press, 2003.
Martin, Steven. "Women's Changing Attitudes toward Divorce, 1974–2002: Evidence for an Educational Crossover." *Journal of Marriage and Family* 68, no. 1 (2006): 29–40.
Mayer, Cornelius, et al. *Augustinus Lexikon,* Vol. 1. Basel: Schwabe, 1986–.
McAllister, Robert J. *Living the Vows: The Emotional Conflicts of Celibate Religious.* Cambridge, Mass.: Harper and Row, 1986.
McCarthy, David Matzko. *Sex and Love in the Home: A Theology of the Household.* London: SCM, 2001.
———. "Cohabitation and Marriage." In Cloutier, ed., *Leaving and Coming Home,* 119–46.
McMillan, Douglas J., and Kathryn Smith Fladenmuller, eds. *Regular Life: Monastic, Canonical, and Mendicant Rules.* Kalamazoo, Mich.: Medieval Institute Publications, 1997.
Merton, Thomas. *No Man Is an Island.* New York: Sheed and Ward, 1965.
Methodius of Olympus. *Symposium: A Treatise on Chastity.* Translated by Herbert Musurillo. New York: Newman Press, 1958.
Migne, Jacques-Paul, ed. *Patrologiae Cursus Completus.* Series Latina. Paris, 1844–91.
———. *Patrologiae Cursus Completus.* Series Graeca. Paris, 1857–66.
Milbank, John. *Theology and Social Theory: Beyond Secular Reason.* Cambridge, Mass.: Blackwell, 1990.
Miller, Donald A. *Concepts of Family life in Modern Catholic Theology: From Vatican II Through "Christifideles Laici."* San Francisco: Catholic Scholars Press, 1996.
Miller, J. Michael. *The Post-Synodal Apostolic Exhortations of John Paul II.* Huntington, Ind.: Our Sunday Visitor, 1998.
Moloney, Francis J. *A Life of Promise: Poverty, Chastity, Obedience.* Consecrated Life Studies 1. Wilmington, Del.: M. Glazier, 1984.
Muller, Earl. *Trinity and Marriage in Paul: The Establishment of a Communitarian Analogy of the Trinity Grounded in the Theological Shape of Pauline Thought.* Frankfurt: Lang, 1990.
National Association of Catholic Family Life Ministers. "Resources." http://www.nacflm.org/displaycommon.cfm?an=1&subarticlenbr=27. Accessed February 7, 2011.

Bibliography

National Commission on Children. *Beyond Rhetoric: A New American Agenda for Children and Families*. Washington, D.C.: U.S. Government Printing Office, 1991.

National Fraternity of the Secular Franciscan Order. *The Rule of the Secular Franciscan Order*. http://www.nafra-sfo.org/sforule.html. Accessed February 8, 2011.

———. *General Constitutions*. Rome: National Fraternity of the Secular Franciscan Order, 2001. http://www.nafra-sfo.org/index.html. Accessed May 10, 2013.

Nau., F., Johannes Rufus, Severus Antiochenus et al. *Patrologia Orientalis*. Paris: Firmin-Didot, 1912.

Nédoncelle, Maurice. "L'Intersubjectivité humaine est-elle pour saint Augustin une image de la Trinité?" International Augustinian Conference. In *Augustinus Magister*. Vol. 1. Paris: Études Augustiniennes, 1954.

Nisbet, Robert. *Twilight of Authority*. New York: Oxford University Press, 1975.

Noonan, John T. *Contraception: A History of Its Treatment by the Catholic Theologians and Canonists*. Rev. ed. Cambridge, Mass.: Harvard University Press, 1986.

Norris, Thomas. "Why the Marriage of Christians Is One of the Seven Sacraments." *Irish Theological Quarterly* 51 (1985): 37–51.

Obach, Robert E. *The Catholic Church on Marital Intercourse: From St. Paul to Pope John Paul II*. Lanham, Md.: Lexington Books, 2009.

O'Donovan, Oliver. *The Problem of Self-Love in Augustine*. New Haven, Conn.: Yale University Press, 1980.

Olphé-Galliard, M. "From the Fathers of the Desert to St. Basil and St. Benedict." In *Obedience*, translated by Lancelot C. Sheppard. Religious Life 3. Westminster, Md.: Newman Press, 1953.

Okholm, Dennis. *Monk Habits for Everyday People: Benedictine Spirituality for Protestants*. Grand Rapids, Mich.: Brazos, 2007.

O'Murchu, Diarmuid. *Poverty, Celibacy, and Obedience: A Radical Option for Life*. New York: Crossroad, 1999.

Ordo Praedicatorum. *The Rule of the Lay Fraternities of St. Dominic*. Rome: Analecta of the Order, 1987. http://curia.op.org/en/index.php?option=com_docman&task=cat_view&gid=41&Itemid=102. Accessed February 8, 2011.

Osiek, Carolyn, and David L. Balch. *Families in the New Testament World: Households and House Churches*. Louisville, Ky.: Westminster John Knox, 1997.

Otten, Willemien. "Augustine on Marriage, Monasticism, and the Community of the Church." *Theological Studies* 59 (1998): 385–405.

Ouellet, Marc Cardinal. *Divine Likeness: Toward a Trinitarian Anthropology of the Family*. Translated by Philip Milligan and Linda M. Cicone. Grand Rapids, Mich.: Eerdmans, 2006.

Pachomius. *The Rule of the Master*. Translated by Luke Eberle. Kalamazoo, Mich.: Cistercian Publications, 1977.

Bibliography

Parrella, Frederick. "Towards a Spirituality of the Family." *Communio* 9 (1982): 128–41.
Perdue, Leo G., et al. *Families in Ancient Israel*. Louisville, Ky.: Westminster John Knox Press, 1997.
Peters, Edward N. *Annulments and the Catholic Church: Straight Answers to Tough Questions*. West Chester, Penn.: Ascension Press, 2004.
Phan, Peter C. "Possibility of a Lay Spirituality: A Re-Examination of Some Theological Presuppositions." *Communio* 10 (Winter 1983): 378–95.
Phipps, William E. "The Heresiarch: Pelagius or Augustine?" *Anglican Theological Review* 62, no. 2 (1980): 124–33.
Pierlot, Holly. *A Mother's Rule of Life: How to Bring Order to Your Home and Peace to Your Soul*. Manchester, N.H.: Sophia Institute Press, 2004.
Pikaza, Xabier. "En communidad: Como la familia del Dios-Trinidad." *Vida Religiosa* 66 (1989): 57–66.
———. "Trinidad." In *Diccionario Teológico de la Vida Consagrada*. Madrid: Publicaciones Claretianas, 1992, 1758–77.
Pinckaers, Servais. "An Encyclical for the Future: *Veritatis Splendor*." In *Veritatis Splendor and the Renewal of Moral Theology: Studies by Ten Outstanding Scholars*, edited by J. A. Di Noia and Romanus P. Cessario, 11–72. Princeton, N.J.: Scepter, 1999.
Pontifical Council for the Family. *Preparation for the Sacrament of Marriage*. Rome: Libreria Editrice Vaticana, 1996. http://www.vatican.va/roman_curia/pontifical_councils/family/documents/rc_pc_family_doc_13051996_preparation-for-marriage_en.html. Accessed January 13, 2011.
———. *Enchiridion on the Family: A Compendium of Church Teaching on Family and Life Issues from Vatican II to the Present*. Boston: Pauline Books, 2004.
Pontifical Council for Justice and Peace. *Compendium of the Social Doctrine of the Church*. Rome: Libreria Editrice Vaticana, 2004. http://www.vatican.va/roman_curia/pontifical_councils/justpeace/index.htm. Accessed February 8, 2011.
Popenoe, David. *Life Without Father: Compelling New Evidence That Fatherhood and Marriage Are Indispensable for the Good of Children and Society*. New York: Martin Kessler, 1996.
Power, Kim. *Veiled Desire: Augustine's Writing on Women*. London: Darton, Longman, and Todd, 1995.
Provencher, Normand. "Vers une théologie de la familie: L'Église domestique." *Église et théologie* 12 (1981): 9–34.
Rees, B. R. *Pelagius: Life and Letters*. Rochester, N.Y.: Boydell, 1998.
Rémy, Gérard. "L'analogie et l'image: De leur bon usage en théologie." *Recherches de science religieuse* 92 (2004): 383–427.
Riley, Patrick G. D. *Civilizing Sex: On Chastity and the Common Good*. Edinburgh: T. and T. Clark, 2000.

Bibliography

Rinere, Elissa. "Error Which Causes the Contract." *Studia Canonica* 38, no. 1 (2004): 65–84.

The Rites of the Catholic Church: As Revised by Decree of the Second Vatican Ecumenical Council and Published by Authority of Pope Paul VI. Translated by the International Commission on English in the Liturgy. New York: Pueblo, 1978. Originally published in 1969.

Ross, Susan A. "The Bridegroom and the Bride: The Theological Anthropology of John Paul II and Its Relation to the Bible and Homosexuality." In *Sexual Diversity and Catholicism: Toward the Development of Moral Theology*, edited by Patricia Beattie Jung, with Joseph Andrew Coray. Collegeville, Minn.: Liturgical Press, 2001.

Rubio, Julie Hanlon. *A Christian Theology of Marriage and Family.* New York: Paulist Press, 2003.

———. *Family Ethics: Practices For Christians.* Washington, D.C.: Georgetown University Press, 2010.

Russell, Kenneth. "Loves in Conflict: Maritain on Marriage and Contemplation." *Église et Théologie* 7, no. 3 (1976): 333–40.

———. "Marriage and the Contemplative Life." *Spiritual Life* 24, no. 7 (1978): 48–57.

Rutba House, ed. *School(s) for Conversion: 12 Marks of a New Monasticism.* Eugene, Ore.: Cascade, 2005.

Ryan, Peter F., and Germain Grisez. "Indissoluble Marriage: A Reply to Kenneth Himes and James Coriden." *Theological Studies* 72 (2011): 369–415.

Schaff, Philip, and Henry Wace, eds. "Council of Ancyra." In *Nicene and Post-Nicene Fathers 2.* Translated by Henry Percival. Vol. 14. Buffalo, N.Y.: Christian Literature Publishing, 1900.

Scheeben, Matthias. *Mysteries of Christianity.* Translated by Cyril Vollert. St. Louis, Mo.: Herder, 1946.

Schelkens, Pius. "De Ecclesia Sponsa Christi." *Augustiniana* 3 (1953): 145–64.

Scheppard, Carol. "The Transmission of Sin in the Seed: A Debate Between Augustine of Hippo and Julian of Eclanum." In *Doctrinal Diversity: Varieties of Early Christianity,* edited by Everett Ferguson, 233–42. New York: Garland, 1999.

Schillebeeckx, Edward. *Marriage: Human Reality, Saving Mystery.* Translated by N. D. Smith. New York: Sheed and Ward, 1966.

Schmitt, Émile. *Le mariage chrétien dans l'oeuvre de saint Augustin: Une théologie baptismale de la vie conjugale.* Paris: Études Augustiniennes, 1983.

Schneiders, Sandra M. *Finding the Treasure: Locating Catholic Religious Life in a New Ecclesial and Cultural Context.* Religious Life in a New Millennium 1. New York: Paulist Press, 2000.

———. *Selling All: Commitment, Consecrated Celibacy, and Community in Catholic Religious Life.* Religious Life in a New Millenium 2. New York: Paulist Press, 2002.

Bibliography

Schroeder, David. *Die Haustafeln des Neuen Testaments: Ihre Herkunft und ihr theologischer Sinn.* 2 Anmerkungen. Hamburg: Universitaet Hamburg, 1959.

Scola, Angelo Cardinal. *The Nuptial Mystery.* Translated by Michelle K. Borras. Grand Rapids, Mich.: Eerdmans, 2005.

Scott, Kieran, and Michael Warren, eds. *Perspectives on Marriage: A Reader.* 3rd ed. New York: Oxford University Press, 2007.

Sheppard, Lancelot C., trans. *Obedience.* Religious Life 3. Westminster, Md.: Newman Press, 1953.

———. *Poverty.* Religious Life 4. Westminster, Md.: Newman Press, 1954.

Sherba, Jerry M. "Canon 1096: Ignorance as a Ground for Nullity." *Canon Law Society of America, Proceedings* 59 (1997): 282–99.

Shivanandan, Mary. *Crossing the Threshold of Love: A New Vision of Marriage in the Light of John Paul II's Anthropology.* Washington, D.C.: The Catholic University of America Press, 1999.

Shorter, Edward. *The Making of the Modern Family.* New York: Basic Books, 1977.

Silanes, Nereo. "Trinidad y vida consagrada." *Comunidades* 17, no. 66–67 (1989): 47–65.

Smith, Janet. "Conscious Parenthood." *Nova et Vetera* 6, no. 4 (2008): 927–50.

Splett, Jörg. "Evangelical Counsels in Marriage?" *Communio* 31, no. 3 (2004): 404–18.

Stanley, Alan P. "The Rich Young Ruler and Salvation." *Bibliotheca Sacra* 163 (January–March 2006): 46–62.

Stegemann, Ekkehard W., and Wolfgang Stegemann. *The Jesus Movement: A Social History of Its First Century.* Minneapolis: Fortress Press, 1999.

Stegemann, Wolfgang, Bruce J. Malina, and Gerd Theissen, eds. *The Social Setting of Jesus and the Gospels.* Minneapolis: Fortress Press, 2002.

Stevenson, Kenneth. *To Join Together: The Rite of Marriage.* New York: Pueblo, 1987.

Stone, Lawrence. "The Family Crisis Today." In *The Family, Civil Society, and the State,* edited by Christopher Wolfe, 17@72. Lanham, Md.: Rowman and Littlefield, 1998.

Suggit, John. "The Eucharistic Significance of John 20:19–29." *Journal of Theology for Southern Africa* 16 (1976): 52–59.

Tabbernee, William. *Fake Prophecy and Polluted Sacraments: Ecclesiastical and Imperial Reactions to Montanism.* Supplements to Vigiliae Christianae 84. Boston: Brill, 2007.

Talbot, Alice-Mary. "The Byzantine Family and the Monastery." *Dumbarton Oaks Papers* 44 (1990): 119–29.

Teske, Roland J. "The Image and Likeness of God in St. Augustine's *De genesi ad litteram liber imperfectus.*" *Augustinianum* 30 (1990): 441–51.

Therrien, Michael. "The Practice of Responsible Parenthood, NFP, and the Covenantal Unity of Spouses." In Cloutier, ed., *Leaving and Coming Home,* 173–205.

Thomas, David M. "Home Fires." In *The Changing Family: Views From the Theology and*

Bibliography

the Social Sciences in the Light of the Apostolic Exhortation "Familiaris consortio," edited by Stanley L. Saxton. Chicago: Loyola University Press, 1984.

Traina, Cristiana L. H. "Papal Ideals, Marital Realities: One View from the Ground." In *Sexual Diversity and Catholicism: Toward the Development of Moral Theology*, edited by Patricia Beattie Jung, with Joseph Andrew Coray, 269–88. Collegeville, Minn.: Liturgical Press, 2001.

U.S. Catholic Bishops Conference, 2013. *For Your Marriage*. http://www.foryourmarriage.org. February 7, 2011.

U.S. Catholic Conference. *The Consecrated Life and Its Role in the Church and in the World*. Washington, D.C.: United States Catholic Conference, 1992.

U.S. Council of Catholic Bishops. *Love and Life in the Divine Plan*. November 17, 2009. http://www.usccb.org/loveandlife/MarriageFINAL.pdf. Accessed February 7, 2011.

U.S. Census Bureau. *2009 Statistical Abstract*. http://www.census.gov/compendia/statab/. Accessed 19 August, 2009.

U.S. Department of Health and Human Services. Administration for Children and Families. "Healthy Marriage Initiative." http://www.acf.hhs.gov/healthymarriage/index.html. Accessed February 7, 2011.

Van Bavel, Tarsisius. *Recherches sur la christologie de saint Augustin: L'humain et le divin dans le Christ d'apres saint Augustin*. Fribourg: Editions universitaires, 1954.

Vatican Council. *Documents of the II Vatican Council*. Rome: Libreria Editrice, 1966. http://www.vatican.va/archive/hist_councils/ii_vatican_council/index.htm. Accessed February 7, 2011.

Verbraken, Pierre-Patrick. "Le sermon LI de saint Augustin sur les genealogies du Christ selon Matthieu et selon Luc." *Revue Bénédictine* 91 (1981): 20–45.

Verheijen, Luc. *Nouvelle approche de la Regle de saint Augustin*. Collection spiritualite orientale et vie monastique. Godewaersvelde, France: Editions de Bellafontaine, 1980.

Von Balthasar, Hans Urs. *Mysterium Paschale: The Mystery of Easter*. Translated by Aidan Nichols. San Francisco: Ignatius Press, 1981.

———. *The Christian State of Life*. Translated by Mary Frances McCarthy. San Francisco: Ignatius Press, 1983.

———. *Theologik II: Wahrheit Gottes*. Einsiedeln, Switzerland: Johannes, 1985.

———. *The Laity and the Life of the Counsels: The Church's Mission in the World*. Translated by Brian McNeil, with D. C. Schindler. San Francisco: Ignatius Press, 2003. Originally published in 1993.

Von Hildebrand, Dietrich. *Marriage: The Mystery of Faithful Love*. London: Longmans, 1942.

Wallerstein, Judith S., Julia M. Lewis, and Sandra Blakeslee. *The Unexpected Legacy of Divorce: A 25 Year Landmark Study*. New York: Hyperion, 2000.

Bibliography

Ward, Maisie. *Be Not Solicitous: Sidelights on the Providence of God and the Catholic Family.* New York: Sheed and Ward, 1953.

Ware, Kalistos. "The Monk and the Married Christian: Some Comparisons in Early Monastic Sources." *Eastern Churches Review* 6, no. 1 (1974): 72–83.

Whitehead, Kenneth D., ed. *Marriage and the Common Good.* South Bend, Ind.: St. Augustine's Press, 2001.

———. *The Church, Marriage, and the Family: Proceedings from the 27th Annual Convention of the Fellowship of Catholic Scholars, September 24–26, 2004, Pittsburgh, Pennsylvania.* South Bend, Ind.: St. Augustine's Press, 2007.

Wilcox, Bradford, ed. *The State of Our Unions 2009: Money and Marriage.* The National Marriage Project. Charlottesville, Va.: University of Virginia, 2009.

———. *The State of Our Unions, Marriage in America 2010: When Marriage Disappears; The New Middle America.* National Marriage Project. Charlottesville, Va.: University of Virginia Press, 2010. http://www.stateofourunions.org. Accessed February 7, 2011.

Williams, Daniel H. "The Origins of the Montanist Movement: A Sociological Analysis." *Religion* 19, no. 4 (October 1989): 331–51.

Wilson, William J. *When Work Disappears: The World of the New Urban Poor.* New York: Random House, 1996.

Wolfe, Christopher, ed. *The Family, Civil Society, and the State.* Lanham, Md.: Rowman and Littlefield, 1998.

Wood, Susan K. "The Marriage of Baptized Nonbelievers: Faith, Contract, and Sacrament," *Theological Studies* 48, no. 2 (1987): 279–301.

Wright, Wendy. *Sacred Dwelling: A Spirituality of Family Life.* New York: Crossroad, 1989.

Yoder, John Howard. *The Politics of Jesus: "Vicit Agnus Noster."* 2nd ed. Grand Rapids, Mich.: Eerdmans, 1994.

INDEX

Acts of the Apostles, 59, 63, 146
Ambrose of Milan, 52n46, 97n19, 98–99, 112
Analogy: husband/wife to Christ/Church, 200n29; of the Trinity, 78–84, 95; virgin as bride of Christ, 110
Annulment, 4, 18
Anthropology, 12, 55–56, 73, 158n76
Aquinas, Thomas, 9n9, 77n59, 158n76; on vows, 44n26, 45, 189
Augustine of Hippo: on family and Trinity, 78–79; on friendship, 147, 206; historical context, 94–107; on marital chastity, 115, 119, 120, 189; monastic rule of, 143n27, 146; on obedience, 147, 206; on relationship between states, 93–94, 107–21, 223; on sexuality, 48n36, 50n41; on stability 158n76.
Asceticism, 53, 69, 88, 89, 91, 96, 99–100, 106–9

Baptism, 15, 27, 32, 35–36, 40–42, 44, 55–56, 67–68, 98, 102–3, 105, 110, 118, 171, 187, 195
Bennett, Jana M., 3n9, 16, 26–33, 48n37, 116n79, 121n99, 153–57, 159n80, 165–66, 214
Bonhöffer, Dietrich, 153, 156, 158, 161n90, 163n93, 168–69, 174–75
Bourg, Florence Caffrey, 37n8, 160n84

Breidenthal, Thomas, 140n17, 143n28, 153, 157n72, 158n76, 160n87, 162–63, 166, 169, 193
Bridegroom: Christ as, xii–xiv, 12–13, 17, 19, 34. 55, 73, 86, 95n13, 110

Cahill, Lisa Sowle, 3, 7, 10, 11–12, 18–30
Canon law, 16, 42–43, 67–68, 73, 127
Capon, Robert Farrar, 218n37
Casti connubii, 8
Celibacy, 38, 45, 52, 63, 65, 91–93, 96–97, 98, 106–7, 109, 111, 117, 119–20, 154, 190, 214–15
Chaste married sexuality (CMS), 191–93, 196, 198–99, 212
Chastity: as evangelical virtue, xi, xiv, 5, 34, 36n5, 40, 47, 57, 63–66, 76, 77n57, 83, 87, 90, 114, 120, 150, 171, 188–99, 208, 212, 217, 219–24; as good internal to a practice, 23–25
Christology, 12, 13, 32–33, 55–56, 103, 209
Chrysostom, John, 85
Church: as bride of Christ, 18–19, 33–34, 36, 55–56, 64, 72, 95, 110–14, 121, 130, 136–37, 140n16, 202; Eastern Orthodox, 71n40; Episcopal, 4n11; general use of term, xii; as household of God, xiii–xiv, 15–16, 27, 30, 33, 41, 132–39, 143, 150, 170, 179, 197, 215, 224

243

Index

Coloe, Mary L., 133, 135–38
Communio. *See* Communion of persons
Communion of life, 14–16, 23, 28
Communion of persons, xii, 9, 20, 21, 28, 67, 77, 84; within the Trinity, 34, 55, 67, 84–85, 136, 171
Community: consecrated religious, 48, 60, 70–71, 73, 74n47, 76, 79n65, 141–49, 151–52, 154, 157–58, 166; early Christian, 59, 63, 77, 139; ecclesial, 19, 21, 67, 73, 100, 112, 134, 136, 140, 150, 165, 167, 216; in general, 6, 11–12, 17, 22, 24–25, 29, 48, 62, 68, 83, 104, 133, 151–52, 156, 159, 164, 167–69, 174–75, 180, 188, 215, 218, 221
Complementarity: in general, 54 156, 169, 223; in marriage, 8n16, 121–22, 188; relationship between religious and conjugal life, 30, 129, 154
Consecration: common baptismal, xiii, 35, 40–41, 171; in marriage, 42, 53; to religious life, 41, 54, 66
Consent, marital, 9, 20, 31, 42–6, 49, 72, 73n44, 84, 127, 128n116, 181, 188, 195, 206, 216
Consummation of marriage, 8n17, 9, 16, 20–21, 31, 50, 72, 73n44, 90, 127, 129, 195
Continence. *See* Chastity; Virtue
Contraception. *See* Natural family planning
Contract: in general, 26, 29, 174, 182; marital, 5n12, 6–7, 42, 43
Covenant: Abrahamic, 72; of marriage, 3n9, 6, 8, 46, 157, 158n76, 191n19, 199n27
Cruciform, 31, 119

Divorce, 1–2, 4, 18, 127n11
Domestic church, xiii, 3n8, 12, 30, 37–38, 86, 160n84, 166n98

Eschatology, 15, 26–27, 30, 47, 57, 64, 76n55, 116, 125, 129n119, 130, 136–37, 139, 163
Eucharist, 29, 31, 45–46, 66, 73, 91, 138n15, 139, 154–55, 161n90, 163, 168, 178, 195, 216
Evangelical counsels (virtues). *See* Chastity; Obedience; Poverty
Exclusivity, 155–56, 162, 164, 189

Familiaris consortio, 9n24, 86, 119n95, 158n76, 165
Familiarity, 155, 160–64, 166, 176, 193–96
Family: Church as family, 76; crisis in family, 1–7, 10–12, 28, 167; as evangelizing, 86; family values, 10; in first century, 135–36; in general, xii, xiii, 11, 16, 17, 26–30, 33, 34, 47n32, 70n37, 91, 107, 113, 162, 165, 173–79, 182–83, 185–86; influence on religious life, 141–43, 147–57; spirituality of, 51–52, structure of, 11–12; and the Trinity. *See also* Communion of persons; Domestic church; Trinity
Formality, 155, 162–63, 176, 193, 195

George, Robert P., 3n9, 7–8
Givenness, 155–56, 158
Gospels: John, 69, 78n61, 133–39, 153, 202, 223; Luke, 69; Mark, 202; Matthew, 59
Grace: in general, xii, 20; 36, 39–40, 61, 66, 76, 89, 101, 158, 161, 215; of matrimony, 8, 15, 20, 68, 75, 161, 217; of other sacraments, 31, 118, 195
Gratissimam sane, 83n73
Grisez, Germain, 3n9, 7, 8n16, 9n22, 31n74

Hauerwas, Stanley, 10, 166n102
Hogan, Margaret Monahan, 7–10, 14–15

Index

Holmes, Paul A., 4n11, 215–16
Hospitality, 29, 61, 85, 91, 139–40, 163, 167, 169–70, 175, 178, 183
Householding: as Christian practice, xiii–xiv, 5, 28, 33, 37n8, 45–46, 56, 68–69, 153–79, 182, 187, 193–94, 208, 211–12, 214, 217, 221–23; in John's Gospel, 133–52
Humanae vitae, 7n15, 119n95, 158n76, 192n20
Humility, 67, 70–71, 91–92, 108
Hunter, David G., 48n36, 50n41, 97n18, 99, 109n59, 110n62, 125n108

Indissolubility, 6–8, 14, 18, 31, 45, 72, 73n44, 76, 131, 205
Intimacy: personal, 17, 161, 194, 195; sexual, 6, 20, 194, 196–98, 212, 216–17

Jerome, 94, 97n19, 98–99, 106n49, 108n54, 109, 112
John Paul II, 7, 9, 20, 24n52, 27n63, 35n2, 39n11, 57, 62n16, 68, 73, 75, 76n55, 80n68, 83–86, 120, 129n119, 160, 165, 169n109, 198–200
Joseph, husband of Mary, 61, 69, 103–4, 126–30, 187
Jovinian, 48n36, 52n46, 93, 94, 95, 97, 98–99, 105–9, 112, 125

Kinship, 11, 27, 32, 47n32

Lawler, Michael, 4n11, 7, 164n97, 215
Leckey, Dolores, 35n2, 143n28, 157n74, 158–61, 168–69
Lee, Patrick, 7–8
Liguori, Alphonsus, 208n34
Lonergan, Bernard, 31n75, 166n101, 180

MacIntyre, Alisdair, 16–25, 32, 172–77, 206–7
Magisterium, 8, 106, 216, 187
Manicheans, 93–99, 102, 103n44, 113n70, 125
Mary, Mother of God, 66, 69, 71–72, 118–19, 125–30, 137; as New Eve, 78, 103–4
Matzko McCarthy, David, 16, 26–29, 32, 149n50, 159n80, 167n103, 174n3, 182n11, 194n24
Moloney, Francis J., 59–60, 64–66

Natural family planning, 19, 190–93, 198–99, 220, 222
Non-voluntary. *See* Givenness
Novitiate, xi, xiv, 34, 164n97, 170–71, 215–16, 223–24

Obedience: as evangelical virtue, xi, xiv, 5, 34, 36n5, 40, 57–58, 66–71, 76, 77n57, 80, 97, 108–9, 114–15, 121–22, 139–40, 170, 200–208, 211, 212, 214, 220–24; as good internal to marriage, 24–25, 29
Ordo Celebrandi Matrimonium, 41–42
Ouellet, Marc Cardinal, 3n9, 73, 78, 79n65, 86n80

Paul's letters: 1 Corinthians, 196; Ephesians, 46n31, 89n79, 133, 200; Timothy, 133
Parrella, Frederick J., 52, 88, 107
Permeability, 156, 164–65, 168, 173
Phan, Peter, 52–53, 88, 107
Poverty: as evangelical virtue, xi, 5, 23, 24n52, 35n1, 36n5, 39–40, 48, 55–63, 67, 76, 83, 86, 171, 179–89; 199, 212, 214, 217–24; as unwilled lack of needs, 26, 213

Index

Practice: general definition, 16–26; marriage as, 1–7, 12, 13–33
Preparation for marriage, 2n7, 3n8, 4n11, 33, 43, 171–72, 215n36, 216, 219–20, 223–24
Priesthood: of all believers, 37, 41; ordained, 216
Promise: God's promise of the kingdom, 128, 135–36; as to vows, 31n47, 41–45, 148n48, 151, 159

Reciprocity. *See* Virtue
Relationship: between consecrated and conjugal life in modern theology, 35–54, 153–70; as marital paradigm, 7–14, 20, 22–26, 29, 30–32, 34; in monastic rules, 140–52; in patristic thought, 89–94, 101, 104, 107, 115–30
Riley, Patrick, G. D., 15n35, 150n52
Rite of Christian Marriage. *See* Ordo Celebrandi Matrimonium
Ross, Susan, 7
Rubio, Julie Hanlon, 32n76
Rule: Augustinian, 146; Benedictine, 70, 143–45, 146, 169; Dominican, 148; Franciscan, 77, 148–49; in general, 57, 153–55, 158; of Pachomius, 140–42; as part of a practice, 22; spousal, xiv, 163, 171, 208–15, 221–23
Russell, Kenneth, 52, 53n48
Ryan, Peter, 7–9, 31n74

Sacrament: Church as sacrament of Christ, xii; of marriage, 4n11, 5–6, 8, 15, 20, 28–31, 37, 41, 44, 50
Schneiders, Sandra, 64, 152
Second Vatican Council: *Gaudium et spes*, 7–8, 13–15, 20n46, 41n17, 50n40, 53n50, 56n1, 60n12, 106n50, 158n76, 192n21; *Lumen gentium*, xii, 35–41, 60, 68, 73, 76, 105n47, 223; *Perfectae caritatis*, 41n15, 57, 63–64, 66n30, 68, 74–75, 77n60
Sex and sexuality. *See* Chaste Married Sexuality; Chastity; Virginity
Sheppard, Lancelott, 106n48
Shivanandan, Mary, 198n26
Smith, Janet, 192
Stability, 156, 158–59
State of life, 38–40, 60n12, 107, 166

Theology of the Body, 24n52, 27n63, 76n55, 194n24, 200n29
Trent, Council of, 48
Trinity: related to the Church, 74; related to marriage, 32–34, 53, 56, 78–86, 135–36; related to religious life, 73–78, 135–36

Virginity: in Augustine, 94–97, 107–30; in early Christianity, 47; in Eastern patristic texts, 90; in Eden, 123; of Mary and Joseph, 66, 126–30; as paschal, 66. *See also* Chastity
Virtue: as constitutive of marriage as a practice, 18, 22–25, 26, 32, 176–79, 210–11, 217–23; of continence, 109–10, 119–22, 128; evangelical, 5, 33–36, 39–40, 47, 55–57, 58–75, 97, 104, 164, 171, 179–208, 217–23; of fortitude, 159; in general, 4–5, 98–99, 105, 108–9, 113–14, 142, 147; of hospitality, 29, 61, 85, 91, 139–40, 163, 167, 169, 170, 175, 178, 183; of humility (simplicity), 67, 70–71, 91–92, 108; of patience, 110, 199; of reciprocity, 16, 28–30, 62n17, 174, 182, 186; of religion, 43, 45, 55, 75

Index

Vita consecrata, 36n5, 57, 61, 68, 73, 169n109

Vocation: marriage as, 3, 5, 58, 165, 169, 178n8; religious, 75, 125, 152; universal vocation to holiness, 35–40, 60, 188

Von Balthasar, Hans Urs, 61–62, 65–66, 68, 71

Vows: marital, 9, 18, 20–21, 40–46, 189–90, 220; of religion, 32, 58, 75, 157, 189; religious and marital, 35, 40–46, 55, 57

Wilcox, Brad, 1n1, 2n3

Yoder, John Howard, 46n31, 135n8, 200n28

Vocation to Virtue: Christian Marriage as a Consecrated Life
was designed in Arno and composed by Kachergis Book
Design of Pittsboro, North Carolina. It was printed on
60-pound Natures Book Natural and bound by
Thomson-Shore of Dexter, Michigan.